THINKING AND THE I

THINKING AND THE I

Hegel and the Critique of Kant

Alfredo Ferrarin

Northwestern University Press
Evanston, Illinois

Northwestern University Press
www.nupress.northwestern.edu

Copyright © 2019 by Northwestern University Press. Published 2019. All rights
reserved.

A version of this book was published in Italian in 2016 under the title *Il pensare
e l'io: Hegel e la critica di Kant.*

Printed in the United States of America

10   9   8   7   6   5   4   3   2   1

ISBN 978-0-8101-3938-1 (paper)
ISBN 978-0-8101-3939-8 (cloth)
ISBN 978-0-8101-3940-4 (ebook)

Cataloging-in-Publication Data are available from the Library of Congress.

To Stanley (1929–2014) and Massimo (1941–2015)
Best of teachers, colleagues, friends
in loving memory

This was the last stronghold of the dualism he abhorred. The square root of I is I. Footnotes, forget-me-nots. The stranger quietly watching the torrents of local grief from an abstract bank. A familiar figure, albeit anonymous and aloof. He saw me crying when I was ten and led me to a looking glass in an unused room (with an empty parrot cage in the corner) so that I might study my dissolving face. He has listened to me with raised eyebrows when I said things I had no business to say. In every mask I tried on, there were slits for his eyes.

—Vladimir Nabokov, *Bend Sinister*

Contents

Acknowledgments		xi
List of Abbreviations		xiii
Introduction: The Actuality of Thought		3
1	Hegel on Recognition: Self-Consciousness, Individuality, and Intersubjectivity	23
2	Nonhuman Thinking?	53
3	The Movement of Thought: Spontaneity and Reification	88
4	On Transforming Representations into Concepts	111
5	Kant's and Hegel's Reason	137
Conclusions		195
Notes		201
Index of Names		231

Acknowledgments

This book was originally published in Italian in June 2016 by Carocci Editore under the title *Il pensare e l'io: Hegel e la critica di Kant.* Elisa Magrì kindly agreed to translate it into English. Because I was painfully aware of the quite divergent constraints of the Italian and English prose styles and of the problems of translation, I asked her to provide a literal draft that I later reelaborated and rewrote altogether. Which is to say that my gratitude for Elisa is profound, and she bears no responsibility for all possible idiomatic infelicities that might still be present.

I have presented some parts of this book in conferences, seminars, and academic courses over the last four years (starting with Pavia, then Warwick, Venice, Boston, Palermo, Vercelli, Pisa, Luxembourg, Frankfurt, Rome, Dublin, Freiburg, Leuven, Paris, Basel, and New York). I wish to thank the audiences for their questions, comments, and criticisms.

I am thankful to Luigi Ruggiu and Italo Testa, Dietmar Heidemann, and Luca Fonnesu and Lucia Ziglioli for allowing me to reproduce here some pages taken from my contributions to their edited books and journal issues: "Hegel on Recognition: Self-Consciousness, Individuality and Intersubjectivity," in *I That Is We, and We That Is I,* ed. L. Ruggiu and I. Testa (Leiden: Brill, 2016), 253–70; "Reason in Kant and Hegel," *Kant Yearbook: Kant and German Idealism* 8 (2016): 1–16; and "Spontaneity and Reification: What Does Hegel Mean by Thinking?" in *System und Logik bei Hegel: 200 Jahre nach der Wissenschaft der Logik,* ed. L. Fonnesu and L. Ziglioli (Hildesheim: Olms, 2016), 81–104.

I wish to thank Trevor Perri at Northwestern University Press for his generosity and support.

List of Abbreviations

Works by Descartes

AT René Descartes, *Oeuvres de Descartes*, edited by Charles Adam and Paul Tannery (rpt. Paris, 1996).

Works by Kant

Collected Works

Ak *Akademie-Ausgabe—Kants gesammelte Schriften*, edited by Preussischen Akademie der Wissenschaften zu Berlin (Berlin, 1902–). Citations in the text refer to the volume and page number, respectively.

Single Works

Anthr. *Anthropologie in pragmatischer Hinsicht* (*Ak* 7); translated by R. B. Louden as *Anthropology from a Pragmatic Point of View*, in Kant, *Anthropology, History, Education*, edited by Günter Zöller and Robert B. Louden (Cambridge, 2007), 227–429.

GMS *Grundlegung zur Metaphysik der Sitten* (*Ak* 4); translated by M. Gregor as *Groundwork of the Metaphysics of Morals*, in Kant, *Practical Philosophy*, edited by M. Gregor and J. Timmerman (Cambridge, 1996), 37–108.

KpV *Kritik der praktischen Vernunft* (*Ak* 5); translated by M. Gregor as *Critique of Practical Reason*, in Kant, *Practical Philosophy*, 133–271.

KrV *Kritik der reinen Vernunft* ("A" following the abbreviation refers to the 1781 version; "B" refers to the version of 1787); translated by P. Guyer and A. W. Wood as *Critique of Pure Reason* (Cambridge, 1998).

ABBREVIATIONS

KU	*Kritik der Urteilskraft* (*Ak* 5); translated by P. Guyer in Kant, *Critique of the Power of Judgment*, edited by P. Guyer and E. Matthews (Cambridge, 2000).
Log.	*Logik Jaesche* (*Ak* 9).
"MAM"	"Muthmaßlicher Anfang der Menschengeschichte" (*Ak* 8).
Prol.	*Prolegomena zu einer jeden künftigen Metaphysik* (*Ak* 4).
Refl.	*Reflexionen* (*Ak* 14–19).
"V-Lo/Dohna"	"Logik Dohna-Wundlacken" (*Ak* 24)

Works by Hegel

Collected Works

GW	*Gesammelte Werke*, edited by Rheinisch-Westphälischen Akademie der Wissenschaften, in collaboration with the Deutschen Forschungsgemeinschaft (Hamburg, 1968–).
JA	*Sämtliche Werke*, anniversary edition, edited by H. Glockner (Stuttgart, 1927–40).
W	*Werke in zwanzig Bänden*, edited by E. Moldenhauer and K. M. Michel (Frankfurt am Main, 1969–71). Citations in the text refer to the volume and page number, respectively.

Single Works

Diff.	*Differenz des Fichte'schen und Schelling'schen Systems der Philosophie*, in *Jenaer Kritische Schriften*, edited by H. Büchner and O. Pöggeler (*GW* 4).
EA	*Enzyklopädie der Philosophischen Wissenschaften im Grundrisse* (1817) (*JA* 6). Citations in the text are followed by § (section number), A (*Anmerkung*, remark), or Z (*Zusatz*, oral addition).
ENZ	*Enzyklopädie der philosophischen Wissenschaften* (*W* 8–10).
	ENZ 8 is translated by K. Brinkmann and D. O. Dahlstrom as *Encyclopaedia of the Philosophical Sciences in Basic Outline, Part I: Science of Logic* (Cambridge: Cambridge University Press, 2010); also translated by T. F. Geraets, W. A. Suchting, and H. S. Harris as *The Encyclopaedia Logic: Part 1 of the Encyclopaedia of Philosophical Sciences with the Zusätze* (Indianapolis, 1991). *ENZ* 9 is translated by M. J. Petry as *Hegel's Philosophy of Nature*, 3 vols. (London, 1970). *ENZ* 10 is translated by M. Inwood as *Hegel: Philosophy of Mind* (Oxford, 2007).

ABBREVIATIONS

Erdmann	*Vorlesungen über Philosophie des Geistes 1827/28: Nachschrift von Johann Eduard Erdmann und Ferdinand Walter*, edited by F. Hespe and B. Tuschling (Hamburg, 1994); translated by R. R. Williams as *Lectures on the Philosophy of Subjective Spirit 1827–8* (Oxford, 2007).
FK	*Faith and Knowledge*, edited by W. Cerf and H. S. Harris (Albany: State University of New York Press, 1977). English translation of *GuW*.
G/J	*Vorlesungen über die Geschichte der Philosophie*, vol. 2, edited by P. Garniron and W. Jaeschke (Hamburg, 1989).
GPR	*Grundlinien der Philosophie des Rechts* (*W* 7); translated by A. W. Wood as *Elements of the Philosophy of Right* (Cambridge, 1991).
GuW	*Glauben und Wissen*, in Kant, *Jenaer Kritische Schriften* (*GW* 4), edited by H. Büchner and O. Pöggeler; for the English translation, see *FK*.
Hoff	*Briefe von und an Hegel*, 4 vols., edited by J. Hoffmeister (Hamburg, 1952–60).
JSE 3	*Jenaer Systementwürfe III* (*GW* 8).
LL	*Lectures on Logic*, translated by C. Butler (Bloomington, 2008). English translation of *Logik 1831*.
Logik 1831	*Vorlesungen über die Logik: Berlin 1831*, supplement by Karl Hegel, edited by U. Rameil and H.-C. Lucas (Hamburg, 2001); for the English translation, see *LL*.
PhS	*Phenomenology of Spirit*, translated by A. V. Miller (Oxford, 1977). English translation of *W* 3.
SL	*Science of Logic*, translated by G. di Giovanni (Cambridge, 2010). Unless otherwise noted, I use this translation, but see also *Hegel's Science of Logic*, translated by A. V. Miller (London, 1969).
VGPh	*Vorlesungen über die Geschichte der Philosophie* (*W* 18–20; for example, *VGPh* 3 is *W* 20).
VPhG Lasson I	*Vorlesungen über die Philosophie der Weltgeschichte*, vol. 1, edited by G. Lasson (Hamburg, 1920).
VPhR	*Vorlesungen über die Philosophie der Religion* (*JA* 12), part 1, *Begriff der Religion*, edited by G. Lasson (Leipzig, 1930).
WL I, II	*Wissenschaft der Logik* (*W* 5–6).

I have tacitly corrected the above-mentioned translations whenever improprieties or mistakes were present.

THINKING AND THE I

Introduction

The Actuality of Thought

Die Gedanken sind frei, wer kann sie erraten,
Sie rauschen vorbei wie nachtliche Schatten.
Kein Mensch kann sie wissen, kein Jäger sie schiessen,
Es bleibet dabei: die Gedanken sind frei.

Thoughts are free, who can guess them?
They fly by like nocturnal shadows.
No person can know them, no hunter can shoot them
and so it will always be: Thoughts are free!
— "Lied des Verfolgten im Turm" ("Song of the Persecuted
in the Tower"), from *Des Knaben Wunderhorn*

Are Thoughts Free?

We do not know who wrote this lied, which was published in 1780 in a form similar to the current version (in four stanzas rather than five) and whose original core dates back to the Austrian minnesingers of the twelfth century. Achim von Arnim and Clemens Brentano included this song in the third volume of *Des Knaben Wunderhorn* (*The Boy's Magic Horn*) in 1805, and at the end of that same century Gustav Mahler set the song to music in his homonymous cycle.

Thoughts are free; they flow like nocturnal shadows that no hunter can ever hope to shoot, is what these verses say. Reducing such a sense of freedom to the naïveté of denying thoughts any constraint, as Adorno argues, would be to misunderstand them.[1] It would entail a concern with the origin and alleged foundation of thoughts—a matter of causality—whereas the lied refers to the very being of thoughts. These are free not because they are not rooted in something that can precede or constrain them, but because they cannot be subjugated to the thinker. Thoughts can escape us, dominate us, exceed our control. They seem animated by a logic of their own and a spontaneity that is difficult to comprehend and yet is irreducible to the will of the subject who thinks them.[2] If thoughts may happen not to know themselves, it is because they are not the product of a self-transparent I who controls and dominates them.

With regard to this elusive character of thoughts set against an I that supposedly owns them, Hegel partly shares the critique of the I that we find in Rousseau. The natural man lives in himself, whereas the I depends on the power of reflection which leads to self-estrangement and replaces self-love (*amour de soi*) by egocentrism (*amour-propre*). The I always arises as the resolution to take charge and possession of oneself. The I replaces the immediate, indistinct, and natural *being* one with oneself with a relationship that is based on the mode of *having*. The property title acquires legal status when I introduce a duality between my several states and natural qualities that I must be able to manage and myself as I. With respect to a conception that regards thinking as the property of an I, I believe that Hegel could paraphrase in the following way the words of Rousseau's *Discourse on the Origin of Inequality* regarding the original enclosing of a plot of land: the first man who took it into his head to say "this thought is mine" and found people simple enough to believe him was the true founder of modern philosophy. Unlike Rousseau, however, the underlying motivation is not the condemnation of the impostor who is responsible for infinite misfortunes and horrors. For Hegel, the act of reducing thought to the property of an I is one-sided, biased, and even false, yet such one-sidedness appears to be indispensable, and Hegel's conception of thinking must be able to account for its necessity. The I of reflection, which if absolutized into a principle is a misleading starting point, is actually an essential and inevitable stage for thinking.

The subject matter of this book is the relationship between thinking and the I in Hegel. We will see how radically Hegel critiques the ordinary view of thinking that reduces thought to a property of an I. As soon as we name the concepts at stake, however, we grow impatient to fill them with familiar meanings in order to make them accessible and comprehensible from the very start, and this creates that feeling of comfortable familiarity which it is our precise task to call into question. For this reason, it is appropriate to specify right away what we must *not* think about when we talk about thinking and the I in Hegel.

The Uncritical Assumptions of the Ordinary Conception of Thought

The ordinary conception of thought (i.e., modern philosophy from Descartes to Kant as well as common sense, which is roughly consonant with it) believes that thought occurs when *I think something determinate.*

There is thought when someone thinks something. Concepts are mental and subjective acts that refer to objects outside us. Whether thinking is the mental act or its content, thought is externally limited by what is outside it, so that this external being is the touchstone of our thoughts and the measure of their correctness. Concepts thus transcend themselves toward what is outside them. They are the way that consciousness, the I, or the cogito gets a grip on the world. Thought is about something; and it is the deliberate and conscious act of an I.

Thought is one activity among others, and is distinct from willing, feeling, and perceiving. It is one faculty alongside others. If the understanding is the understanding that I own, and concepts are understood as products of activities variously described as syntheses, unifications, or modes of grasping a given material independent of thought, it follows that thought amounts to a property, which has to be distinguished from other properties I have.

It also follows that the concept is in itself an empty form. When I have a concept, I have an abstract and universal way of referring to a reality existing as a material singularity outside myself in space and time. When matter saturates the form, this empty form is filled and a contact with the world is established. If abstraction is properly defined by leaving out the sensible qualities of concrete things, concepts are helpful abbreviations that we usually avail ourselves of in order to refer to objects. In short, thought is defined by its not being the thing but its mental elaboration. Thought distinct from the object is residual: it is *just* thought. The I and nature are understood as opposites: the subject of thinking is opposed to the world, like the inner to the outer, the subjective to the given, the form to the content.

If thought is the I's activity of thinking determinate contents about something, it has to be understood not only as the property of consciousness, but also as a form of reflection. Reflection is by its nature a subjective process of hovering over something stable and firm outside us. It does not change or affect its object in the least.

The negation of determinate contents is equally external to the object. When I deny a property, all I do is claim that it does not belong to the object. Whether used as a logical or grammatical function, negation is always the negation posited by an I in a judgment, the assertion of a nonbeing.

As we engage in a philosophical analysis of this conception of thought, we can focus on the content of concepts and stop there (prudently or blindly, depending on the position we are more inclined to) before taking a further step toward the transcendental inquiry of the I-think's positing of its representations. Either way, concepts, judgments, and reflection remain forms opposed to contents and different modes of positing, that is, activities of an I.

In this conception, by "truth" we mean the value of our cognitions and judgments. Truth is an attribute we assign to a judgment after establishing its correspondence with facts. Truth is the result of an attestation, the seal we affix on to the assertion of our belief.

Concepts and judgments have properties studied by disciplines such as logic and psychology which must be able to account for the universality of a concept or the assertion of a judgment. Clarity about the rules and laws of thought is the objective. But laws and rules discipline our thought and impose constraints upon it, so that thought can be said to undergo a necessity that is imposed upon it from without. Its freedom is limited by boundaries that have already been set up from the start. Focusing on a particular concept and on the rules of logic are essentially distinct acts. If in the former we hope to gain an extension in knowledge regarding particular realms of being, the latter aims at the clarification of what is implicit and seems wholly analytical in nature.

Equally external to contents is the method. It can be in turn scientific, analytic, or geometric, but it must systematize beings that are given independently of it. The method actually presupposes them in their givenness. The method must be understood as a form of behaving toward objects; it is a form of organization that bestows an orderly arrangement upon given objects.

Dialectic, understood either as a method of division or as one specific section of logic—the logic of what is probable or the logic of *Schein*, "appearance" or "illusion"—is itself a form of reflection on the thing, unless it is taken in common parlance, such as when one talks about the dialectic between the I and society or among subjects in conflict. Even then, however, as one can see, the dialectic is an external relation between entities that are pre-constituted, presupposed as known, and thereby given prior to the relation itself.

We can further articulate and subdivide this conception of thought. For example, we could say that forms and modes of thinking must be accurately distinguished so that we could admit a rigorous form of thought only with regard to contents expressed in a propositional form. Differ-

THE ACTUALITY OF THOUGHT

ently stated, we could rule out the possibility that other forms of conscious representation, like imagination or feeling, count as thought; or we could be more liberal. We could consider worthy of counting as thought only those contents expressed in universal and objective concepts, leaving aside all that is private, personal, or the object of an indexical reference. Using another example, we may ask whether dreaming—which is after all another way of having representations—is a form of thought or not. Descartes replied to Gassendi's objection that we can take into account the effects of imagination in dreaming, but realizing that we are dreaming is still a distinct act of the pure intellect unmixed with imagination which alone deserves the title of thinking.

What seems excluded from the aforementioned modes is the possibility of unconscious thoughts. Even more outlandish is a thought that is not mine.

For Hegel, not one, not some, but *all* of these theses on thinking represent unproven assumptions that a self-respecting critical philosophy that takes to heart its claim to scientificity cannot accept. Strictly speaking, these theses are not wrong in the ordinary sense of the term. They are one-sided; in other words, they have a range of plausibility and application that is limited and does not exhaust the concept of thinking. Reducing thought to the formal and subjective activity of an I-think is a far-reaching assumption of modern philosophy that jeopardizes its power.

For Hegel, the modern philosophy of reflection is the meeting point of common sense and understanding on the shared ground of what Hegel calls representation (*Vorstellung*). Representation is a way of reflecting on contents and objects presupposed as known and reciprocally external that takes for granted too many unexpressed and arbitrary theses.[3]

The presuppositions accepted uncritically by this conception can be easily identified. In assuming that thought is a form opposed to its content as the mental is to the real, we behave as if we already had a definition of form and reality that is valid and binding for all subsequent development. Thought is understood by reference to its other, but the concept of otherness or the relation between inner and outer are understood as little as the transcendence of consciousness. Relations are employed without clarifying their connection to the relata. This conception takes for granted that thought is the faculty of abstract and discursive reflection without considering alternative possibilities; for example, that thought may pervade through its rational connections what this conception calls the lower faculties—as if there were no rationality in the lived body, in intuition, desire, and feeling.

When we reduce negation, dialectic, method, and even truth to forms external to the thing, we empty them out and condemn them to inaction because we are already intimately convinced of their powerlessness. They become superfluous for the object, whose consistency is not affected in the least by our vain hovering over it. Likewise, once it is reduced to a subjective form of reflection, thought is incapable of actualizing itself, because we take it for granted that reality and thought fall asunder.

In this way, we fail to realize that we constantly raise rubber walls against our questions. By rejecting and pushing our interrogations back on to familiar and beaten paths, we censor our questioning. In other words, we do not realize that we exclude from our examination of conceptual determinations certain categories in favor of others. For example, there is no way we can account for the relation between concepts and laws of thought precisely because we assume that what is binding for thought is imposed from without. Thus, we do not raise the question about the relation between thinking and its laws. We consider principles such as that of identity or noncontradiction as natural necessities that are simply given, just as we take negation to be the opposite of affirmation without wondering where it comes from. We accept all these conceptual relationships in the same way in which we accept that it rains, and we rest content with the analysis of some of their functions and operative applications. Still, these are conceptual relationships, and thinking should be able to verify the value of its concepts in their reciprocal connections as well as to understand itself. Thinking can certainly fail at this; yet this conception of thought assumes from the very start that it cannot even try, because certain constraints are given and prescribed to thought once and for all.

In this way, thought is limited from without. But it is also limited and articulated internally, in a plurality of concepts which is also assumed as immediately given. One of the most sneaking and fundamental theses of this conception holds that the imperative of determinacy goes hand in hand with the plurality of thought. That is, for a concept to be one it must be distinct from other concepts, so that we can only speak of concepts in the plural. But when we say we think determinate contents, what do we mean by content, and how do we distinguish it from the form it supposedly is opposed to? Where does determinacy come from? The question that is not asked is how plurality arises: we simply give it a name, as does Aristotle when he says that being exists as determinate being and divides itself immediately (*euthus: Metaph.* Gamma 2, 1004a4–5) into genera, or as Kant does when he assumes a table of twelve categories overarching the concepts that the I-think goes on to form on its basis. Thought is here pluralized from the outset, but we do not ask ourselves why or how. If thoughts are only in the plural, as self-subsisting determinacies, we do not realize we have already taken them as finite.

THE ACTUALITY OF THOUGHT

Above all, we take for granted important theses about the I and self-consciousness. As original concepts, these are taken as fixed poles that remain self-identical as their predicates change. As such, these concepts are given independently of the body and inferior functions (think of the Cartesian cogito or the Kantian I-think, which are arrived at by difference from the body and inner sense respectively). The identification between subjectivity and the I-think is no less presupposed. However, this conception also fails to question the relation between thinking and thoughts. The relation between the I and its thoughts is a presupposition that falls outside thought. It is an external relation between concepts and the I, which, having objectified concepts in the first place, finds them again like ready-made products whose constitutive genesis it then assigns to logical reflection the task of clarifying.

If the problematic aspects of this philosophical conception are hardly noticed, it is because we have become impervious to Hegel's diagnosis. The rigidity of the understanding is the symptom of the defense mechanism of a thought that feels insecure of itself and powerless. The understanding, in its unwitting passive-aggressive attitude toward reason, does not realize that it constantly cuts corners and relies on the uncritical acceptance of presuppositions—from the externality between thinking and thought and the impossibility of transcending the finite to the derivation of thought from the object.

While it may be clear enough what the arbitrary assumptions of this conception of thought are, it would be surprising if it were equally clear how Hegel can offer different starting points or criteria of analysis. We now turn our attention to that.

The Ellipse and the Squirrel

All logical determinations must be treated homogeneously and systematically precisely because they are all equally conceptual. If it is possible (and we must show how) to conceive of self-consciousness as one subject of thought among others, we cannot accept any uncritical assumption or start out by denying implicit or unconscious thoughts the status of thought. We must recognize the essential difference between explicit thoughts and those implicit forms of representation and thinking that drive and motivate us in our everyday life. We need to retrieve a broader conception of thought, which must be able to refer both to mental states and to those forms that are irreducible to our particular subjectivity, even to what is human.

This invitation might sound disconcerting. In order to lessen its oddity, let me consider two examples. We know mathematics is a human construction; among the constructions that obtain through the variation of the angle of incidence of a plane on a cone, we know different conic sections; we know ellipses to be one of them; after Kepler we also know that planets have elliptical orbits. Now, what is the relation between the geometrical figure of the ellipse and the orbits of planets? We cannot accept the subjectivist view that ellipses are geometric means we use to refer to something that is beyond us anyway, as if we had an elaborate language and then did not dare say it applies to things. Ellipses are somehow *embodied* in the heavenly rotations, while at the same time they cannot be reduced to them. The concept is both in the thing and independent of it: the concept of ellipse exists regardless of orbits, and yet it is actual, that is, it is not the result of an operation of measure in the scientist's mind. It has been real all along, while the fact that it occurred to Kepler in 1603 in order to explain the anomalies and irregular speed of the earth's rotation is a historical fact. So one thing is the cultural reality the concept at some point acquires for us, while quite another is the objective reality of the ellipse as a specific curve accounting for the mathematical order of the solar system. As we can see, different concepts of reality are exhibited along with the traditional assumption about the sensible reality (or physical presence) of objects like the table upon which I write.

Take now the squirrel outside the window. Every organism is a specific relation between parts and whole, which is different from the relation that applies to inanimate objects. An organism keeps itself alive on the basis of an interaction with the environment: the squirrel assimilates the world outside through eating, reproduction, and so on. Hence, we could say that the squirrel embodies a certain relation between means and goals. But if so, then the squirrel is the subject of a life, that is, it subordinates to itself the means it uses to promote itself and realize its ends. An identity maintains itself through its relationship to an alterity. It pursues its own goals, both as an individual and as a species, in everything it does. The squirrel negates what it finds, which it uses and consumes. The world is *for it*, that is, it is relative to its survival. This is an instinctual form of assertion of itself as a subject within its own dynamic and incessant relation to its other.

The squirrel is an example of subjectivity; and subjectivity for Hegel already exists in nature. The squirrel is in the way of a universal that maintains itself through its particular forms (the behavior and functions made possible by its anatomy, the morphology of its organs, etc.). The squirrel, Hegel says, is the actuality of its concept. We must think of the organism as the actualization of a concept, the embodiment of a structure that can be expressed logically—that in fact becomes comprehensible only when it is expressed in terms of the concept. In the organism, the concept actualizes itself through goals. All of this is in contrast to the *timid* conception of Kant's *Critique of the Power of Judgment*, which denies with one hand what it had introduced with the other and cannot assert the objectivity of its principle. If nature as it is known and determined by us is a mechanism, Kant wants us to suppose that organisms are governed by a form of teleology that we, however, have no right to claim is rooted in the object because it is nothing but our own way of reflecting upon it.

These are two examples regarding the actuality of thinking. While the former pushes us to reconsider our vocabulary regarding reality, the latter raises the question of the meaning of subjectivity. There are subjective activities that are not human or cannot be brought back to an I. Thus, subjectivity applies to both animal forms of movement and life as well as to inferior human forms which precede the rise of the conscious I (for example, desire, self-feeling). In other words, subjectivity or self (*Selbst*) occurs when a movement or a process takes place by establishing a center and an active form of self-relation through the negation of alterity (and in turn, the absence of subjectivity is exemplified by mechanical interaction among mutually external forces).

These two examples have been introduced to highlight a notion of thought that cannot be reduced to the subjective thinking of a self-conscious subject. If we now focus on their difference, we can say that the ellipse stands for the mathematical structure of nature, its objective intelligibility, while the squirrel is the active and negative production of a self in its interaction with the world. In the former, rationality is only in itself, that is, in a way that is implicit and hidden in appearance; in the latter, rationality is in the way of an instinct that pushes to assert itself, that is, as a realized end. In the second case we find a teleology that is absent in the first and is in turn different from the intentional teleology by which I realize an end willfully when I go out to see a friend, read a book, or strangle my neighbor.

Before this self-conscious teleology, thinking is unconscious in two different ways. In one sense, thinking can be unconscious *to the I* when the I does not know it, and this indicates the various non-reflective activities with which Hegel's Philosophy of Subjective Spirit thematically deals (thinking is operative in myself without my noticing it, from its most elementary psychophysical forms up to pre-linguistic intelligence). Here the unconscious can be understood when it is translated into known conceptual determinations. Even though unconscious thought cannot be exhausted without residue through the process of becoming conscious, nonetheless it is transformed through its being known. Otherwise, and this is the second sense, unconsciousness can be a form of thought that is at work everywhere, in nature as well as spirit. In this case, thinking is unconscious because it is the substance and truth of the world, and this is what Hegel's *Science of Logic* and his *Encyclopaedia* call objective thought. Here knowledge includes the unconscious, yet this remains the soul of things: for example, in nature, the contradiction between the conceptual inner and the accidental outer, between intelligibility and appearance, persists, and it is not resolved or transformed when it is understood and conceptualized (*ENZ* §248 A).

We unconsciously employ the categories of thinking in everything we do. If Hegel pokes fun at the idea that logic must serve the purpose of learning to think (an idea which is as inappropriate as the claim that we learn how to digest by studying physiology: *WL* I, 14, *SL* 8), it is because we think instinctively just as we digest naturally. There is a natural logic at work in our every act. It is up to conscious thinking to highlight the unconscious logic of the world.

If these are all thinking's modes of being, then they cannot be considered separately from each other. Our philosophical task is in fact that of investigating the relation between the ellipse, the squirrel, and our intention in conceptual terms: we must treat them as bound by a relation among thought-determinations. If thought must constitute the object of a unitary examination, it must focus on the difference among its forms, and in particular and most fundamentally on the difference between the unconscious life of reason that asserts itself instinctively in the world and its self-conscious life in its knowledge of itself.

As it turns out, however, it is not enough to say that there are different modes of thought. We need to *invert* the perspective and argue that it is thought that gives itself different forms of existence by acting in different ways. In particular, thought divides itself into objective intelligibility, which works as passive reason, and self-knowledge, which is the highest form of rational activity. If the different forms of thought must be examined as conceptual determinations included between these two extremes, and if the development of thought-determinations from the simplest to the most complete must be construed as a deductive system governed by inner necessity, then we must say that it is thinking that exhibits and articulates itself in such a concatenation.

This is why Hegel writes in the *Encyclopaedia* that philosophy must show the conceptual necessity of its objects, which are also the laws and the concepts of particular sciences (*ENZ* §9). In this sense, the second preface to the *Science of Logic* reads:

THE ACTUALITY OF THOUGHT

> *There is* a multitude of concepts. . . . But *a* concept is also, first of all, in itself *the* concept, and this concept is only one concept, the substantial foundation; it is of course also a *determinate* concept, and it is this determinateness that appears in it as content even though, in fact, it is a form determination of the substantial unity of the concept, a moment of the form as totality, *of the concept itself* which is the foundation of the determinate concepts. This concept . . . is only subject matter, the product and content *of thought*, the fact that exists in and for itself, the *logos*, the reason of that which is, the truth of what we call things; it is least of all the *logos* that should be kept outside the science of logic. (*WL* I, 29–30, *SL* 19)

It is the concept over which nothing external and given can exercise any authority that determines and divides itself ("The concept must show that it itself holds the source of the determinations," *WL* I, 57, *SL* 38). The concept divides itself into being and subjective concept, namely, into thinking as it is and thinking as it knows itself. It follows that Hegel's philosophy, which is the self-understanding of the concept, must grasp the concept's most estranged and unconscious forms. As a result, Hegel's philosophy is a theory of thinking in its widest sense.

Another fundamental point concerns the fact that, precisely because such a theory does not presuppose anything as given, it cannot even presuppose the difference between theory and practice. Those who expect a speculative analysis of merely theoretical concepts, like those of pre-Kantian metaphysics and ontology, would be surprised to find, among Hegel's most important categories, the concept of life. They would be no less surprised to find out that the term "chemism" is indifferently used to speak of natural compounds as well as of a scientific approach to psychology; that mechanism applies to natural forces as well as to certain conceptions of right, physiology, and pedagogy (*ENZ* §195 Z); that the idea of the good is examined after the idea of the true (the true and the good are actually the two forms of the activity of the idea, *ENZ* §225); and that Hegel's main example of the understanding's procedure is not the fixed and reciprocally isolated concepts of natural science, but rather the firmness of a goal-oriented character (which returns at *W* 3, 36, *PhS* 18–19; *WL* II, 285, *SL* 538; and *ENZ* §80 Z and §467 Z).

The premise to this move is a straightforward one: the transformation, which Hegel ascribes to Kant, of metaphysics into logic.[4] A philosophical logic must be able to examine every position that uses logical categories and conceptual organizations. For the logical element constitutes the warp and the weft that weave together all forms of nature and spirit. However, the logical element must be investigated independently of such forms of actualization and self-estrangement.[5] Thus the logic, as a theory of thinking and of all the conceptual connections organizing being, takes the place of the old metaphysics and ontology, but only as it is purified from the substrates of representation, that is, devoid of the reference to special objects it purports to describe in conceptual terms (God, the world, the soul, being).

Hegel's Philosophy as the Systematic Reversal of the Familiar

Speaking of metaphysics, I would like to dwell for a moment on one peculiar sense of that word. I am not going to comment on the recent debate concerning the metaphysical or anti-metaphysical import of Hegel's logic. It seems to me that it takes speculative acrobatics to deny the obvious and not to concede that we are ascribing to the terms at stake meanings foreign to Hegel.[6] On the other hand, a metaphysics or a logic that applies uncritical restrictions and obstructs the fluidity of thought cannot be a solution. If scholastic metaphysics, most notably the pre-Kantian German metaphysics, was precisely the logic of the understanding which takes its objects from representation (*ENZ* §30) and proceeds dogmatically, the reason is the presumption that it is possible to grasp the in-itself without undertaking an examination of the dialectical development of concepts. This is an approach that pre-Kantian metaphysics shares with Kant (*WL* I, 131, *SL* 119; *ENZ* §124 Z). In this sense, Hegel criticizes the presupposition of a metaphysics whose attitude is to grasp being in itself regardless of thought (which it turns into a reflection external to being).

I would like instead to introduce another sense of metaphysics: a metaphysics of negativity, of an imagination that displaces and wreaks havoc in sedimented habits of thought as it subverts what is familiar and counts as obvious. If all immediacy is an appearance that hides a mediation, and if all givenness must be examined in light of the becoming that has generated it; and if philosophy, rather than simply marking a distance from common sense, must be the systematic pursuit of the reversal from within of what is familiar from representation, then Hegel is a stern metaphysician in this sense—in fact, the most metaphysical thinker I know. Where others look at the surface of simple facts in their fixed and unrelated externality, Hegel, like a visionary of the real, sees in them the forces that have generated them. He can describe them as processes that refer to one another and the reification of a becoming because he wants to bring back to light an image of the whole. His philosophy owes much to imagination and is the archenemy of positivism: it revokes what is accepted, it negates the obvious, it keeps possibilities alive for the sake of understanding when facts have decided otherwise, it turns the gaze away from the given it puts in question in order to enable the conception of an alternative development. Despite all the positive aspects of his philosophy (especially his political philosophy, which for this reason has been considered a justification of the existent), Hegel invites us to question what appears immediately, on the basis of which we build our certainties. His entire philosophy is the reversal and redefinition of the concepts we use. This overturn is more radical, unprecedented, and systematic than the Socratic criticism of *doxa*. To study Hegel means to be unsettled, disoriented, displaced. Without this subjective proneness to reconsider one's own position, retrace one's steps, and subvert what seems known in its obviousness, not only the profound novelty of Hegel's philosophy will go unnoticed, but its very sense is bound to remain elusive.[7] What eludes us is the need to abandon a largely shared ethos through the criticism of the model of thought and the I prevalent in the modern age.

Humboldt complained about the lack of imagination in Hegel's language.[8] Actually, it seems to me that Hegel is the most counterintuitive thinker we can read, to the point that the large success his philosophy has enjoyed for decades cannot stop surprising us. Among all the inversions of the terms of our vocabulary, the re-semantization relative to thinking and the I is the most crucial as well as the most obscure. According to Ricoeur, a paradox disorients, yet it has the effect of reorienting our gaze. It is in this spirit that I think we must interpret Hegel's inversions concerning thought.

In order to understand thinking, we cannot start from the I as if this were the hidden director that monitors, overviews, and manages every thought we have. Quite the contrary, the decision that inaugurates this move is the *prôton pseudos*. The I is but one of the modes that thinking gives itself for its self-actualization. Human consciousness, Hegel says in the *Lectures on the Philosophy of Religion*, is "the material in and through which the concept carries out its plan" (*VPhR* 71). Already in the preface to the *Phenomenology*, we read that the formative education which from the side of the individual "consists in his acquiring what thus lies at hand, devouring his inorganic nature, and taking possession of it for himself" must be then considered from the point of view of "universal Spirit as substance[:] this is nothing but its own acquisition of self-consciousness, the bringing-about of its own becoming and reflection into itself" (*W* 3, 33, *PhS* 16–17).

The identification between spirit and substance in this passage should not mislead us. Hegel does not intend to replace the beginning from the I with a Spinozistic premise. In other words, it does not suffice to change the starting point. Better yet, Hegel is Spinozist only because the only requirement he assigns to thinking is the systematic investigation of a totality that is devoid of presuppositions. The study of logic requires a rationality that develops its own contents thoroughly in the form of a progressive generation. All forms of linearity and univocity are ruled out from this procedure just as much as all empirical and positive criteria and all original debt to experience. Hegel's speculative language is animated by thought's relentless return to itself and to the relationship between meaning and expression. If the language of representation maintains its rights, including that of not being bothered by Socrates's gadfly, then speculative language is the constant reconsideration of the concepts we use. This shows that it is not only being that is said in many ways, as in the Aristotelian metaphysics. *All* fundamental concepts are said in many ways, and their different meanings require their continuous going back to themselves. This is their dialectic: a lexicon in the making, a dictionary of all philosophical concepts exhibited in their development, where nouns are provisional designations of knots to be untangled rather than titles of a possible solution. Kant asserts the principle according to which representations have no identity unless they are the result of a synthesis and an active reproduction in the necessary unity of the subject of thought. Likewise, in Hegel the dialectical movement of conceptual determinations shows their identity to be one moment. The dialectic is a synthetic and progressive movement that does not find rest in what is merely affirmative and unrelated to its other. Determinations do not have a definite identity once and for all, but live through the relation to their other. They have a role, a function, and a positional value that changes depending on the interaction with their other. Hence, it is not possible to give a univocal definition of thought-determinations. They must be shown in their use.

Language presupposes an ontology made up of distinct entities as well as grammatical and syntactical structures that are notable for their separateness. Language is thus the work of the understanding insofar as it fixates its objects in their identity, whereas dialectic must be able to show their contradictoriness, their becoming, their movement, their fluidity, their plasticity. In its claim to scientificity the understanding, and the ordinary conception of thinking that shares this attitude, takes meanings literally. It requires univocity, determinacy, stable identity. It seeks normativity, and opposes rules to use. It admits metaphors, analogies, rhetorical tropes, and imaginative figures of speech to the extent that they are devoid of cognitive value. Poets are at liberty to deviate from fixed meanings, but at the price of futility. By contrast, in its sensitivity to different layers in language, meaning-shift, and plurivocity, dialectic recognizes potentialities of meaning where the understanding sees only illegitimate, or playful, divergences from accepted norms. Dialectic, however, does not have its peculiar language. The pages on the speculative sentence in the preface to the *Phenomenology* in particular are the demonstration of the limits of language from a reflection internal to it. Hegel's logic can therefore only use the existing language to subvert it from within.

In Freud, displacement (*Verschiebung*) is one of the mechanisms that makes possible the work of dream. It collaborates with repression and the forces that block access to meaning. In Hegel, something similar to Freudian displacement is the deliberate result of the work of philosophy: dispossession, decentering, inversion of value. For this reason, each concept draws its sense and truth relative to what precedes and what follows it, and each concept must be examined as a movement in light of its genesis and its outcome. This is why we can say that identity is one shape of movement among others.

This reconceptualization, this re-semantization of our whole system of thought, this recasting of our vocabulary is the effect of Hegel's new logic. His logic is not new because it is unprecedented (think of the importance of Aristotle's metaphysics for him), but because it is bound to sound new to those who are not used to stepping out of the habitual styles of thought of modern philosophy and common sense. From another point of view, it is the modern principle according to which we understand best what *we have made ourselves* that Hegel subscribes to when he says that the best a child can do with a toy is to break it.[9] Tearing a toy to pieces is the first test of the object's independence; breaking its mechanism apart is the first step toward reconstructing it. Only thus can we grasp its organization, structure, functioning: its inner principle.

Only in this way does one understand the dynamics of thought and overcome the naive understanding of *theôria* as the faith in thought's ability to reproduce things as they are, unaltered by thinking. If so, however, one cannot help but raise the question anew: Did we really make what we find? In the terms of this book, this is the underlying question: What role does the thinker play in relation to thought?

I have not yet explained why I found it important to write a book on Hegel. I start out from an observation that voices, as I am well aware, my personal impression: although Hegel is used and talked about a lot, he is not studied much. We could learn a lot from him, and yet the appropriation of Hegel's thought is no longer as rich and multifaceted as it was, for instance, in the 1930s or in the 1970s at the hands of different philosophical traditions. What passes for Hegel today is increasingly the result of a cultural and academic operation which is certainly justified in a country like the United States where this tendency was originally introduced, but it is often incidental. In its eagerness to make Hegel more accessible and viable to a philosophical tradition that is naturally hostile to systematic thought, metaphysics, and theology, this interpretation seeks to smooth all that is scandalous and controversial in the inversions and displacements of dialectical thought by polishing its alleged excesses. It thus loses sight of the heart of Hegel's philosophy. This book aims to bring to light some important outcomes of Hegel's philosophy while not engaging thematically with a debate which seems to me misleading, extrinsic, and above all ideological. The inspiration of my work is the Hegelian notion of critique. My hope is that this book could be useful to rediscovering the vitality of a classic that risks getting transfigured and buried by the very desire to update it and render it palatable.

Here is an overview. In the first chapter, I argue that subjectivity and the I are distinct concepts. To begin philosophy with the I is a misconception of modern philosophy. Self-consciousness is not an original given, but must be expounded in its genesis. I dwell on the *Phenomenology of Spirit* and on the concept of recognition which, as I intend to show, is not sufficient to ground self-consciousness. I conclude with the point that in my view sustains the discussion of self-consciousness in Hegel: individual self-consciousness is derivative. What speculative thought must show is the self-consciousness of substance. It is science that has to exhibit itself as a subject; it is the concept that represents the most fundamental form of self.

In this manner I pave the way for the thematic discussion of thought, and in the second chapter I introduce the Hegelian concept of thinking as irreducible to human thinking. I clarify the themes around which such nonhuman thinking is articulated in the *Science of Logic* as well as in the *Encyclopaedia*: objective thought, the logic animating the world as an unconscious nature, the primacy of the concept that makes itself real. Finally, I show the paradoxical character of retrieving the I—now as concrete universality and negative self-relation, no longer as an individual subject presupposed as a self-identical pole—as the logical dynamics internal to thinking.

In the third chapter I propose a reading of the movement of thought in Hegel as a spontaneity which finds its determinate form and reifies itself in it in order to regain itself as self-knowledge. Fluidity of thoughts and arrest in determinate forms are equally constitutive elements of thought's activity. I clarify the concept of the nature of thought, which stresses the importance of its passive objectification, and the productivity of thinking. More than elsewhere, here I draw on the analyses of my previous work, take up some of its conclusions, and offer a new angle to show the importance of the Aristotelian intellect for Hegel.[10] The *nous*, which has no form in itself so as to be able to become each form it thinks in turn, is the model for the self-determination of thought in Hegel. Thought is in itself free, has no content, order, or rules, but if it wants to claim anything at all it must give itself particular contents, an order and rules. The second and third chapters express the necessity to distance ourselves from certain contemporary readings of Hegel's thought and show that Hegel's philosophy is not reducible either to a metaphysical realism or to a new form of transcendental philosophy.

In the fourth chapter I consider the relationship between representation and concept in Hegel. The logic of representation is one of the modes of the self-determination of thought which needs to objectify itself in a second nature in which it is free to move at ease. The logic of language is an essential moment of this process: the critique of the form of judgment and the speculative sentence represent one of the best illustrations of the dialectic and the movement of thought—what philosophy can and ought to do. In this chapter I focus particularly on Hegel's introduction to the *Encyclopaedia* and on the Philosophy of Subjective Spirit, as well as on the final pages of the preface to the *Phenomenology of Spirit*.

The fifth chapter, which is far longer than the others, concerns the relationship between Kant and Hegel and deserves a more extensive comment.

Hegel and the Critique of Kant

In my view, Hegel's critique of Kant is not among the best teachings we can still draw from his philosophy. In it I believe that Hegel does not live up to his extraordinary philosophical sharpness, not only because he is sometimes arbitrary and tendentious, but above all because, if only Hegel had had a less biased reading of Kant, he could have offered a tighter confrontation with him which unfortunately he does not deliver. We will see why in the fifth and final chapter of this book. However, I wish to point out straight away that the subtitle of this book, which is also the title of this section, is intentionally ambiguous. It suggests on a descriptive level the critical reading proposed by Hegel against Kant. But I would like it also, and more provocatively, to suggest that it would be instructive to try to imagine how Kant could have replied to Hegel, an attempt the likes of which in the secondary literature I find to be surprisingly lacking.

For Hegel, Kant reduces reason to the intellect, thinking to the finite I, and so on. Using my earlier terms, we could say that Hegel seems reluctant to venture beyond the familiar to which he lends an idle, curt, and dismissive word. He thereby falls short of his dialectical imagination. His critique of Kant lacks the boldness and the critical attitude one can find, for instance, in his extraordinary reading of Aristotle, for what is basically missing are the generosity and interest pushing him to look beneath the surface. In the case of Aristotle, Hegel aims at bringing back to life after an unfair century-long oblivion the speculative philosopher par excellence. In the case of Kant, by contrast—the father of the philosophical revolution in the wake of which Hegel thinks he is living—Hegel does not make an analogous effort at revitalizing the true philosopher beyond the aporetic developments brought about by Kant's diverse followers in the last decade of the eighteenth century. Moreover, after 1802 Hegel often tends to repeat what he had grasped about Kant and expressed in *Faith and Knowledge* without ever seriously reconsidering the plausibility of his judgments. Of such a reconsideration Hegel proves he is perfectly capable when, for example, in his mature years he revises the verdict of his Jena years on Jacobi (in the review of Jacobi's writings, as well as in the third position of thought with regard to objectivity in the *Encyclopaedia*).

As for Kant, it is also true for Hegel that "the fact that the human being can have the 'I' in his representations raises him infinitely above all other living beings on earth" (Kant, *Anthr.* §1, *Ak* 7, 127; Eng. trans. 239). The I divides itself from itself and overcomes mere self-feeling. In thinking, the I separates itself from itself; the I is actually such duplicity. Like Kant, Hegel avails himself of many meaningful analogies in order to describe the activity of thought.[11] For both, however, these analogies almost never turn around the role of the I. Like Kant, Hegel speaks of philosophy in terms of work. While Kant talks about the need, the interest, the fate, the satisfaction, and the ends of reason understood as organism and system, Hegel emphasizes the concept as restlessness, labor, movement, Self. It is essential that the concept be as much restlessness as Self. Restlessness is an impulse and a force; as such, it does not coincide with itself, but this difference is internal to a unitary subject of becoming that strives to find itself. Philosophy does not begin in wonder and desire to contemplate, but out of division. Only when thinking reconsiders retrospectively its own realization in the form of absolute spirit (or in the shadowy regions of speculative thought) does it contemplate itself, but this is because thinking retreats from the sphere of conflict in which it naturally lives into the calm regions of pure thought. Even though philosophy is not at all a form of therapy à la Wittgenstein, it is the coming

THE ACTUALITY OF THOUGHT

back to oneself from the lacerations of the epoch: it is the willingness to restore the whole.

Among the most meaningful traits of the Hegelian description of the concept's work is the duplicity of assimilation and arrest. While in the former the work of the concept consists of the process of internalizing, digesting, and appropriating, one of the most recurrent verbs to describe the latter is *festhalten*, "to hold fast." Holding fast can be the action of the hand or of the gaze; it indicates the use of force to halt a movement. However, if this is an unnatural or violent act, it also refers to attention, as well as all indispensable concentration that divides, isolates from the context, and lets things stand out against a background. It also refers to the violence we exercise upon ourselves to avoid distraction and the imposition of our opinions onto the matter at stake. Holding fast is the culture of determinacy, wherein—as in every form of work for Hegel—what is cultivated is both the determinate object *and* the subject, who is educated and transformed through work. If, as we have just seen, concepts are nothing but different modes of the concept or thought, then holding fast is the arrest of a spontaneity that is supposed to be original. While the process of assimilation has often been misunderstood as the vain and arrogant impulse to absorb reality, what matters in the arrest is the will and sustained effort at being faithful to the thing itself. As we will see, the work of the concept combines objective thinking—the imperative to let the thing speak for itself without subjective impositions—and the tendency to fixation typical of the understanding. Yet this understanding is not the competitor of reason, but one, if not the most fundamental, mode of reason's function.

In my book *The Powers of Pure Reason*,[12] I focused on an unsolved tension in Kant's philosophy between two pictures of reason included in the Architectonic of the *Critique of Pure Reason*. Reason is a seed or germ (*Keim*), from which an organism stems and develops internally as a systematically articulated unity, and it is also an architect that plans the project of the building of laws, the system of reason's a priori cognitions. The fact, however, that reason is an end to itself and that it sets itself ends are two quite different notions of teleology, just like the purposiveness of humans as natural beings is different from their finality as will beyond nature. This tension underlies a reason that as an organism finds itself with a life it is has not contributed at all to have and a reason that is but the result of its own efforts. Organic and poietic models, life and constructive activity, are indeed similar, but they ultimately point to descriptions that cannot help but contrast with one another. In the organic model, the living body does have its inner purposiveness, but this is established from the start, and each member of the species naturally accomplishes its own course. By contrast, the architectonic model presupposes the individual that stands out from the species in order to produce something new. Among the consequences of such tension is another difficulty. Reason is not the reason of an I, and yet it works by means of an I. The problems of reason and the problems of the I are placed at different levels, and sometimes it is not easy to keep them apart. Most notably, it is not easy to understand to what extent reason is an anonymous force that operates through the I, like a seed independent of individuality, will, and human subjectivity, and to what extent reason is mixed up with the subjectivity of an individual I.[13]

Hegel does not seem to realize that he inherits this same tension. For Hegel reason is not theoretical, but defines itself as the instinct to be at one with itself, at home in the world. Reason is desire, will, and the search for itself in a world that has to become its own second nature. Hence, thought is life and inner force, and at the same time also absolute self-consciousness, the knowledge of its own self-realization in the world. The separation between eros and logos no longer applies, and in fact we find in Kant and Hegel the eroticizing of logos. Naturally, the forms taken on by such affective reason are quite different in the two of them. The Hegelian solution to this tension, as we shall see, is as different from the Kantian one as is the relationship between reason and I. Yet, in order to better understand this difference, I believe it is necessary to go beyond the Hegelian overcoming of Kant as the philosopher of a powerless and empty subjectivity and retrieve in this tension, which is decisive for Kant, the most vital and important core that drives both philosophers.

1

Hegel on Recognition

Self-Consciousness, Individuality, and Intersubjectivity

Se vuol ballare signor contino
il chitarrino le suonerò

If you want to dance, little count,
I'll play the guitar.
— Lorenzo da Ponte, *Le Nozze di Figaro*

Imagining the Other?

By and large, in modern philosophy the social dimension is made possible by an imaginative effort that projects me outside myself and the self-centered horizon of my consciousness. In this view, the other is the result of an inference from our originally self-enclosed mental sphere. Imagination and sociality go hand in hand in Hobbes, Rousseau, Hume, and Smith.

Kant shares this view only in part. For him reason makes itself real by declining itself in the singularity of the first-person perspective and taking on the form of the I-think in the speculative realm, and in the practical sphere in the form of the laws that govern my agency. In both dimensions, I must think for myself and be consistent with myself. However, the maxim of *Selbstdenken* (thinking for oneself), Kant says in the *Critique of the Power of Judgment*, must be tempered with the maxim according to which I ought to think from the standpoint of others (*KU* §40, *Ak* 5, 294, Eng. trans. 174). This is not an alleged intersubjective conception of the I-think, for it is not a problem concerning knowledge but the way of thinking needed to make a purposive use of reason (*KU* §40, *Ak* 5, 295, Eng. trans. 175). A shared way of thinking, by means of which I think in the position of others, is necessary. And yet it is not others like myself that I take into account. The possible judgments of others must guide my reflection, because what I aim at is putting myself in the position of *any other* (*KU* §40, *Ak* 5, 294, Eng. trans. 174). In other words, I do not aim at my other, whether actual or possible, but rather at a form of shared thinking that Kant calls "communal sense." I broaden or extend my own *Denkungsart* not thanks to reason, but through imagination, which orients and guides my power of judgment.

Even though it is imagination that enables me to abstract from my individual perspective, unlike his predecessors, Kant does not presuppose sociability as a disposition, let alone a given reality. He makes it instead the criterion of communal sense, which in turn is but the idea of a measure we try to approximate as we reflect, the aim and ideal of an enlarged mentality (*KU* §40; *Ak* 5, 294; Eng. trans. 174; see also *Anthr.*, *Ak* 7, 139–40).

If we now consider an alternative model to reach intersubjectivity from an egological premise, that is, Husserl's, we soon realize that, unlike the imaginative and empathetic identification we find in Smith, there is a relevant effort to account for the fundamental asymmetry between I and thou. Unlike any form of Cartesianism, the other is not the result of an inference. The purity of the I does not lead back to a cogito, a disembodied ego that stands against the world, but rather to an I-can (*Ich kann*), the substrate of habitualities, the personal history of the intentionalities that inhabit a lived body. Rather than a Cartesian or Kantian I, we have a monad with all windows open.

In the words of the fifth of Husserl's *Cartesian Meditations*, I make an effort to consider alien bodies as expressions of an intentionality similar to my own, so I do not take them as physical bodies but as animated organisms that manifest goals and intentions, that is, as subjectivity. My reality, then, will not consist of the totality of objects that are given to me, but will also include a community of other egos. Hence, the effort is that of opening up a solipsistic perspective so as to make it overcome its boundaries. The other cannot be perceived as such; what makes him or her a person and animates his or her body is apperceived in the form of an assimilation of motives that can never replace the asymmetry between I and thou. For Husserl, the other is not meant on the basis of what I perceive, but also of what is potential in my own experience and by analogy with my own possibilities.

The other is only for an I, and yet he or she is not reducible to my representation, for he or she is transcendent and independent of me. But if so, I can never identify myself with another. Unlike Smith's view, the other is recognized as foreign. Even when he says that I constitute the other, Husserl means that, although I get to the other from the perspective of my own lived body, I cannot objectify him or her. In short, the other is not reducible to the I, but it must be recognized in his or her alterity from the only perspective available to me, that is, my own. In turn, what I imagine is not one presentification of an absent being among others, but a form of apperception, that is, a coincidence that I know is unreachable and that for me always bears the mark of its impossibility. Reciprocity is achieved starting from an asymmetry I can never overcome.

If we now ask why such primacy of imagination in intersubjectivity is so foreign to Hegel, the strong suspicion arises that for Hegel it is precisely the egological perspective that must be overcome. But how? How does Hegel tackle the problem, and how does he intend to go beyond egology? The solution cannot be entrusted to catchphrases such as the famous appeal of his Jena writings to the Aristotelian priority of the polis over the individual.

The subject matter of this chapter is the problem of the relationship between I and we, between subjectivity and the I, between individuality and intersubjectivity, and finally between self-consciousness and recognition. What I would like to do is clarify why the I and subjectivity are quite distinct notions. Furthermore, I would like to focus on the genesis of self-consciousness and explain, through the discussion of Hegel's famous pages on lordship and bondage in the *Phenomenology of Spirit*, why recognition, in contrast to what many interpreters claim, is unable to ground the concept of self-consciousness. Eventually, I want to prepare the ground for the transition to the following chapters concerning thinking in Hegel by showing the necessity that consciousness understand the concept as a self, the subject and substance of its own becoming.

Soul, Consciousness, and Self-Consciousness

We have seen that the Hegelian notion of the subject is broader than that of the I. Subject means the potentiality of being in relation to oneself in the development and interaction with its other. The squirrel is a subject and has a self, but it cannot say "I." Apparently Hegel thinks that for the human being there must be a pre-egological subjectivity, and that the I arises at some point in tandem with the oppositions that consciousness faces, but must not be presupposed at the lower levels in which it has itself as its object. That it is possible to *be a subject* without *having an I* is a theme we can find in the reflections that take shape in the Jena period, but which becomes thematic in the mature philosophy of subjective spirit which brings this knot to the fullest clarity.

CHAPTER 1

To aid the comprehension of these pages, I believe it may be helpful to illustrate this point through a comparison between two models that I would like to present as partially akin: Freud and Husserl. Common to Freud and Husserl is a stratification from an impersonal and anonymous stage toward a personal level up to a supra-personal one.[1] As in the structural model id–ego–superego, we bear witness to a conflict between different demands, and the I is nothing but a compromise formation. Likewise, in Husserl's genetic phenomenology, the I is formed as an active pole starting with passive syntheses in order to get finally to what Husserl calls cultural substructions. For both, the psychic dimension is not identical to consciousness.[2] Consciousness is not identical to the I because the dynamics of becoming conscious are a magmatic substrate in contrast to which the I is already clearly delineated, almost de jure, like the owner of one's own acts. Consciousness and the I must not be presupposed as original and constituted from the outset; rather, they supervene as a later formation on the unconscious as well as on spontaneity in passivity. Since they represent the purpose of a specific development, they are not inborn or granted like a natural right.

For Freud and Husserl, the problem is to explain how a latency becomes an explicit presence that is self-responsible. For both, a form of teleology applies respectively to the Freudian principle *wo Es war, soll Ich werden* (where id was, there shall ego be) and to the I that in Husserl is an awakening and turning toward one's own affectivity (receptivity is the lowest level of the activity of the ego, as *Experience and Judgment* §17 has it). The differences between Freud and Husserl are relevant, but secondary in this context. What needs underlining for our present purposes is that the I is formed starting from an unconscious and affective basis on which it depends. The I seeks to blur such dependency and master its own basis, so that we can define the I as the impulse to rule upon itself. Obviously, in order to feel such a need and willingness to assert itself as its own master, the I must perceive a threat or a state of minority in its dependence on the world, the body, the unconscious. Differently stated, the I defines itself by reference to actuality and is the function of its own weakness or force with regard to it. The I and actuality are correlative functions, but they are derivative of something that is more indefinite and original. In Freud, the id does not know of time or negation, since it only obeys the principle of pleasure, and the I is a demand of reasonableness toward actuality in its relation to possibility. In Husserl, the tendency to objectification that forgets its ties with the life-world in order to produce sciences and cultural formations is defined by contrast with a functioning rationality which precedes objectivity as an anonymous ground (*Boden*).

HEGEL ON RECOGNITION

Something analogous can be found, well before Freud and Husserl, in Hegel's Philosophy of Subjective Spirit.[3] Consciousness is neither the source of meaning nor an origin. The I is a formation of mediation and is defined relative to the objective sphere of which it is itself the condition. More importantly, the I is the stage of a *conflict*: the conflict which at some point occurs against corporeality. Let us see how this happens. In the Anthropology we deal with the soul, that is to say, with the forms of life that belong to the psychophysical being in which spirit finds itself living. This is a stage characterized by lack of distinction and absence of opposition. It is the mode of being of the lived body, which is not one thing in the world among others or an I yet, but rather logos made flesh, meaning embodied in affective dispositions, in which we find ourselves living and on which we depend. When the need to dominate one's own affects occurs, the subject takes a stand and becomes consciousness. It distinguishes itself from the object it relates to, and distances itself from itself. Through various practices of self-governance the soul becomes an I, and this represents the victory of the soul over the lived body ("der Sieg der Seele über ihre Leiblichkeit").[4] This is the soul's appropriation of the lived body, which reduces it to a sign and the permeable tool of its own activity. The I is formed thus: as a *dualization* of the self, as the return to itself from the lived body and opposition to objectivity. At the same time, this can only happen inasmuch as the I forgets it is a result.

The Hegelian unconscious is naturally conceived in a very different way from the Freudian id because it refers to a modality of logos and spirit and is not a demand substantialized into a subject of repression, resistance, and deflection. The unconscious in Hegel is what is not yet an explicit and conscious object of thought. As a result, the unconscious is pervaded by the same negativity that we find everywhere in Hegel. Unlike Freud, for Hegel negation does not happen only in consciousness. In turn, the unconscious is an adjective and not a noun. Any resistances to the self-transparency of spirit in Hegel are set by nature. They do not have to be vanquished through an analytic and personal work or with the aid of an affective transference. The Hegelian unconscious is closer to the anonymous and functioning moment in Husserl, to the latency that is not yet present to consciousness. As in Husserl, in Hegel the I is an awakening and return to itself. The wakeful and philosophical life of reason that is aware of itself takes its own latent and functioning activity as its object and turns those habitualities that appeared to consciousness as given into explicit sense-units and discrete concepts. Both Hegel and Husserl aim at overcoming the traditional dichotomy between the passivity of sense and the activity of consciousness in order to understand the spontaneity at stake in receptivity. Yet, unlike Husserl and Freud, in

Hegel this point is not restricted to human subjectivity, and it soon ends up involving a trans-human dimension that has nothing derivative. For Hegel the greatest problem, as we will see in chapter 2, is precisely the relationship between the I and a trans-human concept of thought.

Let us now turn our attention to the Anthropology, the first section of the Philosophy of Subjective Spirit in the *Encyclopaedia.* Hegel investigates how our immediate life is a psychophysical totality, wherein activities and manifestations are the functions proper to a lived body animated by a subjectivity that seeks to emerge but does not yet own itself. We could aid the understanding of this point by referring (as does Kant at the opening of his *Anthropology*) to the stages of evolution of a human being who during infancy has not yet mastered the use of the first-person pronoun. However, this illustration should not induce us to forget that at *each* stage of human life there are processes and states that can be analyzed without any need to resort to an I (or that there are lapses and suspensions of the I like madness and dream, i.e., possibilities ever-present for any developed adult of losing oneself more or less temporarily). From the unreflective relation to the natural environment to the alternation of dream and wakefulness, from the embodiment of affects to immediate sensations, from proprioception to self-feeling, the soul does entertain a constant relationship to oneself but does not exhibit the division necessary in order to have an I.

With regard to all these forms, Hegel speaks of soul because they are equally pervaded by a subjectivity that remains opaque to itself. The subject that is in immediate unity with its naturalness is not self-conscious. Nevertheless, the lived body, wherein each part is animated by subjectivity, is the basis for the subsequent consciousness, which is therefore not a disembodied cogito but a reflexive coming back to itself from naturalness.

As the soul progressively appropriates the environment by appropriating the body, which thus becomes its tool and the sign of its dispositions, an active relationship develops between the subject and what only then begins to be objectified in the form of an other to be vanquished. Put differently, at first we can refer to a fully developed and self-certain subject only proleptically, by anticipation. More importantly, we cannot speak of an opposition between subject and object until a division in such a natural unity is produced. Only then is reflexivity possible, and only then does a return to itself in the form of an aggregation and subordination of one's own modes to an identical I begin to develop.

When in the *Science of Logic* Hegel criticizes "a more original beginning to philosophy which has recently gained notoriety, the beginning with the 'I'" (*WL* I, 76, *SL* 53), his motive is straightforward: one assumes

(Hegel has in mind Fichte, but also a large part of modern philosophy) a notion with which everybody is familiar without considering that it is an abstraction. Thus, one slips a foreign body into the thought of the thing where it is least needed. For Hegel, the I is abstract because it has become, that is, it is a result and not an original given, which is nonetheless uncritically employed as a first principle.

At the end of the Anthropology, the soul has separated itself from its own immediacy and opposes it in the form of inert matter that must not resist the force with which the soul shapes it. In this way the soul awakens as abstract universality, that is to say, as consciousness or an I which repels from itself the totality of its own natural determinations and turns them into a world of external objects. Thus begins the section entitled Phenomenology, which in turns preludes to the section called Psychology. While specifically we have further subsequent stages of soul, consciousness, self-consciousness, and finally of spirit, in general the movement of this part of the *Encyclopaedia* becomes clear at the end, when Hegel clarifies why he writes that the soul awakens as consciousness and consciousness posits itself as self-knowing reason (*ENZ* §387). Literally, the titles "Phenomenology" and "Psychology" refer respectively to the appearance of spirit in the form of consciousness and to the investigation of spirit as it has internalized its lower stages and knows itself as spirit. Soul, consciousness, and self-consciousness are the modes in which reason appears, as the unity that has become out of its distinct moments (*ENZ* §413). Here too, as we can see, an inversion is necessary, so that the final stage we painstakingly reach starting from the simplest element is actually the unitary subject of its diverse modes of existence. It is reason that appears as soul, consciousness, self-consciousness, and spirit.

While the soul was a unity whose moments coexisted in a relatively indistinct flux and in the form of feelings, consciousness begins when the soul duplicates itself and turns its unreflected distinctions into authentic oppositions between objects that are now taken as independent. Consciousness is certainty both of itself and of a world outside itself. Consciousness manifests the subject's capacity of division by means of which it constitutes itself as a subject-object opposition. It could not be stated more clearly that what Hegel in his diagnosis calls the disease of modern philosophy (the standpoint of reflection that absolutizes oppositions such as subject-object or ego-world) is actually a derivative form that passes for an absolute and original given. It is one stage that presupposes many others, and for that matter does not even represent the final word because it preludes to other stages.

The Phenomenology of the *Encyclopaedia* investigates the position of modern philosophy with particular regard to Kant, Reinhold, and Fichte

(*ENZ* §415 A). Such a position conceives of spirit as consciousness, as an I in relation to something beyond it. The thought of the I that is established by Kant is an important outcome that should not be diminished by anything defective we may find in it: I am the elements in conflict with each other inside myself, and also their unity. I am the opposites, and also their connection. I am simplicity, but as articulation and internal distinction. Hegel recognizes something decisive in this claim, which he calls ideality: "the I, the subject of consciousness, is thinking" (*ENZ* §415). If only an I is for the I, that is, if the I duplicates itself in an active and a passive side, in thinking and thought, then this position expresses a fundamental outcome: pure thinking has the form of the I. If I know myself as an I, I understand myself as an ideality, that is, as a universality that remains identical to itself in its particular and different modes. I know that I am an infinite self-reference.

For Hegel, however, the problem in Kant is that this I is a formal and subjective identity. It neither has made nor can make itself into a world. It is self-certainty without objective truth. If the object of consciousness is the object, the object of self-consciousness at first directed outside itself is consciousness itself, and the object of spirit is the unity of consciousness and self-consciousness, Kant does not get to this level wherein spirit, having overcome and appropriated the oppositions of consciousness, can take only itself as an object. The mirror side of Kant's problem is that the I as consciousness is understood as an I-think. As such, it knows itself as an abstract individual subject, which is, however, not identical to the universal subject. Kant still owes us an explanation, Hegel holds, of the way the I becomes aware that it is always already a "We," the moment of a universal operation, of a collective subject, of a substance that preexists individuals.

For this reason, in the same passage (*ENZ* §415 A) Hegel opposes to the modern philosophy of reflection the only authentic way of conceiving the genesis of spirit. It does not suffice to say that spirit attains to itself starting from consciousness; we must also add that it attains to itself as substance. The subject is constituted starting with the substantial totality in which it lives, and this explains the reference to Spinoza: "As regards *Spinozism,* it is to be noted against it that in the judgement by which *spirit* constitutes itself as I, as free subjectivity in contrast to determinacy, spirit emerges from substance, and philosophy, when it makes this judgement the absolute determination of spirit, emerges from Spinozism."[5]

It is certainly not worthwhile to begin with a misleading premise, and yet it must be shown how the I of modern philosophy represents an essential stage in spirit. At the same time, we must highlight its internal limits: modern philosophy believes it has discovered the I-think, but in truth it has discovered the negativity of the I. We need then to stress that the I is not only thought, but also life, the impulse to assert itself, desire, and self-love. Cogito and *conatus* must be thought together.

If the I is practical in this general sense and not only theoretical, the well-known Hegelian strategies follow: the doctrine of natural right, liberalism, contractarianism, and the ethics of autonomy are opposed to Spinoza's priority of substance over individuals, including in a political sense, as well as to the Aristotelian conception of a political animal. It is from here, as is well known, that Marx took his critique of the "eighteenth-century Robinsonades."[6] In short, there is something residual in the I. When it stakes a claim to count for itself, then it becomes a mosaic tile that disappears from sight, devoid of meaning, as a useless piece that has survived a cracked "We."[7]

Some Methodological Clarifications

It is true that this complex interrelation of distinct moments that are internal to spirit (soul, consciousness, self-consciousness, spirit, each of them investigated in an independent section) is not developed by Hegel until the Nuremberg years, that is, after the *Phenomenology of Spirit*. However, the traits we have just seen—the critique of the individual and theoretical I as derivative abstractions, the distinction between consciousness and self-consciousness, the need to move from the I to the "We," and the progression of consciousness, self-consciousness, and spirit—are already operative in the 1807 breakthrough work.

For Hegel, as for Kant, reason is life. It is practical, albeit not in Kant's sense of the supposed primacy of practical reason, but in a very basic pragmatic sense of life as dynamism and involvement in its interests and activities. In Hegel the dynamism and life of reason reveal it as a subject that wants to find itself in the world. The idea as unity of the concept and reality in which reason consists (*ENZ* §214) is not presupposed as already achieved from the beginning, but must become and posit itself as what it is in itself. This is why reason is at first impulse. It is therefore apt to understand reason in light of the features by means of which Hegel characterizes life. In the *Encyclopaedia* (§359), Hegel writes that need and lack are the privilege of the living. Unlike limits, which define inanimate things like external boundaries that these happen to have and undergo, need and lack are the inner stimulus to overcome lack. The infinity of subjectivity consists precisely in the capacity to endure pain. While instincts are the way in which the concept promotes itself to existence, need is the condition for the concept's self-realization.

CHAPTER 1

In Kant, reason's life involves reason's interests and ends as well as the activities intended to promote and fulfil them. However, Kant's description of reason's life is largely analogical. The declension of reason into a first-person perspective remains quite abstract. At the same time, it refers to the empirical I from which it nonetheless knows it differs. In Hegel, the picture is much more concrete because he strongly insists that reason is embodied in a different way, and empirical and pure I cannot fall asunder. We can now see that the problem with the egological perspective does not concern its monadic core. The problem, I suggest, is that the world is not really shared as long as we start from a theoretical I. A pure I cannot be the answer. Hegel's picture is more concrete because he must not simply postulate an inner relation between individual and universal self-consciousness, but must show how the one *becomes* the other from and through its finitude and embodiment.

We know that whatever assertion or statement Hegel makes changes meaning depending on the stage in the system in which it is embedded. The principle that the true is the whole is so vital that taking anything out of context vitiates irremediably all conclusions. What Hegel says may be true *for* the stage of consciousness or thought-determination he is examining rather than for us or in itself; it can be one-sidedly and incompletely true, an assertion to which its opposite still has to be countered until both are resolved in a more comprehensive unity. So every assertion we make must be preceded by the indication of the work and chapter we refer to. If we place Hegel's points on self-consciousness and intersubjectivity in the entirety of his system, we immediately realize that we cannot extract a univocal thesis to be taken as a truth that is either valid universally or pervasive of all figures. Self-consciousness in the struggle for recognition in the 1807 *Phenomenology* is one thing, while in the *Encyclopaedia*'s Phenomenology it is quite another. Self-consciousness is the truth of consciousness, but also the manifestation of reason. Self-consciousness finds its truth in another self-consciousness, but it also has an independent structure prior to and regardless of the encounter with the other in which it nonetheless discovers itself. And so on.

But as soon as we take these precautions, we realize that more clarifications are needed before we even start to draw our focus closer or to isolate a particular thesis. I propose as a premise of my considerations two elementary points, knowing full well that what seems evident to me is most likely going to be disputable for others.

1. Hegel's conclusions present at least three distinct phases: (a) the development of his earlier views in the Jena period prior to the *Phenomenology* (with the further subdivisions of the *System of Ethical Life,*

the 1803–04 and 1805–06 system projects), (b) the 1807 *Phenomenology* itself, and (c) the later systematic conception to be found in the Phenomenology and Psychology sections of the Philosophy of Subjective Spirit and in the Objective Spirit of the *Encyclopaedia*. The first point that requires clarification is the use of the concept of "recognition" which, preponderant until 1806 at all levels (as Siep and Testa have shown),[8] is thematically central in but substantially restricted to the struggle between two self-consciousnesses in the 1807 *Phenomenology*, and is later further narrowed in the *Encyclopaedia* and in the *Elements of the Philosophy of Right*.

2. This simple consideration indicates that recognition, reciprocity, and intersubjectivity are by no means identical notions. There are spheres of more immediate and natural reciprocity, as well as more complex objective relations of intersubjectivity *between* which the stage where I discover that I am an individual self-consciousness depending on another I's recognition is merely intermediary and instrumental (if not surprisingly problematic, as we will see).

These are methodological points, but they are sufficient to grant a number of preliminary conclusions. As to principle (1), we can say what follows. From his earliest days, Hegel has mistrusted all attempts to begin with a free autonomous subject. His appeal to Aristotle in the Jena period must be read in this light: against the abstraction of a pure I, we must see self-consciousness as rooted in nature, in a community, in institutions which to the I are its constitutive second nature. Ethics cannot be separated from either nature or politics. Individual freedom is nothing without the substance that constitutes its inner core. Accordingly, the pure I cannot come without embodiment or shared practices and activities, that is, without a form of unification. The reconciliation between freedom and substance in the Jena period takes the form of recognition, and this model is dominant for all spiritual and social practices.

In Ludwig Siep's summary, Hegel's Jena philosophy of spirit presents four moments: (i) the constitution of a common consciousness among self-conscious individuals; (ii) the claim that everyone ought to have dignity and worth for everyone else even in his or her division, separation, and distance from them; (iii) the mutual respect of rights, functions, and institutions; and (iv) the awareness that individual and universal consciousness and will are reciprocally dependent. As a result, recognition entails my knowing myself as a moment of the universal substance which in turn is the result of everybody's doing. Hegel's philosophy of spirit is thus the genetic formation of institutions and of consciousness at the same time. Here individual and universal self-consciousnesses arise through one and the same movement.[9]

By contrast, the *Phenomenology of Spirit* tells a different story. This is no wonder, for the *Phenomenology* is a critique of the appearance of knowledge in consciousness's voyages of discovery. Consciousness has to be led upward to recognize the logic that moves it, until it sees that no difference between itself and speculation remains on its way. Truth and consciousness's certainty must become one. Consciousness, self-consciousness, reason, and spirit can appear as separate and independent shapes, however, insofar as the subject of the movement is not aware of what goes on behind its back. Absolute knowledge, or speculative logic (the identity of logic and metaphysics, thinking and being), are therefore not the *product* of consciousness's movement, but are *known* by consciousness at the end of its calvary as the *truth* that had been operative all along.

This new position, made possible in 1807 by Hegel's freshly gained definition of the Absolute and of logic, cannot rest on something like recognition because the experience of consciousness and speculative truth are quite distinct and mutually independent. The conclusion I draw from this point is that in the 1807 *Phenomenology* recognition amounts to acknowledgment and discovery on the part of consciousness. Even if it is the acknowledgment and discovery of a practice we share and thereby contribute to constitute, its productive or constitutive role is limited. For this reason, its latitude is so drastically reduced in comparison with the Jena system projects.

Hegel progressively narrows the role ascribed to recognition in his philosophy of spirit after the *Phenomenology of Spirit*. In Nuremberg, Heidelberg, and Berlin Hegel still uses the concept of "recognition," but he accurately separates theoretical spirit (i.e., intelligence), practical spirit (i.e., will), and objective spirit. As a result, language and spirit's self-realization in the formal moments of the will and in political institutions, which in Jena were equally treated in conjunction with, if not under the aegis of, recognition, are now severed. That is, they are deduced in different sections and are thereby assigned different functions in different thematic scopes. Far from forming the condition for the validation of rational institutions in objective spirit, recognition survives in the much-truncated version of the Phenomenology of the *Encyclopaedia*. But this recognition is independent of language, right, institutions, and the State, since it is appealed to only in order to explain the doubling (*Verdopplung*) of self-consciousness as one moment of subjective spirit. The Phenomenology has become one stage of spirit's evolution. At the same time, it is now a *part* of science, not an *introduction* to science. The *Encyclopaedia*'s Phenomenology is, in other words, a *theory* of consciousness, not a *criticism* of it. In its turn consciousness, which has meanwhile been reduced to the philosophical stance of opposition to objectivity, now forms the condition for spirit's free self-relation and assumes, as we have seen, a well-defined historical connotation modeled upon modern subjectivism.[10]

Hegelians therefore know better than to hoist recognition as a slogan and find in it the seed of a political philosophy, let alone a philosophy of history, the prefiguration of Marx's class struggle, or even a romanticization of desire as desire of the other's desire. In fact, and here I come to some conclusions regarding principle (2) on the difference between recognition and intersubjectivity, recognition first occurs at the level of personal relations.

The natural and immediate form of recognition is love. Love is finding oneself in the other. But the resulting unity is not the simple sum of two. It is a superior unity in which each member finds meaning, purpose, and substance. This relation is reciprocal; the unity is sought for. In it we give up our independence. In the words of the 1805–06 *Realphilosophie* (*JSE* 3, 209), it is the unity of being-for-itself and being-for-other. "By the fact that each one knows him- or herself in the other, each overcomes him- or herself as a being for itself, as distinct" (*JSE* 3, 210). It is a natural dissatisfaction, rooted in the body and sexuality, that moves us to find satisfaction in another. As in Rousseau, then, the first form of sympathy occurs in the form of feeling.

Given the importance of love for Hegel from his Frankfurt to his Jena years, it is tempting to see in this notion the model of Aristophanes's speech in Plato's *Symposium*, but it is a temptation we must resist. For Aristophanes's model of fusion annuls individuality. In Hegel's idea of love, two individuals are not simply looking for a fusion. In fact, they overcome this ephemeral unity through the *intuition of themselves in a third element, an external object* that will presumably survive them: the child. Fusion wastes like a flame that consumes and burns out (Aristophanes's lovers are so engrossed with each other that they die of hunger: *Symposium* 191a–b). An immediate unity has no substance or endurance, whereas Hegel's love pushes to objectify itself in a mediated object, the representation of enduring unity: marriage, family, and its patrimony. Thereby immediacy makes room for mediation, naturalness for ethical life, and narcissism for consciousness of finitude.

We could express this in Aristotle's words and say that in this unity the other is another self and friendship of pleasure may transform itself into a different form of friendship. In Hegel, however, we find an additional point: in this objective bond flesh becomes spirit, as it were. Nature turns into culture: union is instituted socially and symbolically. Crucial for all this is the independence of the other self-consciousness. In reciprocity lovers at first give up independence, but the other's alterity is not effaced. If anything, it is sanctioned officially by the objective rite of marriage.

From this relation between two people the consciousness of a "we" first arises. Still, this remains a natural bond. The satisfaction of finding myself in the other in love must give way to more public forms of recognition and of satisfaction. Importantly, reciprocity between two self-consciousnesses is not the same as the universal self-consciousness, which is arrived at only in the socially shared world: in the plurality of self-consciousnesses that feel and act as one.

Aristotle moved from *oikos* to *polis* through *dêmos* alone (the village). The village is a mere bridge between family and city. In Hegel, the family is not followed by the state without further ado. Hegel needs a further mediation, civil society or more fundamentally its subject, self-consciousness. Another way to make the same point is this: what the I *asserts* in love is the truth of a superior *unity*, which includes lack of independence and its renunciation to self-centered will. Love itself prefigures higher, more complex forms such as ethical life, in which self-consciousness is not only in relation to others like it but also to the whole, a "we": spirit, universal self-consciousness. Before we achieve the recognition of *wills* that *integrate* each other in a *whole*, however, we must pass through the recognition of wills that *assert* themselves as being *independent* from one another. Unity breaks up into separate elements. Conflict is inevitable here.

Before we see why, let me draw a few conclusions from the themes of this section. The first element worth stressing is that *Geist* (spirit) is the proper level at which we can speak of intersubjectivity as the substance and bond of a universal self-consciousness. In Hegel's mature philosophy this is the ethical life of objective spirit, because the phenomenology of Subjective Spirit as well as the first two forms of Objective Spirit, Abstract Right and Morality, concern an individual self-consciousness that is not yet identical with its ethical substance. Shared practices happen at the level of rational institutions in which we freely participate and which shape our very being together. The intersubjectivity of spirit is the "I that is We, the We that is I." In Hegel's mature thought, recognition does not constitute ethical intersubjectivity. Let us therefore distinguish between natural reciprocity, relationships between separate individuals, and ethical life.

If recognition has its thematic place before ethical intersubjectivity, we need to clarify—against the theory widely held nowadays according to which recognition is the source of sociality—that self-consciousness is in turn placed *before* recognition. My second conclusion, then, is that recognition cannot constitute or ground self-consciousness. From social practices of recognition I can never arrive at self-consciousness. The I does find and discover itself in another, but cannot draw its identity from other I's.[11] Social roles and practices, language, normative relations of recognition will never be able to constitute the peculiar relation to oneself that self-consciousness is. They do fill the I's life, give it substance and scope, but only insofar as they are experienced and willed—recognized—by an I. However, demanding that they give rise to an I and at the same time that the I recognize them—that is, that the I constitute them through social interaction—is circular.[12]

I would like to illustrate this point in two different ways: as a theoretical discussion of this reduction of self-consciousness to recognition (a) and as a critique of Brandom's and Pippin's interpretation (b).

(a) Self-consciousness is a self-relation, but this type of relation cannot be grounded by recognition. If anything, it is recognition that is made possible by two self-relating subjects. It seems to me that reducing self-consciousness to recognition is a category mistake. Recognition is treated as a relation that makes possible its relata through their reciprocity. This amounts to mistaking, in the words of the *Science of Logic*, the thought-determination "Something and other" taken as a universal bond with the determination "Being-for-itself" (*Fürsichsein*). While the former is a finite relation to another, the latter is the true infinity of self-relation. *A reciprocal relation is not a reflexive relation.* The two poles of a magnet are in a reciprocal relation but are no self-consciousness.

Recognition is considered not only as a relation that gives rise to relata, but also as an act that creates its object. It seems to me that social ontology mistakes the genesis of social objects for that of social subjects. Recognition accounts for the sociality of objects, not of subjectivity. Let me explain this with some examples. The Dow Jones exists only to the extent that it is recognized: without the generalized consensus on which it rests, the Dow Jones would not have any basis. It is absurd to suppose the Dow Jones on a desert island, whereas the same does not hold for self-consciousness. A United States law applies in the United States to the extent that it is recognized by all participants in the social covenant, whereas self-consciousness is such everywhere and independently of conventions, contracts, and of the recognition upon which these are grounded. A right exists only insofar as it is recognized, but this does not hold for self-consciousness.

If we now consider that many contemporary theories of self-consciousness, especially in analytic philosophy, take their bearings from language, indexicals, and the ability to say "I," then we can realize another aspect of this problem. The I is a personal pronoun because it is used by self-consciousness. Interpreting the first-person perspective exclusively in terms of the possibility of using the indexical "I" amounts to annulling the very phenomenon we seek to explain. The reflexive pronoun does not make possible self-consciousness; it is the I as a subject that uses the "I" as a pronoun in a reflexive sense. Indeed, other reflexive uses of pronouns do not have the ambition of explaining self-consciousness or the specific reflexivity at stake. Self-movement, self-destruction, self-combustion, and so on are self-relations, but they are not reflexive relations like self-consciousness. On the basis of such uses of the pronoun we can never arrive at the I as subject.[13]

In conclusion, the legitimacy of self-consciousness is grounded differently than that of other objects. From this brief discussion one could also infer that self-consciousness is a primitive term that cannot be derived from anything else. Actually, the opposite is true for Hegel, as we will see more clearly presently. Self-consciousness must become; only, I suggest, it does not become through recognition, but out of consciousness.

(b) Brandom and Pippin share the view that self-consciousness becomes only through recognition. For them the "we," the logical and social space of reasons as it is now customary to call it, grounds the I. In Brandom's account, self-consciousness is "a social achievement"—which, for the reasons just seen, strikes me as unintelligible.[14] There are, however, further reasons of a textual nature. According to Brandom, a being is self-conscious when what it identifies with or takes itself to be is what it is in itself. He takes self-consciousness to be the subject of normative positions,[15] as a formal structure separate from its embodiment, that is, separate from its practical being. Brandom's I does not come about as, or is in any way linked to, desire. Brandom's I depends on what it thinks of itself, and this is discontinuous with the sphere of desire. For Brandom, desire is on the same level as need and animal impulse, and in fact, it is modeled after appetite and eating. Thus Brandom egregiously suppresses the blatant difference between animal need and specifically human desire which these Hegelian pages on the struggle for recognition are explicitly meant to bring to light, alongside the whole Hegelian discourse on the struggle to overcome the other's resistance (for Brandom these pages are veined with what he deplores as a martial rhetoric). For Brandom, it is surprising[16] that the Hegelian self-consciousness is desire for recognition, whereas this should constitute the starting point of all explanation—or at least so it is in Hegel.

While Brandom's is a particular usage of Hegel, Pippin aims to provide an internal commentary on these Hegelian pages. Yet he seems to me equally arbitrary. Pippin's starting point is that freedom is not naturally given, for it consists in assuming the responsibility to respond to reasons. This is an obviously Kantian trait, according to which a command is valid only if I recognize it as binding (for Pippin, Hegel draws out of Kant's autonomy the most coherent philosophical consequences). But

Pippin gives this Kantian point a constructivist slant: the normative status of a free agent depends on its being recognized as such. In this way Pippin gets a conventionalist Kant (this position is devoid of the fundamental Kantian requisite for rationality, i.e., universality and necessity), and a thesis that is stronger than the idea according to which I exist only within a polis or by participating as a citizen in a shared world: the thesis is that an agent is such only because others confer this status on him or her.[17]

My hypothesis is that Pippin comes to this conclusion because he has in mind the sociality of ethical life in which "the *disposition* of the individuals is *awareness* of the substance and of the identity of all their interests with the whole; and when the other individuals are actual and reciprocally aware of themselves only in this identity, this is *trust*, the genuine, ethical disposition" (*ENZ* §515). But if so, Pippin transfers to the totality of objective spirit what applies only to its final stage; he conflates ethical life and recognition. In ethical life recognition is the substance of shared life, yet the recognition between two self-consciousnesses he is talking about precedes such a stage (and recognition can be at stake in the struggle between self-consciousnesses or in civil society and abstract right: see the *Elements of the Philosophy of Right*, §71).

In my view, the self-consciousness that is the protagonist of the struggle for primacy in the chapter Lordship and Bondage is not yet spirit, to use the distinction of the 1807 *Phenomenology*. Actually, self-consciousness must fight to become precisely that, "the I that is 'we' and the 'we' that is 'I.'" The "we" is not a collective mind or a metaphysical substance that is independent of individuals. It is instead shared work and action, the activity of each and everyone. Therefore reason is life and subjectivity which *appears* in the form of self-consciousness and *to self-consciousness*. In other words, self-consciousness can be understood in terms of reason, not vice versa. It is the manifestation of reason as it becomes thematic to self-consciousness. Self-consciousness is not an absolute origin.

I do not mean thereby to relativize self-consciousness, but I do intend to relativize both the general widespread habit of reading Hegel as if the *Phenomenology of Spirit* were his final word, and the specific thesis according to which the struggle for recognition at stake in the 1807 book should be, as Pippin instead writes, "the most important chapter in all of Hegel."[18] The problem does not concern an opinion about the relative rank of one Hegelian passage or chapter as opposed to another. The problem, as with Brandom, is partly theoretical (the weakness of the constructivist thesis) and partly textual. Pippin's evaluation rests on a misguided foundation: his belief that in this chapter Hegel presents the overcoming of the Kantian notion of apperception.[19]

CHAPTER 1

Self-Consciousness as Desire and Recognition: The Chapter on Lordship and Bondage of the *Phenomenology of Spirit*

Let me clarify what I mean by this relativization. What I seek to do with the struggle for recognition in the 1807 *Phenomenology* is to comprehend this chapter in its context, certainly not diminish it. In fact, its appeal remains intact, for it is one of the most memorable examples of Hegel's genius as well as of dialectic as reversal. I would like to dwell on it in this and the next sections.

The first three chapters of the *Phenomenology* have shown to consciousness (to the understanding) the dawning of infinity. In it, consciousness sees its own process of generating, holding fast to, and destroying conceptual distinctions. Consciousness's object, which at first was other than itself (*W* 3, 137, *PhS* 104), turns out to be thus nothing but itself. Hegel expresses this point in the following words: to consciousness, it and the object are separated by a difference that is not one. Consciousness becomes *self*-consciousness: no more consciousness of another, it now becomes self-certainty.

This, however, means that self-consciousness is this return to itself—which is indeed its most apt definition ("die Rückkehr aus dem *Anderssein*," *W* 3, 138, *PhS* 105). Thus it contains in itself consciousness as sublated, and consciousness's world as negated and inwardized.[20] Self-consciousness thereby brings with itself a contradiction: it looks for itself but finds its other. The contradiction naturally takes on a dynamical form. Self-consciousness realizes it must begin with the object, remove it, and turn back upon itself. In this return to itself, it regards the other as subordinate, a sheer semblance. The sensible world must be negated in self-consciousness's pursuit of its own self.

Still, insofar as self-consciousness understands the sensible as the negative from which it must return to itself, self-consciousness realizes that it is self-affirmation. It understands that *identity and negativity go together.* Self-consciousness is life; but life is impulse and desire. Self-consciousness's reflection onto itself is inseparable from its self-affirmation, and hence from the quest for satisfaction of desire, which, as we have seen, is essentially lack.[21] Self-consciousness understands that it can affirm itself to the extent that it reduces things to its own instruments or consumes them. Some things lend themselves easily to such self-affirmation. If I am hungry and eat nuts to feed myself, this is the end of the story. But the self-affirmation that constantly consumes and destroys the object so as to fuel the identity of the subject cannot ground true individuation, for each satisfaction is temporary and the appetite repeats itself ever the same. Self-consciousness realizes that it needs the independent subsistence of the object. It does not know what to do with an object as a mere subordinate and vanishing semblance. However, if along the path of its satisfaction self-consciousness meets some resistance from the object, then it senses a challenge and an obstacle.

Thus the other begins to acquire a relevance that has so far been unsurmised. The truth of self-consciousness's desire is that self-consciousness can achieve its satisfaction only insofar as it relates to another, which is now *recognized as independent.* This other in turn negates itself at the same time and in the same way. Only another consciousness can do this, that is, negate its own natural and sensible determinations and maintain itself in and through this negation.[22] Because it is desire, self-consciousness must relate to another self-consciousness. As a result, "self-consciousness achieves its satisfaction only in another self-consciousness" (*W* 3, 144, *PhS* 110).

Self-consciousness doubles itself (*Verdopplung*), that is, it exists as a relationship between two self-consciousnesses: "Self-consciousness exists *in and for itself* when, and by the fact that, it so exists for another; that is, it exists only in being acknowledged" (*W* 3, 145, *PhS* 111). Self-consciousness exists only in the plural.

If, then, there is an essential relation between desire and reciprocity, it is worth emphasizing precisely because it reveals a fundamental aspect of self-consciousness neglected by many: the inner connection between the identity of self-consciousness and the negativity of desire. Indeed, it is vital to understand that, before recognition, self-consciousness is searching for itself. If we want to make understandable this side of self-consciousness through a reference to historical antecedents, we may think of the notion of *conatus* in Hobbes, Spinoza, or Leibniz. For many of us, it is natural to think of ourselves as centers of impulse, will, self-affirmation. We are driven by self-love, from Hobbes up to Hegel.[23]

In Hegel self-consciousness arises, even to its own eyes, as desire and is in search of itself. It is not the theoretical reflexivity of a cogito, but the perception of a lack that it must fulfill in order to assert itself as independent. Self-consciousness is *desire of itself* precisely because it is lack of itself.[24] Self-consciousness is eros before being logos. I am aware that I am thus arguing the opposite of what Lacan maintains with regard to Hegel's view of self-consciousness.[25] I am doing so because for Hegel the individual self-consciousness's desire is nothing but the manifestation of reason's desire to make itself world. As we will see in the next chapters, reason's need to realize itself—the logical element that strives to become thing—is for Hegel the fundamental thrust of which the desire for recognition is an epiphenomenon. Naturally, in the eyes of self-consciousness, desire for recognition is instead the primary datum.

In all this, the most important thing is that the relation between reason and desire, eros and logos, traditionally understood from Plato to the eighteenth century as reciprocally alternative, begins to change in Kant. In Kant, for the first time, reason's desire appears: reason is the motivation to realize itself. Hegel brings this thought to even more radical consequences, that is, to the concept of reason as an instinct for self-actualization.[26]

After this remark, let me go back to the text and resume the argument from the doubling of self-consciousness. This movement, which has been presented as if it were the action of one self-consciousness, is in truth the action of both self-consciousnesses involved. Recognition is this doubling by means of which I find myself in the other who mirrors me, and vice versa. But if this is the aim of the movement, that is, an I-thou relation which prepares the birth of a "We," it is not the shape in which it first appears *to self-consciousness*. At first, we have inequality in a struggle (*W* 3, 147, *PhS* 112).

Self-consciousness realizes that it strives to affirm itself *at the expense* of independent others like itself. This is why conflict necessarily arises from desire. This is not, as it were, a struggle *for life*, but a struggle in which each party shows that it wants to be superior *to life* by risking it in order to prove itself. What each wants is the recognition that its own self-certainty has truth, that is, that it prevails over the other and thus gets an objective proof of the value of its own identity.

Life and the I are separated (*entzweit*, *W* 3, 139, *PhS* 106). But faced with the sudden concrete risk of death, one of the two capitulates and prefers life over independence. This is a submissive and slavish resolve in the eyes of the lord who has meanwhile prevailed, for the slave is more attached to life than to his I (to his dignity and freedom). That is, for the lord, only his being-for-self counts. For the bondsman, instead, dependence upon the lord (i.e., being-for-other), life, and self—demoted though it may be—are intertwined.

The lord's life is reduced to futile enjoyment and consumption, that is, the consumption of goods prepared for him by the bondsman (the epigraph of this chapter is "il chitarrino" that Figaro intends to play for the Count in the *Marriage of Figaro*). The stage of consumption falls back on to the previous stage of indefinite repetition of satisfaction without any progress in the lord's being at home in the world. His being-for-self progressively thins out and becomes insubstantial. The lord relates to the bondsman as to an inferior whose recognition can hardly gratify the lord. He also relates to things through the bondsman. "The aspect of its [the thing's] independence he leaves to the bondsman, who works on it" (*W* 3, 151, *PhS* 116). Thereby the recognition shows itself to be one-sided and unequal.

This is a problem for the lord because his independence is recognized by a slavish self-consciousness. He is mirrored by an inessential self-consciousness, and now this relation appears to him as the truth of his self. But a worse problem, and the reason why the relation begins to be dialectically inverted, is that the lord who enjoys things through the mediation of the bondsman has estranged himself from them. While for the lord things have no independence, for the bondsman they have to be vanquished through labor.

Desire Held in Check and Fleetingness
Staved Off: Work and Fear

Work disciplines desire and puts a stop to fear. Work "is *desire held in check, fleetingness staved off*; in other words, work *forms and shapes* the thing. The negative relation to the object becomes its *form* and something *permanent*, because it is precisely for the worker that the object has independence" (*W* 3, 153, *PhS* 118). As in Kant's "Conjectural Beginning of Human History" where the checking of desire is the beginning of culture, here work is a formative activity through which self-consciousness begins to consider itself in its products. The bondsman recognizes himself in the products of his labor ("*I* made you!" is his subdued but proud cry to tomatoes and the plow). Work, even as it is imposed on him by the lord, acquires for the bondsman the sense of a self-objectification. It is his freedom become thinghood. The bondsman finds himself in the thing, and in this intuition it becomes explicitly for-himself. As is clear, work is not *banausios*, the intrinsically servile activity that for Aristotle forced workers to deal with others' needs and made it impossible for them to devote themselves to virtue (which is why Aristotle excluded workers from the rank of citizens in some constitutions). While Aristotle interpreted work in light of its product, for Hegel work has value insofar as it stands for the self-objectification of the I who transforms and educates itself in the process of transforming its product.

Now what is the point of these famous pages? They can be compared to the *Phenomenology* as a whole: incredibly rich and complex, they can be read on multiple levels for the sake of historical narrative or as a description of subjectivity with important psychological, psychoanalytic, and existential overtones. And yet, they are confusing enough that one must disentangle the philosophical systematic lesson Hegel wants us to draw from the otherwise less essential conclusions it *also* grants. The philosophical systematic lesson is this: Hegel is showing generally *how for consciousness the presuppositions behind its back first present themselves to its consideration.* In these pages in particular he is showing the bare truth of self-consciousness's

CHAPTER 1

experience: how reason enters the world practically and negatively through the shaping of recalcitrant things, how subjectivity acquires an objectivity and a permanence that can only be established through the mediation of— through the bondsman's labor on—things, how the bondsman posits himself as this negativity and eventually acquires a higher self than the lord.[27]

No such thing as feeling with or imagining the other has yet surfaced, for at first each self-consciousness takes its selfhood as itself alone. The other self-consciousness in its independence comes up as a sudden shock, and the struggle for recognition grows out of the unexpected check following the discovery of the other's independence and threat. The struggle is a transition from a solipsistic I to an independent world, whereby the solipsistic I is still well before and quite far from Smith's self or Husserl's ego (it is almost autistic rather than solipsistic).

More importantly, the relation is an *abstraction*. For all the richness of its implications, it is the barest and emptiest relation. We know nothing of the two self-consciousnesses' life other than this: the lord is a being-for-self, while the bondsman is a being-for-self, being-for-other and work. It suffices to try to figure out these two self-consciousnesses more concretely to realize just how abstract this relation is. Do the lord and the bondsman have a family (parents, children, a wife)? If they do (and nobody was born in a void), does what Hegel calls the natural form of recognition they must have experienced *before* the struggle have any bearing on it? That is, does it teach them anything about what to expect or fear or anticipate? Was not the family—a unity of individuals that are in reciprocal relations, not atoms—supposed to prefigure a "we" to come? Also, if self-consciousness finds satisfaction in another self-consciousness and desire is the desire for recognition, and hence an appeal constituted by words exchanged with the other, is it not strange that the two self-consciousnesses do not talk to each other in these pages? It seems obvious that these are not questions that it is interesting, pertinent, or even possible to raise because all that matters to Hegel is the truth of the experience that each self-consciousness makes in the struggle. The truth is that work is one way in which reason makes the world its home and freedom makes its first appearance. This philosophical systematic lesson is all that Hegel cares to establish. The appeal is not met or answered, because it is for us philosophers, not for the self-consciousnesses involved in the struggle, that spirit is in itself present.

Still, this is not the end of the story. If the bondsman realizes that he is free even in his servitude (in a way that his lord cannot achieve because to him freedom comes with estrangement from the world), what bears stressing is that the bondsman's freedom is *won*. It is won at the expense of fear. The quote from the Psalms, "The fear of the lord is indeed the beginning of wisdom,"[28] seems to come out of nowhere, but Hegel's biblical references hardly ever do, and this is no exception. It seems to me that interpreters have rightly insisted on work, but upon closer reading of the last paragraph of this chapter, it is the couple *fear-work* that together calls for a commentary.

Fear must be taken as "absolute fear," the fear to lose one's life that infects the bondsman's being through and through and jeopardizes "the entire contents of its natural consciousness" (*W*3, 154, *PhS*119). "The two moments of fear and service . . . are necessary, both being at the same time in a universal mode" (ibid.). Without work, fear is not objectified. It remains "inward and mute, and consciousness does not become explicitly *for itself*" (ibid.). The inner must become outer. Conversely, without fear, that is, if moved only by "a lesser dread" or generic anxiety, work produces "only an empty self-centered attitude" (ibid.). Work is the absolute command dictated by fear of death.

Fear and work are not simply two sides that happen to be conjoined. Fear is internalized in work and in turn achieves its form in work. In Stanley Rosen's words, "work disciplines fear *into* self-consciousness."[29] Negativity must be a dramatic form of negativity in which *everything is at stake*. Nothing less than that constitutes the bondsman's self-consciousness.

Echoes from Hobbes are numerous here. In both Hobbes and Hegel, self-consciousnesses are naturally antagonistic: in Hegel because self-assertion is desire and a negative relation to others, in Hobbes because "in the nature of man" we find competition, diffidence, and glory, which all lead to war.[30] In both, fear, desire, and freedom are inseparable. Work disciplines fear for Hegel, while for Hobbes work (and age) correct vainglory.[31] In both, fear is fear of violent death and, because it advises prudence, the beginning of wisdom.[32] Like in Hobbes, for Hegel desire is not a feeling among others, but a passion I take as essentially pertinent to, if not definitive of, my identity and consideration of myself. For desire is not something I happen to feel, but a subjective stance of self-consciousness which, if challenged, must be defended. If it is legitimized, it is what I take myself to want, so it becomes an object I invest with my sense of self, something worth fighting for and standing by. Desire becomes a claim I make to which I may want to commit myself.

There is a major difference, however. Unlike in Hobbes, in Hegel fear can be quenched and desire can be cultivated and deflected. Consider how desire is channeled. In Aristophanes, the satisfaction of eros gave way to concern for the other needs of life in the city (*Symposium* 191c); in Hegel, after being realized in the family as love, desire is realized in work; in Hobbes, it must be directed to the work of building the city. But the sovereign *controls* fear. That is, he or she can never take it away from us or alter desire. Hobbes must do without a second nature. For him, it is a pious self-delusion that you can cultivate desire or improve human nature.[33] By contrast, in Hegel desire is the first manifestation of self-consciousness. Starting from this, it knows itself and develops to the point that it successively becomes free will, which objectifies itself in forms of actuality such as right and ethical life.

One last difference between Hegel and Hobbes concerns equality. In Hegel, it is true for us, not for the self-consciousness in the struggle, that the I is a We. It is for us that recognition is mutual and free, whereas for the self-consciousness in conflict the initial inequality is never removed (*W* 3, 147, *PhS* 112). On the contrary, Hobbes takes his bearings from a situation of equality but never allows atomic individuality to become a We (i.e., to feel and act as a we, thereby finding itself in the other). In fact, the pride that he finds ingrained in us is precisely the failed recognition of everybody's equality.

I would like to conclude this section by drawing some consequences from what I have argued. Hegel's self-consciousness is not a social achievement. This is not to say, along with many contemporary philosophers, that the I is a primitive notion or that the irreducibility of self-consciousness to social practices entails its primacy. There cannot be any ambiguity about that. Self-consciousness arises out of consciousness in the 1807 *Phenomenology*, and spirit emerges out of nature in the Philosophy of Subjective Spirit of the *Encyclopaedia*. That is, the I *becomes*, as does the We. They are constituted and are not a natural given (or a transcendental condition or metaphysical first principle). If we cannot conclude that the I should enjoy a primacy, I think we must realize that it is no less impossible for the We to constitute the I.

The struggle for recognition in the 1807 *Phenomenology* in particular cannot be the ground of sociality. Recognition in the two self-consciousnesses' struggle is too much of an abstraction to be a paradigmatic, let alone foundational, social phenomenon. The struggle is not only too abstract. Worse still, recognition is, strictly speaking, *absent*. True, self-consciousness exists only as recognized and finds satisfaction only in another self-consciousness; later, in chapter 6 on Spirit, recognition will have produced the basis for the interaction of persons at the ethical, juridical, and religious levels. My point, however, is that this does not happen in the Lordship and Bondage chapter. The satisfaction hoped for and aimed at is not achieved there. The Lordship and Bondage chapter of the 1807 *Phenomenology* stands to intersubjectivity as a prophet to a messiah: it is an announcement of a kingdom come.

Universal self-consciousness is not the result of that chapter, either. Self-consciousness discovers it is not simply desire or singularity. It discovers the problem of dependence, and with it the problem of a *universality that transcends its singular* point of view. But this does not make it a *universal self-consciousness* yet.

The chapter is the moment where the thou first arises in the isolated self-consciousness's horizon, and with it the incipient realization that I depend on others as others depend on me. But it is a rudimentary stage well before any imagination of or involvement with the other. As sense-certainty began with no more than the "this" (here-now), so at the beginning for self-consciousness there is only an "I" (here). The effort at putting myself "there"—in another's shoes—is ahead of us still. Correspondingly, we are still far from all talk of an interiority as constituted in relation to others and from the risk feared by Rousseau that in society we live in the opinion of others. Several further mediations are required to get to that level of artificiality.

For Rousseau, death and foresight were unknown in the state of nature and had to be entertained in imagination. For Hegel's self-consciousness, death is lived as a concrete real danger; the other is a shock because he is a suddenly independent rival and a threat; terror is self-consciousness's experience. Something like foresight or a representation of the future is yet to dawn on this self-consciousness.[34]

There is then a major difference between self-image, which does become relevant in these pages, and imagination. While the self-image that the lord receives back from the bondsman is disappointing and insubstantial and the image in which the bondsman mirrors himself is the product of his work (the things he has shaped and transformed), imagining another can only happen at a more complex stage, when a relation is in principle possible. No genuine relation is established between the lord and the bondsman. Their experience, their *Umkehrung des Bewusstseins* (reversal of consciousness), is not made possible *through* their relation. Each makes his own individual experience. They do not interact; they react to the other's threats and actions. We must conclude that recognition, which is the aim of the struggle, is not reached at its end. Neither the lord nor the bondsman can find himself in the other.[35]

Recognition strikes us for its failure, or to say the least, its conspicuous absence. The lord cannot find himself in the lowly image of the bondsman. For him, recognition can at most mean the bondsman's tribute to his superiority.[36] For the bondsman in turn, recognition is the homage he pays to the lord's pride before his eventual downfall, but it is one-sided, not lasting, shallow. The experience that is decisive and foundational for him has nothing to do with recognition, for it is the acknowledgment that his attachment to life has been transformed. It is now his involvement in the world through the negation of his natural being. The superiority to life that the lord had displayed turns out now to be as proud and vain as the insubstantial negativity of his unlimited enjoyment and consumption. The bondsman who dirties his hands in things instead is the rational and concrete negativity of self-objectification removing the otherness of nature. Still, neither one finds or imagines himself in the other.

We can now better understand why for Hegel imagination is hardly decisive and why he would not frame the question of recognition in terms of imagination to begin with. As we have just seen, Hegel's struggling self-consciousnesses are not in a real relation that transforms them. What Hegel sees in their struggle is only a conflict that must be recomposed and overcome until reciprocity sublates asymmetry. But when it does, it is not because of an acknowledgment of the other in imagination, for recognition is nothing mental or subjective. What counts for Hegel is the establishment of a second nature of shared practices, activities, and institutions. What counts for him, that is, is not how individuals imagine others like themselves, but that they share a solid objective basis for their common life. For Hegel, something like an imagination of the other is still limited and insufficient insofar as it pertains to subjective spirit alone. It has not yet shaped spirit's objective life as it must. For Hegel, individual self-consciousness must become universal self-consciousness.

If recognition is not the experience that each self-consciousness makes in the struggle, it plays a role in intersubjectivity once it is *assumed as achieved*—and it is achieved as the certainty that pervades objective relations. In 1807, Hegel does not show how recognition arises; he shows it in action in later chapters of the *Phenomenology*. Rather than an explicit and deliberate act on the part of self-consciousness, then, recognition is the basis and life-pulse which permeates intersubjective relations. In it, the demand that the I be recognized as an independent agent is at the same time the certainty active in shared practices, institutions, and beliefs—a *Sollen* that is a *Sein* (an ought that is a being).

It is therefore one thing to claim that a norm counts as such only by being endorsed, and that only in the context of a shared life does what we do count as meaningful. It is quite another, which seems mistaken to me, to draw the generalized conclusion that for Hegel one is a self-consciousness or an agent by being recognized as one.

The Concept as the Self

The goal of this chapter in the context of the *Phenomenology* is to show in what sense individual self-consciousness is not an original starting point.

HEGEL ON RECOGNITION

Hegel criticizes the very intention to begin with the I, as well as all preliminary and unjustified divisions between theoretical and practical I. I have not focused on Kojève's interpretation of the struggle between self-consciousnesses, however interesting and famous (or even groundbreaking, having marked the interests of a whole generation of French philosophy and beyond). Others have already shown its one-sidedness, its misleading assumptions and arbitrary conclusions.[37] What is left to do now to prepare the next chapters on thinking and the I in Hegel is to draw attention to other passages in the *Phenomenology* by pointing out one of the most fundamental flaws of Kojève's reading: the reduction of the Hegelian discourse to an *anthropology*. The reduction of absolute idealism to human action in history as a project and a creation of time is unable to account for the goals for which Hegel wrote the *Phenomenology of Spirit*.

As we have seen, the *Phenomenology* is a work of extraordinary richness which can be used and approached for particular purposes and from different perspectives. It comes as no surprise that a theologian focuses on the "Unhappy Consciousness," or a philosopher of language focuses on "Sense-Certainty," or a classic philologist focuses on the pages devoted to Antigone (or a philosopher with a sociological penchant on recognition). They find in these topics the pole against which other themes, which meanwhile have become accessory, revolve like different planets and satellites. This is tantamount to a tribute to Hegel's impressive versatility and learnedness and to his gift for speaking to different readers. However, if we wonder about the reasons why Hegel wrote the *Phenomenology*, our approach has to become a stereoscopic and global vision.

While the *Phenomenology* is certainly the narration of consciousness's journeys of discovery, such a description still misses some essential elements. The notion of journeys is an apt characterization, if only because it shows how consciousness discovers something it has not produced which antedates it. But it does not say that the journeys are tied to each other; indeed, they are expounded so that each of them descends necessarily from the others. The destination we attain through each journey becomes the departure station of the next one, which at that point turns out to be necessary. Furthermore, this description does not say that "narration" is not a mere storytelling, for it must take upon itself the very cogency that sustains the succession of the journeys. Finally, it does not say what consciousness discovers in its journeys.

What consciousness discovers is that there is a certain rationality in things, an objective reality of thought. For instance, there is rationality in the succession of shapes that consciousness takes on, and everything that consciousness believes it encounters in its experience is actually structured according to an inner movement of categories. What appears as contingent

CHAPTER 1

and found is in truth the autonomous deployment of a rationality that has to be better understood. Consciousness discovers progressively the categories it uses in everything it does or says without knowing it simply by reflecting on what it takes to be true. For this reason, as I said, the *Phenomenology* is not a theory of consciousness, but rather a critique of consciousness's knowledge. Its result, the goal of the entire discussion, is to show how consciousness realizes that the categories it uses are immanent in both being and itself, and that it is not an absolute origin but the appearance of something that preexists it. To put it differently, the goal is for consciousness to look beyond the appearances with which it begins and to reach the speculative point of view, a level of discourse in which the oppositions assumed as preliminary do not apply any longer and thinking and thing are the same. The *Phenomenology* is then the production of absolute knowledge, that is, a philosophical knowledge that has removed all presuppositions, wherein consciousness is more than the self-certainty it appears to itself: it is reason and spirit, that is, actual self-knowledge and appropriation of its own history.[38]

Initially, consciousness was self-certainty in opposition to something external and given, its other. Then consciousness discovers that it is the return to itself from the other and negative self-identity, that is, self-consciousness. In the subsequent stage, consciousness becomes reason, which finds itself in the object and is thus certain that it is everything actual. It finds universality in the individual because it believes it is the individual that realizes universality. Spirit, instead, reverses the perspective of phenomenological reason[39] by understanding that it is the universal which realizes itself in individuals. This takes place in different facets and contexts until the identity between human self-consciousness and absolute being is shown in Christianity. At that point there are no more differences between consciousness and God, who has manifested, embodied, and sacrificed Himself. We are at the level of science, of knowledge in which thinking and being are the same.

At the end of the *Phenomenology*, the ordeal of consciousness that has meanwhile become self-consciousness, reason, and spirit is run through again as the memory in which all shapes are regarded in their conceptual essence. If we consider retrospectively the whole process of discovery in its form, we realize that this is "the form of the self [*die Form des Selbsts*]" (*W* 3, 582, *PhS* 485). The self, in other words, is not just the I or self-consciousness, but it must become the self-knowing of the whole, that is, the substance that becomes a subject. Absolute knowledge, as conceptual knowledge and the identity of certainty and truth, is science and self-knowing spirit. Yet spirit ("spirit that traverses [*durchläuft*] its own self," *W* 3, 583, *PhS* 486) achieves self-knowledge only in the form of the return to itself from the other, leaving nothing relevant outside itself. For this reason, at the end of the *Phenomenology* Hegel speaks of science in terms of a "*comprehensive knowing [begreifendes Wissen]*" having "the shape of the self [*die Gestalt des Selbsts*]" (*W* 3, 583, *PhS* 485). Science is this "self-like form" (*in dieser selbstischen Form, W* 3, 588–89, *PhS* 491).

From these pages there transpires yet another conception of the self and of subjectivity, *the self of science itself as substance and subject.* In light of this, we understand why individual self-consciousness is nothing but the manifestation of a logic that is immanent in each of the determinations behind its back. We also understand why Hegel at this point begins to use the term "self-consciousness" with a new meaning. If we contrast it with the familiar notion of self-consciousness as the individual ego common in the language of representation, self-consciousness now acquires in philosophy the meaning of the substance that knows itself as concept and spirit. God, being, substance, the whole, must be conceived as the implicitly active basis that develops until it understands itself as spirit and concept bringing itself forth to existence. If speaking of the self-life form of the concept is unintelligible to representation, philosophy must precisely show that being has an inner movement and is concept, initially as object and finally as subject. At each level, then, we must recognize a unique substance that is driven to become real and actualize fully and knowingly what it is potentially or in itself.

This thesis about the concept that has a self-like form is more "surprising," in my view, than self-consciousness's desire. Yet it is not an occasional mention at the end of a complex work. It is a fundamental point— perhaps for Hegel the most decisive of all philosophy. Hegel returns to it in the preface to the *Phenomenology* when he writes that science organizes itself by the life of the concept by surrendering to the object's life. Knowledge does not supervene from without on the content; rather, "its activity is totally absorbed in the content, for it is *the immanent self of the content*" (*W* 3, 53, *PhS* 33, italics mine). Hegel returns to this key point again five years later in the introduction to the *Science of Logic* when he writes that speculative and pure science presupposes the path described in the *Phenomenology* as well as the liberation from the opposition of consciousness: "As *science*, truth is pure self-consciousness as it develops itself and has the shape of the self, *so that that which exists in and for itself is the conscious concept and the concept as such is that which exists in and for itself*" (*WL* I, 43, *SL* 29).

One might think that Hegel assigns the same logical movement of self-consciousness (identity, negativity, return to itself) to both substance and knowledge. Actually, once again a more radical stance is required and the perspective must be reversed. Thought is the very activity of substance;

knowledge—the concept, science—coincides with the self because substance is subject. Since substance is subject, it avails itself of individual self-consciousness and the I in order to advance and know itself. Absolute knowledge is thus not the swollen and triumphant rhetoric of a delusion that neglects finitude. Absolute knowledge is instead self-understanding as the self-consciousness or self-knowledge that being, actuality, and substance achieve.

In the *Science of Logic* substance will become actuosity, inner activity (*WL* II, 220, *SL* 490), the self-moving cause of its process of self-adequation (*WL* II, 224, *SL* 494), the positing of what it is in-itself and reflection into itself (*WL* II, 246, *SL* 510), the actualization of the basic matter [*Sache*] in which subjectivity is immanent (*ENZ* §147 and Z), and thereby the transition from necessity to freedom: the liberation that, taken as existing for itself, we can call I (*ENZ* §159 A).

Self-consciousness is the substance's self-consciousness. This is what speculative thought is about.

2

Nonhuman Thinking?

> Is Ahab, Ahab? Is it I, God, or who, that lifts this arm? But if the
> great sun move not of himself; but is an errand-boy in heaven;
> nor one single star can revolve, but by some invisible power;
> how then can this one small heart beat; this one small brain
> think thoughts; unless God does that beating, does that think-
> ing, does that living, and not I.
> —Herman Melville, *Moby-Dick*

Objective Thought and Speculative Logic

In the introduction we have seen the necessity of an inversion of the ordinary conception of thinking. In the first chapter we have analyzed the
reasons why Hegel criticizes the demand that philosophy begin with the I.

The possibility of nonhuman thinking, that is, a thought irreducible
to human consciousness, is the topic it is urgent to discuss now. I have
intentionally chosen a negative expression because "nonhuman thinking" must be able to stand for divine thought as well as for subhuman
and unconscious thought. After all, the reference to a hypothetical divine
thought must have some meaning independently of our beliefs in the
supernatural. I believe it would be equally difficult to deny the work of
some thought or other in, for instance, dolphins' and crows' purposive
behaviors, and even more so in actions we perform habitually which we
dub as "done without thinking."

More fundamentally, and this time in a positive sense, this negative expression—nonhuman thinking—refers to a thought that does not
depend on any alleged author or privileged actor, but rather unfolds according to a spontaneity that is alien to any will or design we may impose
on it. In this chapter, we must deal with this issue by focusing on three
aspects of such nonhuman thought: objective thought (1), the logical
element that animates the world (2), and the difficulty in understanding
how there can be a concept that as an original and first principle proceeds to become concrete in the world (3).

53

CHAPTER 2

Invoking an objective thought is another of Hegel's deliberate provocations.[1] If the I is one of the shapes that thought takes on; if every finite being is a one-sided way of the infinite; and if thinking is the self-determination of one and the same thought into the most diverse determinate concepts, then distinctions like subject and object represent the inner division of thinking, not an original opposition. The fundamental subject of the whole process, including its own splitting into a particular subject and object, into being and subjective thought, is nothing but thinking itself.

Actuality is no longer an external givenness that dictates to our thought its moves. Objective thought implies that thinking and being cannot be conceived of as originally different. Just as we must reconceptualize thinking, we must also reconceptualize being. Thinking frees us from the notion of a given reality that appears to us like an alienness beyond reach. Nevertheless, the aim of this process, far from inducing us to believe that the world is shaped at will by thinking, consists in fact in retrieving a true relationship between thinking and reality.

In this respect, we need to beware of the temptation to identify thinking and actuality simply. Not every thought deserves the title of actuality.[2] Subjective opinions are a good example of the unreality of some forms of thought. Conversely, only that kind of actuality which has concrete effects is rational. For example, an essence that does not appear in any form is empty and not actual. Accidental and possible beings do not constitute that actuality which Hegel calls rational (*ENZ* §6 A). Hence, it is not true that for Hegel nothing exists outside thought. Thought deals with the *Sache*, not with *Dinge*: not with things, but with what is essential to them.[3] In one of the most eloquent formulations of this thesis, Hegel writes: "It is only in the concept that something has actuality, and to the extent that it is different from its concept, it ceases to be actual and is a nullity; the side of tangibility and of sensuous self-externality belongs to this null side" (*WL* I, 44, *SL* 30).[4]

This is essential for Hegel as well as for his concept of philosophical truth, which consists, rather than in the relation between our judgment and a state of affairs, in the congruence between the thing and its concept. Clearly, we cannot take this congruence for granted, as we would be entitled to do if everything coincided with its concept (and the finite will be defined precisely as the gap between the thing and its concept). It is not the case that each thing coincides with its concept. Obviously, if the concept can actualize itself to different degrees (*WL* II, 517–18, *SL* 712), it is not in itself identical to its actuality.

Hence, we need to keep in mind two requisites: we must understand the plurivocity of the concepts of actuality-reality and rationality, and we must deal with them selectively, that is to say, by ruling out some of their senses. And we will also have to return to this seeming circularity according to which the actual is defined by reference to the rational, and vice versa. What actuality do possibility and accidentality, "the side of tangibility and sensuous self-externality" (*WL* I, 44, *SL* 30), enjoy if they are neither actual nor rational? Why does every thought that is not a thought of actuality have to be devoid of actuality?

If the logical element weaves together the world, the concept of objective thought is a tangled bundle of different elements that need to be unraveled. First of all, there is the idea that the philosopher's I must be effaced in order to let the thing's development acquire center stage. The polemics against the romantics' individuality, which Hegel considers an expression of vanity and futility, is as well-known as the episode of the dinner party at which Hegel replied to a question asked by a lady that everything personal that could be found in his philosophy is *falsch*, namely both false and wrong. We may object to the impoliteness of the joke or else appreciate Hegel's modesty and wit, maybe recalling the precedent of Plotinus, who insisted on his loyalty to Plato and Pythagoras as a way to defend himself from the charge of originality (*Enneads* 5.1.8–10). We can also raise the question, to which I will come back later, concerning the possibility of dissociating the personal I from the philosophical I and possibly concluding that thinking seems thus to consist in rising to a universal and objective reason that has cut all ties to the I. What matters is to understand the meaning of such effacement of the I: in philosophy we cannot impose anything arbitrary on the analysis of the thing itself. We must rather use discretion and look on the unfolding of the thing without tampering with it or bringing in any impertinent remarks, preferences, opinions, or assumptions.

Accordingly, the first, and least controversial, sense of the expression "objective thought" arises polemically against the subjective conception of thinking. Thinking is objective in the sense that anything true of its object does indeed pertain to the object, and such movement does not owe its unfolding to our subjective action, but is rather the progressive emergence of those aspects of the thing that manifest themselves during its investigation. This is unequivocally the meaning of the passage where Hegel introduces objective thought in the *Science of Logic*.[5]

It is not the thinking of our particular I but thinking for-itself that examines its own aspects and unfolds the way it does. We need to strip away all particularity and contingency in order to let the thing speak. In the preface to the *Phenomenology* Hegel writes: "Scientific cognition demands surrender to the life of the object. Or, what amounts to the same thing, confronting and expressing its inner necessity" (*W* 3, 52, *PhS* 32). If concepts are "pure self-movements" and "souls," "this refusal to intrude into the immanent rhythm of the Notion" is the "continence" expected of the philosopher (*W* 3, 56–57, *PhS* 35–36). This was the attitude, adds Hegel in the *Encyclopaedia*, that Aristotle encouraged us to take up and which "consists precisely in letting go of its [consciousness's] *particular* beliefs and opinions and letting the basic matter *hold sway* in itself" (*ENZ* §23). Such liberation from the particularity of thought is the condition for understanding Hegel's logic at its every step.

However, this picture of objective thought gets immediately complicated when we move on to the consideration of one of its consequences: the inner force of objective logos and reason as the drive to become reality.

The beginning of the Preliminary Conception to the *Encyclopaedia* Logic and the introduction and second preface to the *Science of Logic* run parallel. They employ various images that overlap, when they are not repeated literally. Hegel writes in the *Science of Logic* that "logic has nothing to do with a thought *about* something" because thought's necessary determinations "are the content and the ultimate truth itself" (*WL* I, 44, *SL* 29). Thinking is not an act of consciousness: "inasmuch as it is said that *understanding, that reason, is in the objective world,* that spirit and nature have *universal laws* to which their life and their changes conform, then it is conceded just as much that the determinations of thought have objective value and concrete existence" (*WL* I, 45, *SL* 30). In the parallel passages of the *Encyclopaedia*, Hegel explains that thought must be understood as the substance of things as well as the substance of their subjective thought. Hence, it is the *nous* (intellect) that is the ground of everything, including the inner activity of things and our subjective thought (*ENZ* §24 and Z 1). If we go back to the *Science of Logic*, the text reads: "The profounder foundation is the soul standing on its own, the pure concept which is the innermost moment of the objects, their simple life pulse, just as it is of the subjective thinking of them" (*WL* I, 27, *SL* 17). This is "the logical nature that animates the spirit, that moves and works within it" (ibid.).

The only difference between these passages concerns the fact that the second preface is pervaded by a theme that sounds like an obsession, Hegel's very last one (it was completed one week before Hegel's death), that is, the insistence on the force of thought which first appears as a drive and an urge to actualize itself. After all, if concepts are nothing but determinate forms of thinking and if thinking is not subjective, then there is only one answer: every movement, every progressive determination, every *dialectic* of concepts is not imposed from without, but is internal to the thing as drive and force.

Naturally this theme is not new, yet Hegel's emphasis here sounds unprecedented. In the 1812 introduction, Hegel writes that the system of concepts "is above all in this way to be erected—and it has to come to completion in an unstoppable and pure progression that admits of nothing extraneous" (*WL* I, 49, *SL* 33). This force of logos features strongly, like a new protagonist, in the 1831 preface.[6] Here Hegel speaks incessantly of the logos that "animates everything" that is, "the activity of thought at work in us across all representations, interests, and actions" which is "unconsciously busy." The logos is the "simple life pulse" of "categories [that at first] do their work only instinctively." "The logos, the reason of that which is," "instinctively and unconsciously pervade our spirit everywhere" (all quotations are concentrated in *WL* I, 27–30, *SL* 16–19). The task of logical science is to bring to consciousness such an objective and unconscious logos.

I was saying that this picture of objective thought complicates its initial meaning because this anonymous force seems to postulate a liberation from all human consideration, not just from particularity. While earlier on it was a trans-individual conception of thinking, now it appears as a trans-human view. The reference that often occurs when Hegel speaks of objective thought—perhaps in fact the most frequent reference—is Anaxagoras's concept of *nous* (intellect), which first posited thought as the principle of the world (*WL* I, 44, *SL* 29). The *nous* (and the Aristotelian discussion of the intellect is for Hegel the ultimately developed truth of Anaxagoras's seminal introduction of the intellect) is the cause of the world (*ENZ* §8 A). In the *Philosophy of History*, Anaxagoras's *nous* is employed by Hegel to explain the cunning of reason and the divine providence that presides over the world's events and governs the course of history.[7] It is symptomatic of Anaxagoras's naïveté about the forms of manifestation and work of the intellect that for him the *nous* confines its action to the natural world.

Despite what it may look like, the *nous* does not rule the world as the divine governs a totality of external material entities, whether ordered or even created by the *nous*. The intellect is not a cause in relation to which the world would be an effect. Having then dispelled this first impression which proves to be a misunderstanding,[8] the question regarding the relation between the *nous* and human subjectivity is still awaiting an answer.

Anaxagoras expresses very well the core of Greek metaphysics as Hegel interprets it. In the *Lectures on the History of Philosophy*, the *nous* that governs the world is the principle common to the philosophy of Plato, Aristotle, Plotinus, and Proclus. It means that there is reason in the world or, to put it in clearer terms that are possibly more congenial to some readers, there is an objective intelligibility that is irreducible to subjective thinking. In the preface to the 1831 *Science of Logic*, Hegel approvingly quotes the Aristotelian passage where Aristotle says that the science of

CHAPTER 2

thought, which is pursued as an end in itself independently of its scopes and interests, namely the free science of pure thought as Hegel intends it, "appears not to be a human possession" (*Metaph.* A 2, 982b28–29, in *WL* I, 23, *SL* 14).

How could we not conclude that thinking must transcend humanity? Indeed, we have seen that, in the case of the ellipse, rationality is actual independently of us. But if we assume the unity of thought (the homogeneity between thinking or self-conscious reason and objective intelligibility), are we forced to conclude that objective thinking is the first form of a movement that is in itself *independent of and untouched by human thought*? Or is this an impasse we must resist, based on a misleading reading of objective thinking—a "realist" and foundationalist reading that risks subordinating subjective thinking to a supposed trans-human thought?

A realist reading faces at least three problems that soon become insoluble. (1) *The I.* It is not clear what is supposed to happen to the I. We have seen it limited in many ways so far, but now it seems to be erased from philosophical logic altogether. (2) *Unconscious logos.* Logos as force and drive proceeds independently of our action. In fact, it appears like the soul of the world that preexists humanity and presides over it. (3) *The concept as the first in itself.* The translation of the *nous* that governs the world into speculative language seems, more than a translation, an ideological subreption insofar as it soon acquires the clothes of the traditional religious representation according to which the logos expresses the divine principle that makes itself finite in order to create nature as well as finite human spirit.

As an initial approximation, we can outline the following reply on Hegel's behalf. Each form of thinking, whether objective or subjective, divine, human, or unconscious, must be intended as one and the same activity that underlies both the *nous* and the world. If the logic of the *nous* were incommensurable with the logic of the world, and most notably with human logic, how could we call both of them "logics"?[9] Just as the *nous* must also manifest itself in human history, so there must be a continuity running through all logical determinations, and specifically through the case of the ellipse, the squirrel, and my subjective thinking that thinks both of them as at the same time homogenous and different. This does not mean that the ellipse is a movement that by some inexplicable contrivance at some point *becomes* the squirrel or is forcefully assimilated to it. It means that the logical movement, thinking's self-examination, weaves together the continuity of conceptual forms with its own necessary and immanent development. However, the fact that different objects gradually embody these conceptual forms is a further consideration, which does not fall into the field of logic. I find the ellipse and the squirrel as external objects I run into in my experience in turn, and yet I reconstruct them in their conceptual essence as tied by a relation of continuity because they share categories that speculative logic has purified, that is, isolated from their actualization in the world and examined for themselves, one by one as well as in their internal relations. The guide is not what is found, but thought thinking itself.

Thus we come to a peculiar conclusion. Objective thought is antisubjectivist in the sense we have just seen; it is not reducible to objective intelligibility, for "objective thought" indicates a *methodological* criterion and not one logical section as opposed to others (e.g., the ellipse instead of the squirrel, or both of them but not my purpose). And yet, in the inverted conception that Hegel invites us to adopt and that rules out the ordinary notions of objective and subjective, *objective thought is one mode of development of the subjectivity of thinking.*

For this reason, the realist reading of objective thinking cannot account for Hegel's philosophy. We will see more extensively in the third section of this chapter, on the concept as the first in itself, that the realist reading hypostasizes the absolute idea as the unique and complete agent of every process and contrasts objective thinking to subjective thinking. The problem is that for Hegel thinking must be both objective and subjective, whereby "subjective" refers to the purity of thought of the thing (*Sache*) which in one of its forms must also comprehend the particular subjectivity of the I. And the transition from objectivity to subjectivity is a transition that falls within logical science (it is not something that happens in the world) from a conceptual totality that forms the essence of the thing, while remaining external to it, to a totality articulated within conscious thought.[10]

We could say that thought without the thing is empty, and the thing outside thought is blind. Such identification between being and thought, however, is not something given that we can assume and take for granted, but is rather a process we must bring to life: speculative logic. It shows that objective thought is itself posited by thinking, so that once again it is thinking as independent of anything given that determines itself freely. Thinking does not have a ground outside itself that makes it possible. While it is certainly true that the logic has to do with metaphysics and ontology, it is more fundamentally the logic of pure thinking that thinks itself.

The ellipse and the squirrel do exist as unrelated, but their conceptual determinations are tied together by internal relations that it is the logic's business to reconstruct. The ordinary conception of thinking takes various particular concepts, from the ellipse to the squirrel, as *designations* of independent objects and *therefore* as separate concepts. Here we see as best we can how the ordinary conception of thinking corresponds to the typical procedure of the understanding (*ENZ* §80 and Z) which identifies its abstractions with self-subsisting entities. In other words, it is by virtue of the subjectivism imposed on thinking, which conflates the independence of objects and that of concepts, that the understanding identifies determinate concepts with mutually isolated universals.[11] The fatal vice is forgetting the activity that has given rise to determinate concepts. It is noteworthy that what is at stake here is not mere oversight: the understanding suppresses what is most essential about determinate concepts, the concept.[12]

We must take very seriously the Hegelian inversion of the ordinary conception of thought and show that concepts are moments of the self-determination of the concept. We might possibly want to add that what Hegel calls "the concept" (*den Begriff*) could be more helpfully named "conceiving" (*das Begreifen*), suggesting a verb rather than a noun, an activity rather than the determinate and plural products with which the ordinary view usually identifies the concept. Concepts are not external to the activity that produces them. The diverse universals produced by thinking appropriate what is essential to the movement of the concept: namely, the active subject that forms and modifies itself, thereby resulting in determinate concepts. In this inverted perspective, on the one hand, concepts are nothing but the concept in its determinacy and plurality, that is, in its self-determination. On the other hand, thinking exists only in thoughts, in determinate concepts. This must be kept in mind when we seek an answer to the question about the concept as the first in itself.

Concepts are the concept in a finite mode, the concept as it develops and makes itself determinate. The concept is a substance, a universal that manifests itself in the particular and individual modes of its being. As Aristotle stated in *De anima* that it is the same soul that makes us live, move, and think, likewise for Hegel the concept is literally "the soul of the concrete" (*WL* II, 276, *SL* 531). By contrast to the ordinary view, conceptual differences are the concept's inner differentiations. The concept understands particularity and individuality as the result of the becoming of the universality preexisting them. In this way, universality is the negative, the free activity of self-formation that remains at one with itself (*WL* II, 277, *SL* 532).

Kant distinguishes the idea of reason from the concept of the understanding in that the former has a formative power and presents a relation between whole and parts that is altogether different from the relation that applies to concepts. In the idea, the whole precedes the parts and organizes them architectonically. Thus, the whole lives in each of its parts, and each part is a particular reflection of the whole.[13] The same applies to Hegel's concept. The concept is not the transition to something else, but self-development insofar as "what are differentiated are at the same time immediately posited as identical with one another and with the whole" (*ENZ* §161). "Each moment of the concept is itself the entire concept" (*ENZ* §163 A). The universal is not the extrinsic relationship among singularities assumed as original: the universal is the substance and the root of singularities. Caius, Titus, and Sempronius are what they are by virtue of the universal that is individuated in them (*ENZ* §175 Z). Without their universal, they would no longer be what they are. This is the immanence of the concept in all its particular determinations.

Like cells, like every organism, the concept is a unity that determines itself by dividing itself. In Hegel's words, the concept realizes itself as judgment. It follows that those representations that are the starting point for the ordinary conception of thinking, that is, subject and predicate, are the self-division of an original concept which inevitably comprehends itself through the relation of those opposites. Hence, the judgment, which is the fundamental form of predication and assertion for the ordinary conception of thinking, is the result of the concept's self-division in two relata that are posited as existing per se and as self-identical. Yet the ordinary conception that takes subject and predicate as reciprocally independent believes that it is its own external reflection that connects them and attributes properties to them through the copula.[14] Kant holds that judgment is an act of the I-think which connects two independent representations by means of the copula. In truth, it is not I that institutes the unity; it is the concept that generates an objective production. The connection lies in the object, so that the judgment is the immanent movement by means of which a unitary determination divides itself. As a result, each thing is a judgment: an individuality that has its own nature or universality in itself, "a *universal* that is *individuated*" (*ENZ* §167). Each thing is at the same time the identity and difference of singularity and universality. Far from belonging to a different dimension than that of concepts, as in the case of Kantian intuitions, singularity is the progression of the universal toward the concrete.[15]

The ordinary conception of thought conflates understanding and representation. The concept itself is a representation, literally the way something is present to the mind. Kant summarizes this view when he writes that a concept is the *repraesentatio communis* representing its object mediately, that is to say, by means of characteristics that connect the concept to the object in a universal sense (*KrV* A 69/B 94; *Logik Pölitz, Ak*

24, 565–66). The twofold problem this conception takes it upon itself to solve is the connotations of concepts (how they are composed as simple totalities out of partial marks) and, above all, their denotation (how they refer to objects: their meaning).

Hegel does not deny that the concept can be a representation, but he strongly objects to reducing it to representation alone. The problem of representation is that it does not know itself, for it ignores its limits. Representation is unable to account for its genesis because it assumes that it must mirror whatever it finds and expresses through universals. It does not recognize its inner differentiation (the relationship between universality and particularity, between concept and example). Above all, it does not recognize the problem of its alterity and plurality (its relationship to other representations, that is, the dialectical relation among concepts). By taking marks as the matter or the ground of the concept, this view takes it as a result.

For Hegel instead, the concept can be a result only in the sense that it results from its own activity, and this is what is first. The problem of the concept in Hegel is therefore not reference, but its complete justification; the totality of its own self-relation and self-determination. If the concept is not *of something*, it is its content that has value and significance. If it is not *someone's concept*, that is, it does not belong to me, it is not a mental representation. As a consequence, Hegel's logic is neither a semantics, nor a transcendental philosophy, nor a philosophy of mind.

In this Hegelian perspective, what is inverted is the Aristotelian priority between first in itself and first for us. The ordinary conception takes concepts to be mental reproductions of things. Here things come first, and we translate them into mental constructs. Confident that it can generate and control thoughts, the ordinary conception considers concepts as our products. It is convinced that it is we who reflect, whereas in truth it is reflection that goes beyond immediacy toward the universal (*WL* II, 30–32, *SL* 350–51). It believes we confer objectivity on the connection *we* establish between subject and predicate through the copula, whereas in truth it is the concept that divides itself in a judgment (*WL* II, 304, *SL* 552).

In the context of the critique of subjective idealism which claims to turn concepts into the I-think's tools of knowledge, Hegel writes some lines of great importance that I wish to recall here. In our everyday life, we use categories as abbreviations by virtue of their universality in order to discover objective relations. Yet, when we realize that we are a universal in which feelings, desires, goals, and representations inhere, we realize that it is not we who employ categories; it is they that use us.[16]

> Such determinations of mind and spirit, when contrasted with the universality which we are conscious of being and in which we have our freedom, quickly show themselves to be particulars. . . . It is all the less possible, therefore, to believe that the thought determinations . . . are at our service; that it is we who have them in our possession and not they who have us in theirs. What is there of more in *us* as against them? How would we, how would *I*, set myself up as the superior universal over them—they that are the universal as such? . . . But still less shall we say of the concepts of things that we dominate them, or that the thought determinations of which they are the complex are at our service. On the contrary, our thought must accord with them, and our choice or freedom ought not to want to fit them to its purposes. Thus, inasmuch as subjective thought is our own most intimately inner doing, and the objective concept of things constitutes what is essential to them, we cannot step away from this doing, cannot stand above it, and even less can we step beyond the nature of things. (*WL* I, 25, *SL* 15–16)

The concept stands over us. When we think, it is the objective concept that dominates and uses us, not we the concept. Our thought moves within the boundaries established by the concept. We cannot escape its dominance any more than we can step out of our skin. Nevertheless, this does not mean that we are dominated by an alien power. Quite the contrary: when we think, we exercise our freedom in the highest sense, because thinking is our own and most proper nature (spirit's "unalloyed selfhood is thinking," *ENZ* §11).

The passage just quoted from the *Science of Logic*, which adds that the categories at work in us are unconsciously busy as a natural logic (*WL* I, 25, *SL* 16), restates the problem of the logos in a renewed form as not only trans-individual, but also trans-human. Perhaps, weary of the dead ends faced by subjective idealism in its various postmodern declinations, we might want to cherish such anti-subjectivism with enthusiasm. Still, it is not easy to see how assigning to the concept every relation of property and dependence we have taken away from the I represents a progress in terms of speculative sobriety. How not to suspect that this is an arbitrary and improbable metaphysical construct?

If truth is the objective truth that produces itself and the concept rules the world, including our own thoughts about it, how should we understand the concept? And how does it relate to the unconscious force of the logos?

Before we move to answer this question, let me summarize this section. Objective thought does not designate one realm of objects, but the method of speculative logic. The concept divides and articulates itself in a plurality of concepts. The concept is higher than and prior to our thought, yet this does not mean that thought is a ready-made substance that is foundational for our thought. It is at once the case that thought transcends us (or is trans-human) and cannot do without our thought.

The Logical Element (*das Logische*) as the Soul of Actuality

We have seen how the concept forms the soul of the things. As this soul, the concept is the substance and actuality of the thing, but it is not yet known as such. In fact, insofar as it is not known, the concept is an unconscious force that animates and moves the world. How should we understand the concept as "life-pulse," drive, and unconscious force? And how should we understand the huge difference between the logical element that animates the world and the logic as thorough knowledge of conceptual relations, that is, the logical element as being and the logic as thought's self-consciousness?[17]

When Hegel describes *das Logische* as a soul, he speaks of it in terms of blood flowing and throbbing in the things' veins as their truth. Without this capillary pulse and the order that this life instinctively follows, the logical element appears as "the dead bones of a skeleton thrown together in a disorderly heap" (*WL* I, 19, *SL* 12) that is familiar from the Scholastic study of logic (i.e., the various figures of concept, judgment, and syllogism in a tradition that goes back to the *Organon*).

And yet the logical element is also what Hegel calls "the realm of shadows [*Reich der Schatten*], the world of simple essentialities, freed of all sensuous concretion" (*WL* I, 55, *SL* 37). This is ideally in line with Walter Benjamin's "ice-desert of abstraction" as well as with the "nocturnal shadows" of the lied from *Des Knaben Wunderhorn* quoted in the introduction. Hegel's latter analogy seems at odds with the vitality and warmth of the former. Here it is as if the speculative philosopher had to descend to a peculiar Hades, which is not the kingdom of the dead.[18] There is nothing chthonic, that is, dark, mythical, or threatening to this Hades. The shadows do not live on as separate like the souls that belonged to people who were once alive and are no more. They must rather be considered in themselves timelessly as the principles animating everything. Precisely because it involves the souls of the living and not of the dead, this Hades is the realm of a truth pure from admixture with the sensible. A truth without veils, free from the concretion of the world, and this spectral rarefaction, "the colorlessness and stark simplicity of its pure determinations" (*WL* I, 54, *SL* 36), must be regarded as philosophy's promised land. Shadows do not pass themselves off as reality, as in the Platonic cave, but are interrogated. Yet the speculative philosopher is not driven by any necromancy of shadows.[19] It is not even a katabasis that leads us to this Hades. We do not reach it by descending, nor, strictly speaking, by rising toward it as if we had to climb a ladder we throw off once we get to our destination, for there is no real separation between essentialities and the world. The speculative philosopher, in other words, must free the logical element pulsing in things from its concretion and investigate it per se without considering it effectively separable from what it animates. In this liberation, spirit knows spirit, that is, its freedom and truth. The concept understands its work, its making itself being, and its self-knowledge.

While "objective thought" was a paradoxical phrase, "the logical" (*das Logische*) is an unusual expression starting from its grammatical structure: it is the substantivization of an adjective in the neutral. It is variously described by Hegel as a drive (*Trieb*, *WL* I, 27, *SL* 17), or as nature (*Natur*, *WL* I, 20, 24, 27, *SL* 12, 15, 17), but also as the logical idea that thinks itself (*ENZ* §574).[20] Therefore, the logical element cannot be one specific category, one determination among others. Nor can it be identified with the logos insofar as this is only unconscious, or with objective thought, which as we have seen has a methodological sense and does not refer to any particular way of being of the concept. The logical element is the content and object of the logic as well as of all philosophy. It has different meanings depending on how it is employed.

Notice a duplicity or ambiguity between inner and outer that is essential for the logical element. The logical assumes two different aspects: there is an ambiguity in the logical element between life and the understanding of life, as well as between nature, which the logical takes on as externality from which it must return to itself, and its complete self-knowledge. In the former, the unconscious force that animates the process is internal; in the latter it is the thorough coincidence free of any external residue at which we must aim in our scientific knowledge. These two aspects are closely related, but must not be regarded as opposed.

Let us consider the duplicity between soul or life and self-knowledge.[21] Life is impulse and force; the understanding of life is not. Life is intensity that seeks its development, the principle that fights to establish itself. Understanding is the principle that retraces itself retrospectively, reflectively. The inner teleology that is essential to the former is sublated in the latter as a wanting form. Naturally, the teleological form is wanting to the extent that it is not yet realized. In the same way, we say that any realization is wanting with respect to reality, and potentiality is defective in relation to the act: for potency has not become act yet, but it is nothing other than the impulse to become it.[22]

A second ambiguity of the logical element revolves around the concept of nature. For Hegel, nature is the idea *outside* itself. And yet, when considered in light of the logical as element, nature, and unconscious force, nature is like Aristotle's *phusis*: the *inner* principle of change, the motor and the very dynamics of the process of thinking.[23]

If so, we begin then to understand why it would be a mistake to oppose soul and understanding, the logical as drive and as self-consciousness. It is only when the logical element knows itself in its determinate forms that it eventually understands itself as the principle that has given rise to the whole movement. The logical is nothing but reason that seeks to know itself. In order to do so, the logical element must give itself an external form—a reality, a nature—in which to know itself. This is why the idea is the drive to seek itself in each of its determinations (*WL* II, 498–99, *SL* 697–98) until it comprehends itself. Therefore, *the logical stands to the logic as the content to its form*: the logic is the systematic form of the logical element, which initially appears as an impulse. The logic is the method immanent in the logical element.[24]

Let me dwell briefly on this point. According to a hylomorphic conception of the soul such as Aristotle's, soul and body work only together: the soul is the form of the body. However, this entails that, if the soul does not exist as a separate entity, there can be corporeity without soul (when the body is deprived of life). The body is a content that at least in principle is distinct from its form. In this Hegelian analogy, by contrast, the logical element is the content of itself. Its form is not even in principle distinct from it. The form is the systematic reflection upon itself on the part of the content. The content pushes to become form. And this explains why Hegel occasionally equates the logical element with the logic: it is about nothing but thought. The distinction is internal to the same subject.

What the form does is methodically run through the determinations of the logical element. But this methodical running-through on the part of the form in search of itself, which takes the shape of the logic as well as of the system, is nothing other than the process by which the logical element, which is at first an instinctual force, becomes self-conscious. This is why I propose to understand the logical element animating reality as reason's drive. Let me explain.

The logic is thought that knows itself. If thinking simply took thought as an object in the same way as ordinary logic does, we could then describe thinking from without. In this case, categories and principles would be given to thinking, without any order or development. Since thinking is instead a system of concepts, thought produces each category from the previous one through *determinate negation.*

Section 79 of the *Encyclopaedia* reads: "In terms of form, the logical domain has three sides: (a) the *abstract* side or that of the *understanding,* (b) the *dialectical* or *negatively rational* side, (c) the *speculative* or *positively rational* side. These three sides do not constitute three *parts* of logic, but *are moments of every real logical content* [*Momente jedes logisch-reellen*], that is to say, of every concept or everything true in general."[25] The logic is not separate from metaphysics and truth, but neither is it separate from dialectics, which no longer is the arbitrary and extrinsic art producing the appearance of contradiction. As we can see from this passage, thinking is the logical that determines itself in each of its three sides, not only as speculation. *Each* concept is a determinate and fixed abstraction that, when examined in light of its demand for absolute validity, realizes its limitedness and aims beyond itself. Yet, in order to function, it need not always do so.

Concepts can actually work insofar as they establish their determinacy and their own limits. The understanding's abstraction is necessary. In order to know rationally, one needs first to distinguish between contingency and necessity, essence and manifestation, universality and particularity. We have seen how the understanding is often exemplified by firmness of character. This is analogous to the capacity of attention of holding fast to its object without being distracted or diverted by anything (*ENZ* §448). It is this "identische Richtung" (ibid.) of the understanding that hands its determinations over to the concept. To put it differently, the shape of the understanding is a straight line. If the shape of reason is the circle, it is because reason has rounded the shape of the understanding onto itself.[26]

It is imperative to acknowledge in full the importance of abstraction, which holds fast to determinacy. Contrary to popular belief, Hegel celebrates the understanding's work. Without it we have nothing to go on. Without it we do not get reason, but irrationality.[27]

Likewise, the formation of certain intellectually ordered systems must be preserved and acknowledged. For instance, it is the "logical drive" of thought *in the form of the understanding* that produces the grammar of our languages (*ENZ* §459 A; as you can see, the logical element can determine itself even as understanding alone). And this is necessary because the elements of our grammar and syntax must be understood as fixed, isolated, and abstract. If syntax were fluent and plastic, its absence of determinacy would not permit any distinction or understanding: it would be a chaos.[28]

CHAPTER 2

The understanding's identity, determinacy, and univocity are indispensable. But identity is itself one moment of rationality, to be thought together with nonidentity. The understanding is one form that reason takes. The understanding is necessary, but as a premise that reason must make fluid and comprehend in its movement. This consideration warns against downplaying the role of the understanding in the context of speculative logic. It also exemplifies the inevitability of the relation between understanding and reason within the logical element (whereby, again, understanding and reason do not stand for human faculties, but rather for ways of intending the concept).

A second consideration is that the dialectic is the movement that belongs to *each* concept. In other words, its logic is not alternative to the ordinary logic. Nor is it possible to dissociate positive and negative dialectic, or skeptical moment and positive moment, as if we dealt with two different dialectics.

A third consideration that refers to this passage from §79 is that thought pulses in things as their heart. This stresses the arbitrariness of all interpretation of negation, dialectic, and truth in Hegel in terms of propositions.[29] Negation, contradiction, and truth in Hegel are objective, not linguistic or epistemic, that is, typical of a method or language that is separate from the world.

The inner negativity of concepts must be understood and valued. As an intellectual and negatively rational moment, the logical element produces the discrepancy between thought and thinking, thereby generating the dialectical movement. This is what sustains and articulates the exposition of categories. To be sure, unlike the previous tradition which distinguished between deduction and exposition and separated method from content, speculative *Darstellung* is deduction precisely because it is the exposition of a thought that is already in itself necessity, movement, and inner articulation, the progressive self-determination of the concept. A gap, a difference between each thought-determination and its capacity of accounting for itself, ensures that this movement develops. It is the content that moves; it is not the method reflecting upon an external object that introduces movement.[30] Determinate negation is not a functional operator brought in by an external examiner. It is that side of each thought which promotes the movement of determinations and generates a new form out of the discrepancy between the meant and the true.

It is owing to such a discrepancy that Hegel understands the logical as instinct. A gap, a defect, a lack are expressions of the negativity that urges to overcome them. Contradiction must be understood in this way. "Contradiction is the root of all movement and life; it is only in so far as something has a contradiction within it that it moves, is possessed of instinct and activity. . . . Self-movement proper, *drive* in general is likewise nothing else than that something is, in itself, itself and the lack *of itself* (*the negative*), in one and the same respect. Something is alive, therefore, only to the extent that it contains contradiction within itself" (*WL* II, 74–75, *SL* 382).

When a finite form turns out to be wanting and limited, it is not nothingness, but rather the nothingness from which it results.[31] Determinate negation has a determinate content, but at once urges to a new form. Hegel describes pain as the privilege of the living, which can endure contradiction and strive to resolve it (*WL* II, 481–82, *SL* 684; *ENZ* §359). Unlike limits, which are external negations, lack is internal. It arises from the feeling of incompleteness and is the drive to suppress it. Thus, the need does not only denote lack, but also and more fundamentally the self-affirmative response to lack; it is subjectivity at work in overcoming negativity. The logical element as drive is then the simultaneity of positive and negative (*WL* II, 75, *SL* 382), or more precisely the negation of negation ("Die Negation jener Negation," *WL* II, 482, *SL* 684).

In the pages on method and the absolute idea, Hegel writes that the method is reason's force and drive (*Kraft* and *Trieb*, *WL* II, 552, *SL* 737). But if all instinct is driven by a feeling of incompleteness, what is it that reason lacks? What drives reason is the desire for satisfaction, and it finds satisfaction when it feels at home in its otherness. As logical instinct, reason is defined by the impulse to be at home in the world. If reason is a unitary force that has both theoretical and practical effects, this takes on once again different meanings depending on the context. For instance, in the Philosophy of Right in the *Encyclopaedia*, reason must establish its own freedom in the dimension of practice and institutions. In the Psychology, reason must comprehend itself in the other it first finds as given. In the Logic, Hegel must show the pure form of this movement in which reason seeks itself in externality which first appears foreign to us, but from which we regain ourselves once the teleology of reason has completed its mission and nothing more remains to be done. We shall see in the next chapter how the dynamics of thought, what Marcuse called its motility (*Bewegtheit*), works according to this model.

Since reason is this calling (*Bestimmung*) to deal with itself in its other, its motivation is internal. Like *erôs* for Plato's Diotima, which is equally *penia* and *poros*, reason's poverty is reason's resourcefulness. Yet, unlike *erôs*, reason's motivation does not come from without, nor does it make us transcend this world in order to point toward a truth that resides elsewhere. It is in this world that reason seeks itself. And the satisfaction that reason desires can be achieved at the end of a long process. Only at the end is truth *bewährt*, shown as real truth.

CHAPTER 2

If so, we understand why for Hegel thought is a movement that is everywhere the same. It is a form of adequation, a search for the coincidence between the concept and being, which is not dictated from without but solely by the need for wholeness on the part of the concept. From this point of view, the dialectic of the Logic is similar to the dialectic of the *Phenomenology*. While in the *Phenomenology* the dialectic consisted in filling the gap between knowledge and truth, in the Logic it is not consciousness that makes experience of this gap between certainty and truth, and yet we have a dialectical movement in its purest form: each conceptual determination is a process of testing itself and proving its validity as capable of exhibiting the thing. The upheaval of consciousness in the *Phenomenology* is the dialectic of conceptual determinations in the *Science of Logic*. While at the end of the *Phenomenology* it was possible to trace back consciousness's journeys of discovery in their conceptual essence, in the Logic it is the idea that in the end retraces all the forms of thought's self-determination. In both cases, the end-station of the process eventually appears to be the motor that has given rise to it—that which has been developing in it.[32]

While consciousness sought to adequate itself and the in-itself, the logical movement rests on this gap between finite determinations and the self-knowing idea. The gap is filled not when consciousness becomes aware of the dynamics behind its back, but when the logical element as soul coincides with the logical element as self-knowledge. As we shall see in the next chapter, in order to work and understand itself the logical element must become drive, unconscious nature, and even more paradoxically, it must know itself as such.

At this point one would be strongly tempted to claim that it is the absolute idea that pulls the strings of all this movement. On the one hand, this is textually undeniable, even trivial. On the other hand, if this principle is not correctly understood, it risks hypostasizing the idea as the unique agent, which appears ready-made and complete before our knowledge. This is how many interpret Hegel's logic. More importantly, it is worth stressing that Hegel himself suggests such a reading. However, this is a reading that not only hypostasizes the idea and is incompatible with other central aspects of the notion of the idea. It is also and above all, much like the realist interpretation of objective thought, a reading that misunderstands the relation between finite and infinite, including the relationship that is at stake in this book: the relationship between infinite and finite knowledge, between thinking and the I.

I am speaking of a fatal risk because in this reading the idea would coincide with the full truth which at some point communicates itself to us for unfathomable reasons, whereby the only gain consists in the fact that something like the jealous God of the Old Testament would be replaced by the no less inscrutable generosity of something like Plotinus's One. The idea would be the thing in itself, of which nature and spirit would be the appearances, the only true protagonist of every saying and doing, to the point of making us irrelevant. I refer to such risk in light of what I believe we can learn from the three final syllogisms of the *Encyclopaedia*, as well as from the relation between the logical element and the sciences.[33]

In the *Phenomenology* we were confronted with a consciousness that progressively discovered what moved it. This discovery was the way consciousness commensurated its beliefs with the truth it uncovered. In the logic as well as in the system, we no longer have a gap between certainty and truth because we have left behind the opposition between subject and object. And yet, even in the logic and in the scientific system of truth, the meaning and value of the logical element depend on how we understand it: how we get to it and how we know it.

Most notably, the logical element has different meanings depending on whether we take it as the result of the sciences or as a beginning. Only when the logical element is seen as the result of the experience of the sciences does it acquire its own value, as one can read in the introduction to the *Science of Logic* (*WL* I, 55, *SL* 37). Hence, it is already within the logic that Hegel underlines the one-sidedness of the logical element. Indeed, if we knew the logical element only in its pure and self-conscious form as absolute idea, we would not yet know how the idea makes itself objective in nature and finite spirit. From this, we must draw the conclusion that what we have learned about thought at the end of the *Science of Logic* concerns the idea in itself, before its realization and finitization, which thus falls short of the understanding we get at the end of the *Encyclopaedia*.

Here, in section 574, Hegel writes: "This concept of philosophy is the *self-thinking* idea, the knowing truth, the logical with the meaning that it is the universality *verified* in the concrete content as in its actuality. In this way science has returned to its beginning, and the logical is its *result* as the *spiritual*." Knowing only the logical idea means to possess its truth, but knowing also how the idea pervades reality means for spirit to possess the certainty that that truth is all there is. In other words, knowing the concept is not yet knowing its congruence with reality. Knowing the idea without knowing the modes of its realization is a formal knowledge. Since the idea can intuit its reality only in spirit, the logic cannot be the exclusive core of philosophy at all, that is, its goal or its presumed end.

In our attempt to understand thinking in its broadest sense in Hegel, we thus realize that the logic does not offer a self-sufficient or complete perspective. However, we must also understand that if the logic does not have the final word regarding thinking, turning to the system as it is exposed in the *Encyclopaedia* is not sufficient either. Indeed, not even the *Encyclopaedia* can be read as a linear and progressive description of the true, because it is one contingent configuration among others. For instance, when we speak of logic, nature, and spirit, we do not talk about parts of philosophy. Nor is there any alleged transition from logic to nature—nor, finally, any priority of one element over the other two. Indeed, idea, nature, and spirit do not stand for separate entities, nor can they be understood independently of each other. Each of these three elements of philosophy is the whole from one particular perspective. The logicality of the idea is one of its guises, one that has not entered the sphere of appearance yet, as the soul of nature and spirit (*WL* II, 550, *SL* 736). The idea manifests and realizes itself in different modes in the logic, in nature, and in spirit. The idea of knowledge belongs in the logical idea, but it is nothing more than a possibility that becomes real only in finite spirit. The immediate presupposition of spirit is nature, from which spirit liberates itself, but the first presupposition of spirit is the logical idea (*ENZ* §574–77, §381 and Z, §182 and Z).

To put it differently, the three moments of philosophy are a self-mediating circle, a syllogism in which the elements take on the meaning they have only in their mutual relation. Each position on the part of one element presupposes its relationship to the others (it is the dialectic of positing reflection as presupposing with which Hegelians are familiar). In this sense, the logic does come first, but such primacy is an initial appearance we must put in question because the system of philosophy is a recursive circle in which progression is not linear, but must be conceived of as the deepening of the logical element in each realm.

This does not mean that the logic can be considered from different standpoints at will. The logic remains the science of objective thinking in the sense so far clarified, and this is its necessity. Still, it does make a difference whether the idea is considered as the realm of pure thought or as spirit's awareness of its own freedom.

In the introduction to the *Science of Logic* Hegel compares the study of logic to that of grammar (*WL* I, 55, *SL* 37). To those who know a certain language well, grammar shows how the spirit and culture of a people permeate and pervade that language. In the absence of such knowledge, grammar seems to contain only abstract and arbitrary rules. The difference is between abstract and empty universals and concrete universals, namely made concrete by a living spirit that shines in and through the details. As you can see, the difference is between a logic understood as a particular formal structure, alongside other structures that may interest and excite us much more, and a logical element that we finally see weaving and pulsing in every living fold of reality.

Something similar applies to the reading of Hegel. The absolute idea is real only insofar as it is thought. Only when it is made true by spirit does the logic reveal itself in its true value. But this means that knowledge—that is to say, the perspective of subjective spirit (*WL* I, 55, *SL* 37), that is, individuals who read and presumably write the *Science of Logic*—determines the value of the logic and enables the transformation of an abstract universal into "a universal that encompasses within itself the riches of the particular" (*WL* I, 55, *SL* 37), "a universal which no longer stands as a particular alongside other particulars but embraces them all in its grasp and is their essence, the absolutely true" (*WL* I, 56, *SL* 38).

In sum, there exists no truth in itself. Without the meaning it has for us, truth is not.

The Concept as the First

We have seen in the previous section that the logical element (*das Logische*) is the soul of actuality and the logic is the systematic form of the logical element. Each concept is a determinate and fixed abstraction, but is also run through by an inner negativity and arises by determinate negation. Identity is one moment of every concept. Likewise, the understanding is one form that reason takes. The logic must not be understood as the foundation of everything, because the idea has different value and being depending on how it is thought. But in itself, that is, if it is not thought, it has no being.

This careful and elaborate methodological criterion is much more than mere contextualization simply warning us to keep in mind the framework in which we move. It is the heart of the theory of syllogism as self-mediation: the system insofar as it is thought. Nonetheless, one of the most famous provocations of the *Science of Logic* seems to undermine this criterion. "Accordingly, logic is to be understood as the system of pure reason, as the realm of pure thought. *This realm is truth unveiled, truth as it is in and for itself.* It can therefore be said that this content is *the exposition of God as He is in his eternal essence before the creation of nature and of a finite spirit*" (*WL* I, 44, *SL* 29).

The helpfulness of this analogy is clear. Thinking is not one particular truth among others but is the only truth, without which nothing has value or meaning. Thinking has in itself something absolute, that is, it is not mixed with representations or anything finite and particular.

CHAPTER 2

It has its inner logic that does not depend on anything else that may be found and experienced independently of it, and such independence is an autarchic movement in its own way. Nature and spirit are concrete and particular forms of this logical element.[34]

From this, however, it becomes clear why I referred to the above-mentioned passage as to a provocation. Strictly speaking, it is an analogy (Hegel introduces it by saying: "it can therefore be said"); doubtless it is neither a description nor a definition. If we took it at face value, its consequences would be as important as counterproductive for Hegel. Logic would correspond to the supposed Platonic land of truth, the unmixed *ontôs on*, or to Leibniz's realm of eternal truths, to which a poietic moment (the creation of nature and finite spirit) would then be added. Philosophy would not simply share its content, namely truth, with religious representation (as *ENZ* §1 has it). Philosophy would be nothing but religion, and as such it would be derivative, subordinate, and parasitic, since it is from religion that philosophy originally gets the image of a divine maker. Furthermore, this analogy introduces through the back door a temporal relationship between before and after which does not belong to logical relations and contravenes one of the most recurrent expressions in the logic: namely, that the idea eternally produces itself. The concept of creation belongs to representation, not to speculative philosophy. In this analogy, truth is established once and for all in God's mind, which proceeds later on to give truth a body.

The independence of the logic and its primacy are reduced in this image to an in-itself, an a priori.[35] We then oppose to such a priori the actual, nature and spirit, in relation to which logic would have a foundational function. In this image categories are then exposed in their truth and completeness in the logic, and come to realization in, if not applied as such to, nature and spirit. This would explain Hegel's affinity with traditional philosophy and also the idea of rising toward a trans-human level, in which we can enjoy the vision of truth without veils. Whether it is divided in the highest genera of the *Sophist* or in the truth value to which every thought can be reduced for Frege, thought does not internally refer to a thinker. It is something to which we conform and rise.

All of this contravenes Hegel's thought because, by taking the logic as separate from being, it misunderstands the concept of a priori and the primacy of the concept. Furthermore, by employing non-dialectical and extrinsic operations such as that of application, this interpretation does not acknowledge the animating character, which is neither foundationalist nor causal, of the logical element within actuality. In this reading nature and spirit are not the actuality of the concept, but at best borrow categories that are defined and exhausted elsewhere. Above all, categories and thought-determinations are understood as complete in themselves: fixed, static, ready-made, available for a use that does not in turn modify them. Indeed, this analogy construes their essence and function as mutually independent. But thinking exists nowhere other than in thoughts, in determinate concepts. One can see that such a "realist"[36] reading misses the dialectical dynamics of thought-determinations. It is not the speculative philosopher but the understanding that conceives in this way of the forms of thinking. Once again the affinity between the understanding and representation is striking, and it is this logic they share that philosophy must call into question when it comes to the concept.

We have seen the problem of assuming the plurality of determinate concepts as originally given rather than as the self-determination of the concept. We can now appreciate in what sense this realist reading takes up the converse thesis, a notion of thinking that is independent of thoughts, as if there could be *thinking in itself without thoughts* and determinate concepts. This is the flaw of this reading, a concept of truth as immutable: univocal, pure, independent, given once and for all, transcendent. It suffices to go back a few lines before the passage in question in order to understand it rightly. The previous paragraph came to the following conclusion: "As *science*, truth is pure self-consciousness as it develops itself and has the shape of the self, so that that which *exists in and for itself is the known concept* [*gewußter Begriff*]" (*WL* I, 43, *SL* 29, trans. corrected).

It is then evident that this realist reading misunderstands what Hegel claims about the eternity of the idea. For Hegel, there cannot be any truth apart from its coming true. Each truth is such, that is, it has meaning and value, insofar as it shows itself at work. Thus truth must be active, living; it must be able to speak to us and convince us. To put it differently, not even God or a supposed Absolute is true if viewed in isolation. Generally speaking, *no in-itself has truth*. Each truth must show itself in its becoming and must be known by us as such. Truth is what is known to be true.

For this reason, we can say that my considerations about nonhuman thinking must respect the fundamental principle that the idea, the absolute, and the true are insofar as they are thought and known. If it is true that it is not just the human being that thinks, it is nonetheless true that it is only as spirit that the true may come to know and realize itself. Hegel means the same thing when, as he speaks of representation, he says that "God is essentially in his community"[37] of believers, and, as he speaks of philosophy, he says that the absolute is what we know about it.

There is no absolute vantage point or view from nowhere that one is supposed to achieve by rising painstakingly to a superhuman perspective. This is not because Hegel glorifies finitude or humanity, but because we

CHAPTER 2

cannot identify philosophy with an ascent that severs ties with the finite and the human in order to disclose the sight of the true.

If there is no truth unless realized, if truth is its becoming real, the first thing to be called into question is the couple of concepts *beginning* and *end*. In material processes, in production commonly understood, linearity includes a difference within itself at many levels: between producer and product, between process and goal, between the initial and the final moment. According to Hegel, Aristotle's greatness lies not so much in his showing these features of the activity called *poiêsis* or production, which are the same for all incomplete movement. Aristotle's merit consists in pointing to the alternative model of complete *energeia*. In the latter, which rules both thinking and human practice and in which no difference between past and present counts, we have a process of self-development, not a movement of becoming other. Here the subject of movement and its end coincide (the subject is *archê kai telos*), as do beginning and end which are no longer separate. This is what Hegel has in mind when he writes with regard to the teleology of the concept that "in its efficacy, it does not pass over [into something else] but instead *preserves itself*. That is to say, it brings about itself alone and is, in the *end*, what it was in the *beginning*, in the original state" (*ENZ* 204 A).[38]

Linearity is alien to philosophy; "progression in philosophy would be rather a retrogression and a grounding," "*a retreat to the ground, to the origin and the truth* on which that with which the beginning was made, and from which it is in fact produced, depends" (*WL* I, 70, *SL* 48–49; *WL* II, 570, *SL* 750). For philosophy, the beginning must act as the basis that maintains and develops itself in further determinations, the universal that is immanent in its diverse modes (*WL* I, 71, *SL* 49; *WL* II, 569, *SL* 749). "In this advance the beginning thus loses the one-sidedness that it has when determined simply as something immediate and abstract; it becomes mediated, and the line of scientific forward movement consequently turns *into a circle*" (*WL*, I, 71, *SL* 49; see also *WL* II, 570–71, *SL* 750–51). The first and the last are the same, and the development belongs to the same subject, except for the fact, far from irrelevant, that the first is abstract and immediate, and the last is the result of the movement. In this way, we must conceive of the first as a result potentially, and the result as the complete explication of the beginning. If the beginning is nothing but the result in its immediacy and abstraction, and conversely the result is the truth of the immediacy with which we begin, then we can better grasp why the absolute idea is the subject of the whole logical process and absolute spirit is the subject of each finite manifestation.[39]

When we get to the end of the logic, the concept has posited what it had presupposed until then. Thus, in the Subjective Logic being and essence appear to have been present at the outset. Yet, while it seems that they produce the concept, in truth they are moments of the self-production by means of which the concept has determined itself. In the end, being and essence are abstract moments of the concept that has returned to itself (*ENZ* §159 A). The concept is the origin of its development; it is self-production and self-specification.[40]

It is possible to express the same point by saying that the concept is being that in the end has understood itself.

If so, it is clear that the primacy of the concept does not lead us to consider it an efficient cause of every process. If anything, thought is cause in the same way as the Aristotelian god: as final cause, which, however, unlike the Aristotelian god, is immanent in the world. It is for philosophy that the concept is the first (*das Prius*). It is for philosophical knowledge that the concept turns out to be the true form that produces its content. It is for reason's knowledge, which does not start with the givenness of things but goes back to the primacy of the concept so as to find itself again in objectivity, that the concept is the first. It is philosophy that acknowledges in the work of the concept the type of causality called the actualization of an end.[41] We have seen that the ellipse and the squirrel have the conceptual form they have independently of human thinking. Thinking is first insofar as it transcends humanity. The logical is at first as soul and life-pulse; but it is known only at the end, in human thinking, as the first. The absolute idea, "the sole subject matter and content of philosophy" (*WL* II, 548, *SL* 735), is first in the sense that only for philosophical knowledge does it come first.[42] Only at the end do we realize how present, pervasive, and active in each determination thought was. Reason is embodied in but does not create the world. Reason that knows itself is the same that moves the world, exists in things as their intelligible core, purpose, and essence. Once again, it is essential not to presuppose any separateness between thinking and being or any particular meaning to thinking.

The absolute idea is not a metaphysical entity, separate and a priori. Strictly speaking, the absolute idea does not add anything further to what precedes it in the order of the exposition of the logic and the system. Nor, once we understand its primacy, is it a full-fledged agent before its development.[43] We get the absolute idea when all the previous determinations become a systematic totality. Here we have again the same theme we have seen in relation to the logical element: it is the whole movement that matters, and everything depends on the way in which we conceive of it. Its meaning and value change depending on that.

> When one speaks of the absolute idea, one can think that here finally the substantive must come to the fore, that here everything must

CHAPTER 2

> become clear. . . . ; the true content, meanwhile, is nothing but the
> entire system, the development of which we have considered up to this
> point. . . . In this respect, the absolute idea is comparable to the old
> man who says the same religious sentences as the child does, but for the
> old man they have the meaning of his entire life. Even if the child un-
> derstands the religious content, what validity that content has for him
> is still of the sort that lies outside his entire life and world. The same
> holds then also for human life in general and the occurrences that
> make up the content of it. All work is only aimed at the goal, and if this
> is attained, then one is astonished at finding nothing else than precisely
> this, what one wanted. *The interest lies in the entire movement.* If a human
> being pursues his life, then the end can appear to him as quite limited,
> but it is the entire *decursus vitae* [course of a life] that is encompassed in
> it. (*ENZ* §237 Z, italics mine)

If thinking is the element of every conceiving, we cannot help but start
with the logical element. Since conceiving includes possible objections
to Hegel, we can say that what appeared in the eyes of Schelling, Trendelenburg, and Kierkegaard to be the arbitrary move of starting with a
being that was already surreptitiously identified with thinking turns out
actually to be a strength. For in the end we necessarily conclude that we
were already moving from the very beginning in an element that was active in and pervaded each determination. The same immediacy of the
beginning proves to be necessary. In Peperzak's words, "only at the end
of the system does it appear that the beginning was in fact already the
whole work."[44]

If truth is what shows itself to be true and if there is no privileged
starting point for philosophy, then we can best understand in its poi-
gnancy the Hegelian answer to the critique according to which it would
have been better to begin with the absolute idea. There is no truth in
itself. Truth consists in its exposition, and this must be concrete, developed, and take the shape of a circle wherein each determination is retrieved and exposed as a necessary moment of the totality. Therefore,
even though the concept is the first, it cannot be taken as a starting
point, as an immediate with which we should begin. Rather, it must be
expounded as a self-mediation.[45] Here is a theme recurrent since the Jena
years, when Fichte and Spinoza were the target: the critique of the positional or thetic beginning in philosophy. "Where it is a matter of knowing
through thinking, *it is not possible to begin with the truth*, because the truth,
insofar as it forms the beginning, rests on a mere assurance while the
truth that is thought has to verify itself, as such, to thinking" (*ENZ* §159
Z, ital. mine; see *ENZ* §83 Z).

NONHUMAN THINKING?

If truth is its own becoming, then we must understand the true as the subject of its self-determination. At this point, it is clear why for Hegel every moment of conceptual determination is a definition of the true or the absolute. Here truth or the absolute (even God in the *Encyclopaedia*) comes down to the ultimate subject matter of philosophical knowledge. Like the absolute idea, they are neither particular entities nor substances that exercise any causality. They satisfy the requisites of scientific validity and totality. The assertion that each determination is a different definition of the absolute[46] must be understood in this light in the logic and the system. The same applies to the beginning of the discussion of each philosopher in the *Lectures on the History of Philosophy*, where we read that each determinate philosophy conceives of *the true* in the modality that Hegel proceeds to expose. When Hegel speaks of the true or the absolute as the only subject of becoming, he means that they can be treated as the final (or first) category, as thought in itself without presuppositions. As a result, the absolute can be hypostasized and reified as little as the idea.

Secondarily, if the absolute is the only object of philosophy, it is immanent in each determination. Therefore, it should not be said that philosophy cannot begin with the absolute, because the absolute is always with us even if we are not necessarily aware of it. The beginning is actually the absolute from the most abstract and immediate point of view; the absolute is initially poverty. The thesis according to which the absolute is with us expresses in more imposing or metaphysical terms the same idea that we have already examined about thought as pervading each thing.[47]

Finally, for Hegel this amounts to showing that the true should not be isolated from the false. In fact, the finite is an integral part of the true. The true must show in itself the nullity of the finite. The true cannot be without a relation to the non-true; it is *index sui et falsi* (i.e., truth is the touchstone of both truth and falsehood). And this is another aspect of Hegel's anti-Platonism according to which the purity of the logic is the result of the philosophical work that frees concepts from their concretion, not an attribute of separate ideas unmixed with the sensible.

By way of a conclusion of this section, it is possible to turn to the concept of nonhuman thinking and to the difference between Hegel and Plato one last time from a different point of view. In his dialogue with Adeimantus in book 3 of the *Republic*, Socrates says: "I do not know yet, but whithersoever the wind, as it were [*hôsper pneuma*], of the argument blows, there lies our course" (394d7–9, trans. Shorey). This image that the discourse *must* go where the wind blows is baffling. It sounds intrinsically contradictory. If we are at the mercy of the wind, what is the use of Socrates's point ("we must go")? It seems that the wind overpowers and governs us without leaving room for any choice on our part, not even

CHAPTER 2

the *amor fati* of accepting its whims while we exclaim that thus we wanted it to be. In other words, it appears that there is no room for mediation between the wind and freedom: the alternative is neat. But it would be so if Socrates meant that we are carried away by the wind like bodies in a storm. Instead, he does not refer to gravity, namely, something that we know is connected with our soul although we wish to break free from it, but to something we recognize as intimately our own, the inner necessity of the logos. We are not passive when we think. Our discourse can second the rigor and objective cogency of thought, or resist it. If we resist it, and we are free to do so, it is because we wish to avoid a necessity that we have not yet recognized as our own. To put it differently, I may prefer a particular opinion to a truth in which I have little interest or which I fear because I feel it could crush or smother me. And the truth that I do not want to acknowledge is not inscribed in a divine decree that is finished once and for all: Socrates ("I do not know yet") has yet to discover the direction in which he will follow the logos.

In my view, much of this sense of necessity is included in the Hegelian concept of objective thought. Nevertheless, the differences from the wind of which Socrates speaks are more meaningful than their affinities. We risk being crushed by the wind of the logos only when we do not realize that it appeals to our most rational part. We are not overwhelmed by it, and yet for Socrates this wind transcends us. Its power is superior to the human. Our most rational choice consists in following it once we have discovered it, but there is no way we can produce it. We free ourselves from our particularity by raising ourselves to it. By contrast, in Hegel our particularity has quite a different meaning. The I, of which we have seen so far all the limits, appears to be as necessary as it was necessary for the idea that we think it.

This point is the object of the final section of this chapter. Before that, however, I would like to recapitulate what we have achieved so far. The logical as unconscious power is nothing but the negativity and inner dialectic of concepts. The logos is first and in several forms unconscious because it must thoroughly establish reason in the world. It remains instinct and force because it is life that pushes forward in order to establish itself and become real. Yet, for the logical element, to live is to know itself, and when it knows and understands itself it is the self-conscious idea. The instinct of the logos is to get to know this result, and this is why it is a force.

The Hegelian conception of thinking can teach us something important provided we do not misunderstand it in terms of successful slogans such as Heidegger's "onto-theology." It is true that thinking is not just a human product. Still, we cannot hypostasize the idea. Thinking is nothing without its self-determination: it is the comprehensive determination of all its determinate concepts. The concept, the absolute idea, the truth should not be considered as complete in themselves and totally developed, like an absolute that is ready-made and that becomes finite at a certain point. The absolute idea is only insofar as it is thought, so that only at the end, when it has run its course, does the idea comprehend what it is. Only at the end can the idea understand that it has been the motor and original soul of the whole movement. The idea is only the result of its own becoming, and it is only retrospectively, when we write down the whole encyclopedic system, that we can say that the idea was the force at work from the very beginning.

For this reason, I believe that whoever cares about Hegel should be wary of the shortcuts and simplifications inherent in both metaphysical realism and contemporary transcendental or neo-pragmatic readings of his philosophy.

The Logic of the I

We have seen that there cannot be any thinking in itself without thoughts.[48] If the true is the subject of its exposition, then truth consists in knowledge that interprets its contents. In this way, we are constantly led back to the thesis according to which the absolute consists in what we know about it. Thus, it is certainly appropriate to stress that the I must surrender to the thing in order to let it speak in its necessity, but it is no less important to wonder who the subject of this knowledge is. Who can think of the infinite if not a finite ego (provided obviously that this is not an ego that imposes its finitude on speculative inquiry)? It is Hegel who writes the *Science of Logic*; and not because he translates an alleged intuition of God's thoughts before the creation into a discursive form. Differently stated, each comprehension is finite and gradual. A deliberate and sustained effort is needed in order to abstract logical forms from reality as well as to give shape to scientific knowledge. The fact that Hegel rewrote the 1812 Doctrine of Being a second time in 1831 and that he was not able to revise the whole work seven and seventy times over as he had hoped (*WL* I, p 33, *SL* 21) indicates that the effort at stake was huge and required "absolute culture and discipline" (*WL* I, 55, *SL* 37). One cannot illustrate any better the necessity to educate the will as it painstakingly works toward what we must recognize as a construction, a complex building.

It is only the finite I that can become a philosopher. If thinking does not depend in its essence or reality on the finite I, still, it cannot be known save thanks to the finite I. Once we have clarified that the philosophizing subject does not add anything to the determinations that he or she sees unfolding under his or her eyes, and we have avoided the misunderstanding according to which the I would reintroduce a phenomenological subject with all the oppositions and presuppositions we have already overcome[49]—once, that is, we are clear that determinations examine themselves (*ENZ* §41 Z) and their dialectic is internal, not imposed—we must still ask what would happen if there were no thinker to think those determinations.

Now we can focus on the paradox of the relation between thinking and the I. I call this a paradox because, despite what we have seen so far, there is a final twist, a coup de théâtre worthy of a film noir by Billy Wilder or Fritz Lang: true thinking is nothing but the I—provided this is correctly understood as the concrete universal. After what we have seen, it might be disconcerting to read that the I is the concept that exists for itself. "The concept, when it has progressed to a concrete existence which is itself free, is none other than the 'I' or pure self-consciousness" (*WL* II, 253, *SL* 514). "As concretely *existing for itself*, this liberation is called 'I'" (*ENZ* §159 A).

The fact is that, like thinking, the logical, reality, and subjectivity, the I is also said in many ways. What do we mean by "I"? Is it the "limit of the world" of which Wittgenstein speaks in the *Tractatus* (5.632)? Or is it the parasite hated by Gadda?[50] Is it necessary to have an I to be an I, that is to say, can I be a subject of experience and action without having a representation of myself as that subject? We have seen that for Hegel subjectivity is much more elementary than individual self-consciousness. We must acknowledge that so far we have taken the I as a finite I, as consciousness, an I-think as opposed to its objects. If the concept is, as it is for the ordinary conception of thinking, a property of the I and refers to an object outside itself, then the I is a consciousness opposed to the world. This conception takes the I as the true universal, and thought as one of its particular attributes. But this amounts to the absolutization of the finite I, and that is contradictory because the I that claims to be absolute is limited by what is outside it. If instead the I is the unity of subject and object, thought that does not just animate but *conceives* of the object, then it is the only truth and nothing further remains to be considered. The I is then reason, in which thing and thought of the thing are the same. When the I thinks of the object, it becomes identical to it: "I am I" (*W* 3, 181, *PhS* 140). I am aware of the nonbeing of the object as well as of my own particularity.

The I is the thought of the thing. We must not therefore say: "I have thoughts," but: "thought thinks itself when it makes itself I." The philosopher, instead of wearing the clothes of the functionary of mankind as in Husserl, is rather the special agent of the logos's self-consciousness. Lest this logos may suggest the idea of a ready-made entity complete in itself which then functions through the service of an individual, let us say more emphatically that the logos would remain an unconscious nature and would not know itself if it did not assume the way of being of the individual. The I is the way in which "the idea enters into the shape of self-consciousness" (*WL* II, 545, *SL* 731).

How can we avoid equivocating between these different I's? Taken in itself, the I is neither particular nor universal, neither abstract nor concrete. These two versions of the I are not original, that is, definite, fixed, mutually opposed, and waiting somewhere to beckon us to choose between them like an existentialist chooses between more or less authentic ways of life. It is the I that determines itself as finite consciousness or as the self-knowledge of logos. As usual in Hegel's conception, the I becomes what it appears to be based on how we take it.

Hegel's reference to freedom in the two above-mentioned passages helps us shed light on the I as the existence of the free concept. If the I of the ordinary conception is particular, the most damaging error would be to conclude that the I finds its true self only by ascending to universal reason. The discretion (these are the words of the *Phenomenology*, *W* 3, 56–57, *PhS* 35–36) that keeps at bay the subjective impositions on the immanent rhythm of concepts wards off arbitrariness: it is not the suppression of the individual I, but its true existence. Hegel is against Stoicism: he is critical of the monkish renunciation to passions in ethics as well as of the uniformation of the individual to the rational order of the cosmos in metaphysics. And he finds Spinoza's consideration of human beings as accidents of the substance "revolting" (*Logik 1831*, 168, *LL* 166).

The difficulty is about understanding that the liberation from the I's particularity is in the name of true freedom, which Hegel opposes to the self-centered subject that does not look past his or her nose. And the liberation is at the same time liberation of the true I, as well as of the logos that knows itself. Like thinking, freedom is also an original in-itself whose being is futile without its becoming. It has no reality save the realization it gives itself in the world; in fact, its forms of realization are all it is. Here Hegel speaks of liberation on purpose. Freedom is not an individual prerogative or a predicate of the particular I, nor is it an original right as in many natural right doctrines. It is rather the result of an effort that the I exercises over itself in order to overcome particularity and make itself a concrete universal. The I is something you have to earn and vanquish, just as freedom had to be vanquished in the struggle of self-consciousnesses in the *Phenomenology*. The I is not an ego-pole that is identical to itself and available from the outset.

The ellipse and the squirrel cannot be the subjects of comparable transformations because they have no I. Humans can free themselves from particularity because the logic of the I that we are grants us that possibility. This logic is a specific movement in which no term is left alone and at peace. By behaving like a particular I or else recognizing its true rational self, the I is modified by its own act.

If particularity consists in the forms of realization of the universal, then particularity is necessary. It is necessary for the I to make itself a particular I. The particular I is not the universal I's flaw or inauthentic fall, but an indispensable moment of its reality. The particular I becomes one-sided and vain when it asserts itself as such, when it wants to stick to particularity by suppressing what is larger than it.

But what does it mean in this case to overcome the particular? If the I in itself is neither particular nor universal but becomes what it appears to be based on how we take it, we must ask what interest we have to lean toward either mode of the I. Why does the I have an interest in asserting its finitude and particularity? By making the finite absolute, the I passes for a resolution to a humble and modest self-restraint what is in fact its pride. By making the universal its own product, the I rises to the privilege of being the exclusive principle because all determination is now posited by it. I as finite am the only essential source of worth and meaning, with respect to which the infinite is an unreachable beyond because it is posited as such by me. Reason's I, by contrast, aware of the nullity of the finite and recognizing objectivity in the infinite, the substantial, the universal that exceed and preexist us, overcomes its particular subjectivity. It negates itself as a this, but this negation is the assertion of its freedom. In overcoming itself as a mere particular, the I produces its true self as a concrete universal and true subject, and is knowledge of the universal: "In thinking the thing itself I get rid of the subjectivity of my thinking" (*VPhR* 143); "I know myself as a particular as I intuit myself as a moment of universal life" (*VPhR* 145–46). In his opening lecture of the encyclopedic course for the new chair in Berlin in 1818 (*W*10, 412), Hegel likewise says that the philosophical I, by renouncing its particular goals, "no longer seeks *itself, its own*, but *honors* itself by virtue of the fact that it participates in something independent of it, something *self-subsistent*."

It is in this sense that the concept exists as an I. Hegel focuses on those moments of the concept that the logic of the ordinary conception of thinking treats in extensional terms, assuming that individuals and classes are naturally given: universality, particularity, and singularity.[51]

To go over Hegel's examples, the sun or the animal are their universal, but they undergo it, that is, the universal is not for them. For example, for the animal only a singular animal exists; universality is a genus, but for the animal this remains only "innerly," its nature. Only human beings remove abstract individuality and know that they are identical to the genus: thus they are spirit (*WL* II, 493, *SL* 693). Only the human being duplicates itself so that the universal is for the universal, and it can do that insofar as it knows itself as I (*ENZ* §24 Z 1; *Logik 1831*, 9–10, *LL* 7).

At first, however, the I understands itself as an abstract universal. On the one hand, the abstract universal is the attribute that external reflection claims is shared by a plurality of occurrences: I am I, but so is everybody else who can say "I." On the other hand, the I is an abstract universal not only as a commonality for reflection, but also for itself as subject, for insofar as it abstracts from all determinacy and knows itself as identical to itself through diversity, it appears to itself as abstraction. Insofar as it is a pure self-relating unity, however, it realizes that more fundamentally it is the negative attitude that contains determinacy sublated in itself. The I understands that its own negativity excluding the other is not a simple abstraction, but is no less the self-relation that constitutes individuality. In other words, the I abstracted from particularity is but the immediate form of the I which in truth is the pure negative self-relation.

This self-relation is asserted in the I's each and every particular mode. In the ordinary conception, the I's particular modes are the various subjective activities and states: thought alongside feeling, willing, and so on. Here the I is placed on one side, and its particular activities are placed on the other. In Hegel's conception, by contrast, I am I in my every act, whether I think or walk or feel. The I pervades everything it does. If the concept is I, then we must understand thinking as the universal that pervades every act of the I. As the concept is immanent in each of its determinations but has no reality without them, likewise the I is in its acts but has no reality without them. If the concept is the I, we must then regard thinking as the universal that pervades every act of the I. Thinking is the being-in-itself that lives in the I's acts and abides self-identically throughout their changing.[52]

In the 1831 logic lecture-notes, Hegel says that "thinking, having concepts, seems far removed from us, but it is in fact what is closest at hand. In thinking I remain absolutely at home with myself. I am myself this thinking. . . . We represent thinking to ourselves as separable from the I, but it is in fact what is most present in it. If we say 'I go,' 'I am suffering,' 'I am pleased,' the I remains ever present in these determinations of my state, of my interest or will" (*Logik 1831*, 10, *LL* 7). Saying that "I *accompany* all these representations" does "not say enough: I am entirely invested in these representations" (ibid.).

In Hegel's view, the I does not ground individuation, but is the pure negative self-relation that constitutes our innermost true self. A logical

CHAPTER 2

relation of self-reference constitutes the I and articulates itself as a universal that makes itself particular and singular. The I subordinates to itself and integrates in its own life each of its moments. In contemporary theories on the epistemic asymmetry of the I, I have an immediate cognition about my aching tooth which has nothing to do with introspection or inferences. This immediate self-awareness is a form of knowledge to which others have no access. For Hegel, however, the fact that the I is also an immediate phenomenal self-consciousness which can be so described depends on its peculiar logic. Accordingly, individual self-consciousness can be an immediate datum on which a theory of self-consciousness can rest only if one presupposes that the dimension of the I has already been isolated in its primacy and separated from its assumptions and logical implications. If, however, we want to be truly radical, we need to recognize that individual self-consciousness as an immediate datum is sustained by the logical mediation of self-reference. No theory of self-consciousness eschewing, in its search for something primitive, underived, and immediate, all reference to something outside itself, beginning with the logical concept of self-reference, can hope to stand on its feet. Without (the logical concept of) self-reference, self-consciousness cannot be.

Naturally, a logic of the I is not an explanation of the I, and individuation is not the aim of Hegel's point. His point is that it is the negative self-relation that is constitutive of the I, and the I is a universal that knows itself in its moments. By realizing that the I is what we make of it, we realize that the true backbone of any possible understanding of the I is the concept of self-reference. Because the particular I distinguishes itself from other I's on the basis of its acts and states, we should not say: "The particular I is the original given, and it *can* rise to universality if it so wills." On the contrary, we should say: "The universal, because it is pure negative self-relation, *makes itself* particular and distinguishes itself from other I's."

This pure relation is called by Hegel the true infinity because it is a form of self-reference that is not limited by anything external. Whatever determination, whether internal or external, is the determination of the I that knows it is both identical to and different from that determination because it abides self-identically in it like a universal in one of its particular forms. With yet another paradox for the ordinary conception of thinking, the true universal is the individual that is understood, that is, the infinite.[53]

Notice that this is the fundamental logical dynamics at work even in Hegel's consideration of language. Sense-certainty presumes it can say what it intends, including the I in its singularity, but discovers that the pronoun does not identify because everybody equally says "I." It discovers that the immediate is in itself mediated and universal; but it is an abstract universal, which stops at the acknowledgment of an indifferent and generic relation that is valid for all I's. It must make itself real, that is, individualize and distinguish itself from the genus, to which it also knows it is identical. Only at the end of the logic and the philosophy of spirit, when it has understood it is the concrete universal, will the I grow to substantial individuality and be able to use the pronoun "I" in its true sense: that is—in the final shocking reversal of the Subjective Logic—as a revisitation of Kant's I-think, now purified from the psychological idealism that made it finite, that is, without the subjectivist aspect of the ordinary conception of thought (*WL* II, 253–63, *SL* 514–17; *WL* II, 489–92, *SL* 690–92).

The logical dynamics is the same because the order of all knowledge consists in the passage from the abstract to the concrete.[54] It is important that even here we understand the terms at stake, contrary to the ordinary view. According to it, the concrete is equivalent to the sensible, finite, and material, while the abstract is equivalent to the empty, mental, and formal. These opposite conceptual determinations are presupposed as already known and fixed in themselves; science must begin with the sensible. For Hegel, instead, abstractness is the initial result of an idealization of sensible singularity ("the simple abstracted from the concrete," *WL* II, 520, *SL* 713), like something undifferentiated that provides our investigation with a starting point. But this gradually becomes more complex and internally articulated as its object becomes ever more concrete and real. Thus, for the ordinary conception, the universal is placed on one side and the singular on the other, so that the latter is taken from the material world and the former is *applied* to the particular. By contrast, in Hegel's view, it is the abstract that becomes concrete and fills itself with determinate content (*WL* II, 532–33, *SL* 722–23).

This logical dynamics is internal to what we must consider the movement of thinking. To that I would like to turn in the third chapter.

3

The Movement of Thought

Spontaneity and Reification

> The essence of philosophy has often been located by those already adept in the things of thought in the task of answering the question: *How does the infinite go forth out of itself and come to finitude?* . . . The answer to the question is therefore this: There is not an infinite which is infinite beforehand, and only afterwards does it find it necessary to become finite. . . . The infinite goes out of itself into the finite because, in the way it is grasped as abstract unity, it has no truth in it, no standing; and, conversely, the finite goes forth into the infinite for the same reason. Or it is rather to be said that the infinite proceeded to finitude from all eternity.
>
> —*WL* I, 168–71, *SL* 122–23

The Self-Determination of the Concept as Self-Alienation

When we seek to understand a situation, whether psychological or historical, our effort is invariably concerned with the genesis of its aspects or elements. We may not be convinced that these are the deterministic effects of some causes, and yet we see them as results. They are produced by something as different as free choice, the manifestation of an abiding character, or the impulsive thoughtless reaction whose blindness we deplore, accidental circumstances, or objective forces larger than the individual protagonists on whom we focus. Regarding them as products is like looking at the snapshot of a becoming, the temporary freezing of a flow in a particular configuration.

The phenomenon to be understood appears as an immediacy, something external given to us. However, we know that it is, at least in

THE MOVEMENT OF THOUGHT

part, the outcome of an intention, a will or process of thought, and we seek for the traces or vestiges of the voluntary or failed acts that have given rise to it. We all are archeologists, as it were. The phenomenon presents itself with a shell hardened by time and externality. Still, whether under its encrusted dust we find the transparent seal of the act that has produced it or its cracked and virtually unrecognizable hint, it is only because we are looking for it. And we look for it because we conceive of this phenomenon as the deposit left in a past time by some purpose or thought.

What matters is not the material presence of the phenomenon but its meaning. We see here the same point that Hegel makes about the word, which is the thing as it exists for our representation. In fact, since thinking is the soul of language, we can say that the word gives thought a body. In it, intelligence *becomes the thing*.[1] Generally this applies to all forms of objectification: we objectify our contents in a public and shared medium, which appears all the more given to us the more estranged we are from it or the less we have penetrated it (this is analogous to what we have seen in the previous chapter with regard to proverbs, grammatical rules, and religious contents as they are initially considered). And when we penetrate the content, we feel it, we intuit it as our own. Again in the words of the previous chapter, reason is then at home in the world.

Hegel speaks of the content that, "grounded in thought, does not at first *appear in the form of thought*" (*ENZ* §2). In everything—any expression whatsoever in a language we command, an article of our country's constitution, the customs of a social group, the life of tropical plants, or the laws of refraction in Newton's *Optics*, but most evidently in religion, right, and morality—"*thinking* has not been inactive at all . . . , its activity and its products are *present and contained* therein" (*ENZ* §2 A).

Just as every phenomenon we encounter is the sediment that must be brought back to its origins, likewise the different conceptual determinations must be brought back to the self-determination of the concept that in them has given itself a particular shape. We have seen that the ordinary view of thinking starts with the temporal order of consciousness, thereby absolutizing its beginning from finitude. By inverting this view, we understand thinking not starting from things, but from itself. For the concepts that appear to us as products are the self-production of thinking. Since thinking is immanent in its products, it seeks in them nothing but a form or a particular objectification of itself.

We must then at once recognize the various determinations of thinking as the products of one and the same activity, and revoke the appearance of alienation by making the concrete thoughts we experience fluid

CHAPTER 3

and plastic. Thought is the movement that makes itself objective and retrieves itself from this objectification. It is the movement that gives itself reality at different levels and comprehends itself in what appears at first as externally given.

We have seen that this holds for all the manifestations of a quite broad view of thought. We must then conceive the movement of thinking—the restlessness of the concept (*die Unruhe des Begriffs*) —as the way in which a subject which in itself is not finite takes up several finite forms. Neither the finite nor the infinite are understandable in their separateness. If I take consciousness to be a particular way of thinking, then I must recognize in it "this necessity of externalizing the form of the Notion" (*W* 3, 589, *PhS* 491). If I take the understanding to be a form of thinking rather than a faculty, then I must consider it as a particular form of agency of the concept: the "absolute power" that holds down and keeps separate the abstract which Hegel describes in the preface to the *Phenomenology*.[2] Thinking must fluidify determinate and solidified thoughts (*W* 3, 36–37, *PhS* 18–20). "Thoughts become fluid" (ibid.) when thinking recognizes itself in them. By means of such movement, "the pure thoughts become Notions, and are only now what they are in truth, self-movements, circles; spiritual essences; which is what their substance is. This movement of pure essences constitutes the nature of scientific method in general" (*W* 3, 37, *PhS* 20).

For philosophy, this effort at fluidification amounts to the realization of the authentic relationship between the finite and the infinite. Philosophy faces a "fully ready and well-entrenched, one may even say ossified, material, and the task is to make it fluid again, to revive the concept in such a dead matter" (*WL* II, 243, *SL* 507). Determinate concepts, like all finite being, must be considered not in their separate reality but as ideal. In this conception the finite is not "*a subsistent existent*, but a *moment*" (*W* 1, 165, *SL* 119; see also *ENZ* §95 A). As a member of an organic whole, the finite exists insofar as it has an ideal, not a real, existence. In other words, the finite is not a given datum we come across in experience, but is a constitutive moment of a conceptually organized whole in which every determination is in relation to the others and to the whole.

It is interesting to see how Hegel expresses this same conceptual point in the representational language of religion. Hegel brings disruption to traditional dogmas. If the understanding affirms God's goodness and justice at the same time, it does not realize that there is a contradiction between the two. As always, we must not stay away from contradiction but conceive it: "Love grants the finite its existence, and justice sublates it as it manifests it as finite" (*VPhR* 121). God's goodness lets the finite be as such, but justice does not allow it to forget its nullity.[3]

THE MOVEMENT OF THOUGHT

Finite and infinite cannot count as opposites. This is the understanding's view that, by thinking of the infinite as existing for itself alongside the finite, turns it into a particular and finitizes it. As we have seen in the previous chapter and in the epigraph for this chapter, the infinite cannot comprehend itself as an abstract unity, as the true in itself. Infinity is but the ideality of the finite.[4] In turn, this ideality is not the pure and simple nullification of what pretends to count for itself: "The true infinite does not behave merely like the one-sided acid, but instead preserves itself. Negation of negation is not a neutralization. The infinite is the affirmative, and only the finite is what is sublated" (*ENZ* §95 A).

Thinking is the only truth for itself, which remains by itself in its becoming other; and the finite is the self-alienation of thinking. I suggest we read this movement as the dialectic of spontaneity and reification.[5]

Spontaneity and Reification

"Spontaneity," which is admittedly more a Kantian than a Hegelian term, has two opposite meanings.[6] Spontaneity can mean the voluntary character of an action, as in its first occurrence in English in Hobbes's dispute with Bishop Bramhall, itself derivative of the Latin *mea sponte*; or else it can mean an event unfolding according to its own nature that it seems impossible to bring back to a clearly identifiable external cause and keep under control (think of phrases such as "spontaneous combustion" or "spontaneous growth"). This meaning presupposes an internal movement or activity, whether natural or human, that is not subject to the will.

We can venture to say that the best model for this meaning is Hume's gentle force, with which imagination makes connections of ideas that are stable, known, and shared. It is the voice of nature that induces us spontaneously to connect what in itself exists separately.[7] This would be reasonable, but it would once again reduce a notion that we need to treat in its generality to one particular meaning. Indeed, behind this Humean anonymous force—which is like the natural, almost mechanical version of Kant's spontaneity, which refers to pure activity—reason is at work, according to Hegel.[8] Although I am aware of the relevance of this double meaning of "spontaneity," my reflections in this chapter are largely based on the word's second sense, an inner movement that can hardly be managed.

Hegel would cherish this double meaning.[9] It is symptomatic of the very double meaning of "subjectivity" itself: as force and movement internal to an underlying subject (actuality, the substance that is also subject), and as the individual finite I with which it is typically identified. Modern philosophies of reflection restrict spontaneity to the activity of an I that is presupposed as original, as we have seen.

In order to exercise itself, an activity must have some character or other and be somehow defined, for example, by the end it is directed to. By objectification or reification I mean how an activity, in itself shapeless and potentially aimed at all objects whatever, takes on a determinate finite shape.[10] If I can think of anything, there are no limits to my thought. My thought is plastic, essentially open, unrestricted, and undefined. In itself it has no definite nature, form, or structure constraining and delimiting it beforehand—except that whenever it exercises itself it must acquire one nature, form, or structure or other. It must arrest itself, condense and give a limited shape to its movement. This means that in order to make coherent sense, thought, which in itself is free, has no content, order, or rules, must give itself contents, an order, and rules: the contents, order, and rules that articulate and bind the exercise of its activity.[11]

In his youthful study on Husserl, Adorno wrote that all reification is a forgetting. I am going to explore this meaning of reification and use it to characterize thought itself. The notion of forgetting implies the past and the idea that what is forgotten can resurface and at least in principle be retrieved. In other words, oblivion must be temporary. It is not the oblivion of the metempsychosis, which is a mythical theory as well as an inference rather than the reemerging of a personal past I can recognize as mine. If we must be able to fluidify what is solidified, the logos that pulses in things must be able to show itself again in its pure vitality, stripped bare and without any mixture (these are the terms of *ENZ* §3). Unlike alienation, reification does not petrify or embalm its object. Alienation dispossesses its object, which finds itself drained and exhausted in the form in which it has been arrested. Reification instead sediments and forgets about its object while preserving its nonidentity with it. In more concrete terms, when thought determines itself, it does not lose itself: its is no exile. In fact, it is necessary for thought to externalize or express itself in an objective and public medium, as for example in a natural language. In this case we speak of subjective thought, which is discursive and finite and could not exist without language. Thought is nothing but its exposition: thought and its exposition (*Darstellung, Auslegung*) cannot be assumed as separate and independent. As a consequence, if we could avail ourselves of an intellectual intuition of the whole or a mystical grasp of a supernatural being but could not articulate it in speech, it would be silent and altogether ineffectual. Thought is its objectivity, and this is all we can judge.

THE MOVEMENT OF THOUGHT

If thought infects all that we as humans do and has the very broad meaning that Hegel attributes to it, then in all our representations, feelings, intentions, and desires, thought is somehow present and active, whether or not we know it. Having a human life comes down to organizing such representations, feelings, and so on, assigning them functions and a rank-order. We also confer upon them a discrete independent existence, even a logical status, by first giving them their names and a function in our judgments and in our deeds. In this way every thought, conscious or unconscious, presupposes a drive to selection and fixation. The grammar and syntax of our natural language are once again an obvious example of a fixed structure in which thought finds a propositional expression, but so are the works of our poets and writers and all historical moments of any relevance in our culture.

When we think, we think determinate contents. However, the finite forms that are necessary to thought are the negation of its infinity. When thought becomes determinate, its determination is of nothing other than itself. It negates its own openness and plasticity. For thought does not conform to or measure itself against given reality as if reality were a ready-made standard. As with Kant's reason (*KrV* A XI), thought cannot recognize any authority other than itself. As a matter of fact, thought not only negates itself; it even *posits* in its self-determination this negation as affirmative (in the words of Hegel's cursory reference to Spinoza in the *Science of Logic* at *WL* I, 121, *SL* 87).

All determinations can be taken as thought's self-determination, a particularization of thinking, the finite form or existence that thought gives itself. In other words, when thought determines itself, it is *in negative relation to itself*, and this means, as we have seen, that it takes on particular forms we typically call concepts—in the plural. In this view, thought is essentially fluid and its finite forms are solidifications or crystallizations of such original fluidity.[12] It is as if thought were a continuum made discrete by its existence, or to be precise, a continuum which only exists in the discrete forms it gives itself.

Thought is an activity which momentarily stops at its stations, and its stations are the products of—are instituted by—its activity. Were we to say that Hegel endorses Heracleitus's *panta rei*, we should immediately add that everything flows only when we have a *peras* (limit), for only limits make the flow possible. Without a bed marked by banks a river would not flow or even be a river, but only water (a river is determinate water, as it were). And certainly we would not even perceive water flowing unless we had fixed points of orientation against a background. These analogies break down, naturally, because thought does not have the spatial and material connotation that stations or banks do. Still, the gist of the analogy is that it allows us to see the flow as a force, a movement: life. Each thought-determination is one pulse in a unitary activity, the negativity of thought.

However, lest we miss the difference implicit in these analogies by insisting on their unity, let me consider another analogy as a frame of reference and a corrective. Husserl speaks of consciousness in terms of a flux. The flux is unitary, so that each act of consciousness is like a wave in the flux.[13] In this image, determinacy is made up of the same element as the whole: the wave is water just like flux is. The wave is the momentary configuration of the same element that makes it possible. Individual acts of consciousness stand out against their continuity because they are isolated and considered by themselves, but do not have an independent existence. In fact, all acts have in common their belonging to consciousness, therefore they reside elsewhere than in actuality, which is separate from consciousness. By contrast, in the movement of thought I am describing, thought makes itself something other than itself, thereby becoming real in a medium or a different element to which it has transferred and embodied itself. Thus thought is not comparable to Cronus who devours his children, but to parents aware that they can only see themselves in their offspring if they let them be and take their own path.

The degrees of stability and fluidity of this movement necessarily vary. If we look for excessive stability, we behave like the understanding searching for univocal definitions. These represent, as Kant puts it in the Doctrine of Method (*KrV* A 730–31/B 758–59), the crowning and conclusion of the understanding's work. Because it aims at capturing the distinct identity of conceptual determinations, the understanding does not realize that it halts at the positive and immediate moment of each concept. The tendency to block the movement is essential for the understanding's behavior.

Then again, excessive fluidity loses in determinacy what it seeks to gain in plasticity. As we have seen, without the understanding, reason does not have any object at all. When thought does not retrieve itself in the determinations to which it has given rise, it fluctuates in vagueness. Such a balance between stability and fluidity must be the polar star for our orientation, especially when we consider the inter-categorical relations within the logic. I cannot go into this problem here, but I would like briefly to mention a few aspects thereof. The categories of Hegel's logic are far from being distinct and self-identical with a univocally defined role. The dialectic of categories cannot be translated into a universal rule of operation or into a method that is indifferent to its object; as immanent in each reflexive determination, it must adapt to each concept under consideration. This is why for each category to relate to and cooperate with other categories is to lose something and gain something else. It is not only this dialectic that makes unsuccessful, if not impossible, the univocity to which the understanding aspires. Take also the recursiveness and vagueness of certain categories; or the fact that identity and difference, which are in themselves categories of essence, inevitably contribute to constituting the boundaries of each category as being both distinct in themselves and related to their other; or consider that some categories are treated thematically in certain places and then employed elsewhere to promote a deeper awareness regarding other categories; or, lastly, consider the fact that some categories are defined in relation to or are applied to themselves.[14]

Translating the conceptual pair "spontaneity and reification" into the other, different, and yet complementary couple "fluidity and stability" allows me to stress another aspect. As understanding and reason are two moments of one and the same thinking, and as the posited, the negative, and the positively rational (*ENZ* §83) are moments of each thought and not the definition of some thoughts as opposed to others, likewise I would like to emphasize that spontaneity and reification can be both distinct sides of thinking (e.g., when I say that spontaneity becomes reified) and different moments of the same conceptual determination. Indeed, each determination has in itself as much spontaneity as reification: as much stability as fluidity, as much being as becoming.

To illustrate spontaneity, let me recur to a particular example which for Hegel counts as the very model of thought: Aristotle's active *nous*.[15] The intellect is defined as *choristhos*, separate from the body, and *apathês*, impassive. True, there is a potential intellect, *nous dunamei*, which can become all forms.[16] But the intellect is spontaneous activity without passivity—or without an original and reflective relation to itself or to an I—in both its potential (*nous dunamei*) and productive modes (*nous tôi panta poiein*). Like the soul, the intellect has no form (in the terms I used earlier, it has no contents or rules) because it must be able to become all forms. It is openness to the world. Indeed, it is the world itself in potentiality. But this openness is not receptivity, for it does not receive but can only think forms. This is why thinking them is compared to inscribing them on a slate. Here, too, what is important is not the material slate, but the function of writing. What has been written in each of our slates will perish with us, but the fact that thinking occurs in us as writing on a slate is nothing individual or perishable. This *nous* is by essence activity, and not an intermittent but an everlasting one. In sum, the *nous* cannot be acted upon. Experience does owe to sensibility our cognitions, but it does not affect thought. When it thinks, the intellect is not passive in any way, even when it thinks forms in images.

I want to argue that unlike for Aristotle, passivity is crucial for Hegel's notion of thinking.[17] But what passivity could possibly mean for thought, if thinking is spontaneous in the terms just defined, remains a mystery. This mystery, which will turn out to be closely linked to reification as forgetting, that is, to the existence thinking gives itself, is what I would like to dispel presently.

If every reality must be understood in light of its concept, the truth that holds for philosophy is the complementary and inverted one that the concept gives itself reality. The logos manifests itself in logic, nature, and spirit. This general thesis finds recurrent applications throughout Hegel's system. (a) In the *Phenomenology* we read that language is spirit's *Dasein* (*W* 3, 376, *PhS* 308–9). Or (b), time is the *Dasein* of the concept (*W* 3, 584, *PhS* 487). In general (c), what appears to consciousness in the form of subject and object, I and world, are the different ways in which the concept manifests itself.

(d) In the *Science of Logic*, the I is the *Dasein* of the concept (*WL* II, 253, *SL* 514).

(e) In the *Encyclopaedia*, nature is "die Idee als Sein, seiende Idee" (§244 Z, *W* 8, 393). After all, "nature and spirit are in general different modes of exhibiting its [i.e., the absolute idea's] existence" (*WL* II, 549, *SL* 735). As we have seen, the concept is the source of its division, including its own partition into being and self-knowing subject (*WL* I, 57, *SL* 39).

This self-realization is evident at best in the Philosophy of Spirit. (f) The soul in the Anthropology is one of the forms of existence that spirit gives itself (*ENZ* §403 A). (g) Language in the Psychology "is a second, higher reality than [the] immediate one, in general an existence that carries weight *in the realm of representation*" (*ENZ* §459).

(h) Objective spirit, which is how freedom gives itself existence, is the realization of a universal and substantial will.[18] (i) I have invested value in my body, the value of what is *mine*, by virtue of which my body is no longer simply a piece of nature, but as the manifestation of my will becomes a juridical person. Because of this it is "the existence of freedom" ("Dasein der Freiheit," *GPR* §48 A), and (j) Right is the *Dasein* of free will (*GPR* §29). In turn, (k) ethical life is the *Dasein* of free spirit that has made itself world and second nature in practice and institutions.[19]

Sichselbstentäusserung, or self-realization, self-determination into particular forms: this appears to be the most appropriate definition of thinking. But what matters philosophically in all this are not the external forms of the logos's existence, but rather that the logos be able to recognize itself in its existence, thereby reappropriating its essence. This is why I said that from a philosophical point of view, it does not suffice to consider each thing in its concept. We must complete the inversion and con-

THE MOVEMENT OF THOUGHT

sider the self-realization of the concept as the necessary form from which thought retrieves itself, dissipating the impression of its alienation once its concrete and actual forms no longer appear foreign to us. Differently stated, the actuality of the concept is the temporary alterity that the concept (spirit, idea, the absolute, etc.) gives itself in order to rejoin itself. It follows inevitably that everything is expressive of this movement for Hegel: everything is some kind or other of thought's concretion that we must fluidify if we want to understand it correctly. We must find everywhere the identity of thought within the difference of its particular forms.

If we go through all the quotations we have just seen, we must now highlight their necessary and complementary textual counterpart. Thus (a), when Hegel says that language is the existence of spirit, we must understand that spirit does express itself through language as in one of its most adequate media, and yet spirit must destroy philosophically the propositional form of judgment through the dialectic of the speculative sentence in order to understand itself.

(b) When Hegel says that spirit has externalized itself in the shapes of time consciousness, he means that spirit does so in order to appropriate itself as spirit. To this end, spirit must destroy the form of temporality. "Spirit necessarily appears in Time, and it appears in Time just so long as it has not *grasped* its pure Notion, i.e., has not annulled Time. It is the *outer*, intuited pure Self which is *not grasped* by the Self, the merely intuited Notion" (*W* 3, 584–85, *PhS* 487). Thus (c), while thought appears as an opposition between I and world, as speculation it must destroy such appearance and show the primacy of the concept, thereby understanding why it divides itself into subject and object.

(d) As we have seen in chapter 2, the concept exists as I in order to regain itself as absolute idea.

(e) The passage where Hegel says that nature and spirit are two forms of manifestation of the idea was preceded by the following words, which frame their fundamental meaning: "Since it contains *all determinateness* within it, and its essence consists in *returning* through its self-determination and particularization back to itself, it [the absolute idea] has various shapes" (*WL* II, 549, *SL* 735).

(f) Likewise, spirit must overcome the form of existence of the soul in order to understand itself better as consciousness. And (g) spirit overcomes the external existence of language and mechanical memory when it understands that it is identical to the thing (*ENZ* §465).

Finally (h–k), objective spirit is able to reflect upon itself and understand itself as absolute, that is, in a trans-political dimension, when spirit knows itself as temporarily sedimented in its practical shapes.

For this reason, focusing on one of these concretions at the expense of others is one-sided. More importantly, it does not understand that they are the concretions that the concept or spirit gives itself in order to pervade them, overcome them, and move on. In my view, it is particularly shortsighted and devoid of the indispensable radicalism to isolate one form of existence against others for exegetical agendas that are alien to Hegel's meaning. Thus, when Brandom takes Hegel's dictum in the *Phenomenology* that spirit exists as language as if this were Hegel's final word, he neglects not only the general thesis about language, but also ends up misunderstanding the particular theme he is most concerned with. It is like suppressing the adverb from the sentence of the second preface to the *Science of Logic*: "The forms of thought are *first* [*zunächst*] set out and stored in human language" (*WL* I, 20, *SL* 12). The necessary outcome is that Brandom proceeds to articulate a totally arbitrary and opaque view of Hegel's philosophy of language. Likewise, Heidegger misunderstands spirit's temporality in light of what he believes is the privilege assigned to the "now." Unlike Heidegger's interpretation (for him the Hegelian notion of spirit is a "lapse into time" to which one has to oppose an original temporalization), spirit for Hegel is not subjected to time precisely because it comes back to itself from externality, thereby overcoming temporal succession in an "absolute present," the totality of time that is its concept (*ENZ* §258 A, §259 Z).[20]

In these interpretations, the concept and spirit do not give themselves a provisional reification in order to understand and intuit themselves in it. They have not lent, but have irrevocably consigned and alienated themselves altogether to an objective existence.

Nature and Passivity

In all the languages I am familiar with, thought is expressed by a verb to which a noun may possibly correspond or by the nominalization of a passive participle (for instance, *thought, pensée, cogitatio*). The duplicity between activity and passivity, act and result, thinking and thought, seems to belong to thinking starting with its lexicon.

We do not need to interpret the process in which thought gives itself reality as if thought were invariably an original and transitive causality that proceeds to make itself an objectified product. Let me reconsider some examples I have mentioned before. We say that thought makes itself understanding when it looks for a univocal answer, gives itself the determinate form of German syntax, objectifies itself in some habitual

THE MOVEMENT OF THOUGHT

practice of a voluntary association. In yet other cases, we say that thought gives itself a determinate reality or appears in a particular form as representation. The sense of the expression that spontaneity reifies itself can be stronger (e.g., when we say that the concept must alienate itself and pass into consciousness, *W* 3, 589, *PhS* 491) or weaker. According to the latter, when we say that thinking appears to our investigation in the form of representation, this does not mean that thinking is a first cause that intentionally dresses itself up in inadequate clothes. Obviously, we must go back to the primacy of the concept in order to make sense of this appearance but, as we have seen in the previous chapter, this does not amount to the identification of the ground or causal action of an original and transcendent principle or to the claim that this is the only agent that shapes the world at will. If thoughts are usually "clothed in and combined with familiar and sensuous content" and "in every sentence with a quite sensuous content—as for instance in 'This leaf is green'—categories such as being, singularity are already part of the mix" (*ENZ* §3 A), the task of philosophy is to examine categories as such without any mixture with the sensible. Thinking appears in different forms in which it does not immediately recognize itself as thought, and these forms range from semblance which melts like snow at the first sun ray to the most rational actuality.[21] Thought must come to grips with externality. Its work consists in assimilation. To pick up again the primacy of thought does not mean that we take thought as being always already actualized and reconciled with itself. Thought gives itself over to different media in which it has to appear, and some of them, as we must now consider, are more foreign and inhospitable than others.

As we have seen, the idea must become substance, nature, passivity. Thinking becomes unconscious to itself. Since we are still speaking of sides immanent in the same subject, it is thinking that splits itself into an active and a passive side. It is as if thinking had to become a slate, an immaterial space for the inscription of its determinations. It must describe its space and leave its marks in the same way in which it stores its logical nature in language. For Hegel, categories are stored in language, but they are no less pervasive in nature, history, and ethical life. Still, language, nature, history, and ethical life are externalities for thinking that it initially finds as given. The logical element, our innermost nature, objectifies itself in what appears to be an externality. If thinking is reified and has forgotten itself in externality, how can it retrieve itself?

There are different ways in which thinking must destroy the solidified form of externality in which it has posited itself in order to reappropriate itself. Consider the cases of education or formation (*Bildung*), of sciences and logic. In a rightly famous passage of the *Phenomenology* (*W* 3,

37, *PhS* 19–20), Hegel writes that we modern individuals are no longer like the natural consciousness that philosophizes on everything to educate itself "into a universality that was active through and through" (ibid.). Nowadays the individual "finds the abstract form ready-made" so that the task does not consist in abstracting the form from sensible appearances, but rather in actualizing the universal and "in freeing determinate thoughts from their fixity so as to give actuality to the universal, and impart to it spiritual life" (ibid.).

It is worth focusing on the presuppositions of this passage. Individuals have to reappropriate the history of what spirit has produced. They do so in an abbreviated form. History has become memory, and the previous stages are now virtual moments stored in tradition that we must retrace for our education. As such, those moments tend to become familiar representations that we passively acquire. The understanding brings trouble into this familiarity, yet it tends to fixate and isolate abstract universals, whereas we have to free them from their fixity. The reified universal lacks vitality, and *Bildung* imparts spiritual life to it by analyzing and reconstructing it in the form of the concept.

A complementary way to show the primacy of the concept is offered by the introduction to the *Encyclopaedia*. Philosophy must learn from the sciences: it recognizes their content, but its task is to develop it and transform their categories (§9). *Development* is key. The universal must not be indifferent to its particularization, that is to say, a principle cannot be repeated as invariant in its parts (§12 A). Experience and the sciences, including the genera, kinds, and particular laws they establish, are the way in which we take up categories, yet thought must dismiss the contingent form in which it finds them and be "impel[led] to *the development from out of itself.*"[22] "Taking up this content" is the same as "bestowing upon [it] the shape of a content that emerges purely in accordance with the necessity of the subject matter itself" (§12). In this way, within an encyclopedia (which is literally the act of forming in a circle, *en kuklôi paideuein*) of the sciences, "it is thinking's free act of placing itself at that standpoint where it is for itself and thus *generates and provides its own object for itself*" (§17).

In both these forms of education and the sciences, however, the concept has still to struggle to find itself again, because it is immersed in externality. In logic, too, thinking has given itself a determinate form (a logical *Dasein* I would call it, if I did not fear it might be equivocated); but here it is otherwise. For Hegel, the unconscious is not a mental content (like Leibniz's small perceptions, which are unknown mental contents), but rather the activity that gives rise to it. We do not realize that what is given has been produced; it is the result of an activity that no longer recognizes itself in it. And in the logic this is the issue: there are unconscious thought processes, which, however, become objects of thought in the absolute idea.

We have seen that nature is an unsolved contradiction (*ENZ* §248 A) between the concept, which is the hidden soul immersed in phenomena, and appearance, which remains insuppressable. In language, history, and ethical life, instead, thought reifies itself into a *second nature*: it appears to itself like culture to the individual who must appropriate it in education. Here appearance continues to be the appearance of externality, but the second nature (word and deed) is the self-objectification of thought and the reified result of its doing. In the logic the appearance of externality is internal to thought that splits itself up; thought appears as a result, when in fact it is the first. In language and history, thought's inscriptions have an independent life. They are stored and have a development in time. But how can logical determinations achieve permanence and an independent life? How should we conceive of the medium in which they maintain and develop their own being?[23]

In Kant, self-affection is the effect of the understanding upon inner sense. The understanding inscribes pure concepts into pure intuition. But these effects do not have any duration or permanence save as a psychological sediment in inner sense. Each constitution is due to the understanding's spontaneity: a subject without substance, an activity that is not only distinct, but also tenaciously and jealously other than its products. Activity and passivity have opposite features. Above all, they fall into two different camps, the I-think and inner sense. In Hegel instead, we have exactly the effort to think of activity and passivity as interactive moments of the organized system of thought-determinations. The subject of activity and passivity is one and the same; and its features are not opposed but rather complementary.

Hegel appropriates Aristotle's thought that the soul is somehow all beings. He translates it in the Philosophy of Subjective Spirit and in the logic in two different forms of ideality or virtuality. In the former, he translates it into the principle that the soul is a featureless mine (*bestimmungsloser Schacht, ENZ* §403), and intelligence is the night or pit (*nächtliche Schacht*) in which all our cognitions that have been passively acquired are preserved unconsciously (*bewusstlos aufbewahrt, ENZ* §453).[24] Intelligence is described as "the existing universal in which what is diverse is not yet posited as discrete" (ibid.). The meaning and purpose of all this for Hegel is spirit's liberation from externality and self-affirmation. Intelligence, which initially is the soul immersed in corporeality and the environment, is the power to stop depending on the given and alienate its products (signs, symbols, language, etc.) in an external medium.

In the logic, by contrast, we do not have a subject that we call soul, consciousness, or intelligence. Here the subject, the universal, or the in-itself being of all its determinations is the concept itself. It is in the concept that thinking stores its categories through determinate negations that organize its movement. This is why we can speak of substantiality with regard to thinking. This does not push us to postulate a speculative memory in terms of a logical space in which thinking inscribes its determinations. Indeed, thought is not conceived of as a discrete act, for it is itself the memory of its past and sublated stages.

In the Subjective Spirit we have an idealization through which spirit posits external contents in space and time within itself and organizes them inwardly in the form of its own representations and concepts. This activity occurs mostly unconsciously. It shapes our life-functions and our body through habit and many other spontaneous pre-discursive activities. By contrast, in the *Science of Logic* we do not have an idealization but an ideality. After all, if things do not count in their reality but are for the concept as moments, how can we explain that they persist? They persist because we move about in the pure element of knowledge which presupposes the sublation of consciousness's oppositions and the independence of external reality as already accomplished. The determinate negation of the concept does not produce entities endowed with existence, but ideal moments. The element of knowledge is "the form of simplicity" in which moments persist (*W* 3, 39, *PhS* 22).

The logical movement takes place in this simplicity and self-certainty of knowledge. Negation is internal to this movement, so that what is negated or evanescent is regarded as essential (*W* 3, 43, *PhS* 27). This means that *what disappears actually lives on virtually as a moment of the concept.* Differently put, in *learning* we must devour our inorganic nature and appropriate it so that spirit's past existence becomes spirit's conceptual property in which it feels at home and certain of itself (*W* 3, 32–33, *PhS* 17–18). In *knowing*, by contrast, existence is already reduced to memory, "the universal spirit," "the bringing-about of its own becoming and reflection into itself" (ibid.). Science is precisely the systematic representation of what "has already been reduced to a moment and property of Spirit" (ibid.). It is noteworthy here that being reduced and being raised are equivalent. When Hegel says that existing determinations "are in their truth . . . reduced to forms" (*WL* I, 58, *SL* 39) and when he says that the term "sublating" (*aufheben*) means that something is at the same time preserved and "removed from its immediacy" (*WL* I, 114, *SL* 84), what he means is that one determination counts as a moment, as an ideality, when it is a determinate negation that retains in itself that to which it simultaneously puts an end. It preserves and overcomes.

THE MOVEMENT OF THOUGHT

In logic we have a different notion of thought's self-externality. Thinking does not have to retrieve itself from the matter in which it has been concretized, because it deals only with itself. The notion of *Aufhebung* is sufficient to preserve the dialectic as well as its results, because each determination contains in itself the movement "to vanish spontaneously" (*WL* I, 93, *SL* 67). In the logic, each concept is the memory of its own becoming.

Yet this persistence is not explicit ("the proposition thus contains the result" but presents "the defect that this result is not itself expressed in the proposition," *WL* I, 93, *SL* 67). For this reason, we need to retrieve thought from its self-forgetting.

I would like briefly to recapitulate my argument by going back to its beginning. Hegel would not agree with my remark concerning the distinction between the intellect's passivity and potentiality. In his enthusiasm for Aristotle's *nous*, it seems obvious to him that if the intellect is the whole potentially and is therefore nothing before thinking, when it thinks, its object can be nothing other than thought itself. If thought does not undergo anything external because it is *apathês*, the relation between active and potential intellect is posited by thinking itself, which "makes itself passive intellect, the objective, the object for itself" (*VGPh* 2, 213). It seems clear to Hegel that if the active intellect is but activity and its essence is efficient causality (*Wirksamkeit*), as *De anima* III 5 claims, then it must be understood as the eternal activity of finitizing itself in the sensible realm as a whole—in the sensible realm as a whole, for the passive *nous* is now finitude in its in-itself rationality, or reality insofar as it is thinkable: objective intelligibility. "That the world, the universe in itself, are rational, this is the *nous pathêtikos*," reads the note of an auditor in Hegel's 1820 class.[25] In the words of the *Lectures on the History of Philosophy*, "passive *nous* is nature, and even what in the soul feels and represents is *nous* in itself" (*VGPh* 2, 216). The rationality of nature and of the soul becomes explicit in thought, which is the identity between the concept and objectivity or between thinking and thought (*Denken-Gedachte*). This can also be expressed as follows: the intellect divides itself into an active intellect and another intellect that must become the object of the former's thinking ("Der nous ist der noêtos, das Gedachtwerdende," G/J 88).

This is why Hegel writes that the soul is "spirit's sleep" (*ENZ* §389). He calls the soul "the passive *nous* of Aristotle" which is potentially all things (ibid.). The leading thread of his argument is this: the totality of all intelligibles, the idea in itself, is mediated by spirit's idealization. Like everything finite, the soul with all its contents is "merely the *dunamis* of thinking" (G/J 91); insofar as it is the object of active thinking,

CHAPTER 3

the soul is *nous pathêtikos* (passive *nous*) starting with its most elementary forms. All thought-determinations are *virtually present* in the soul, apprehended as the progressive stages of the assimilation of reality on the part of spirit.

Aristotle's passive *nous* can include both nature as the idea outside itself and finite spirit because these are the finite existence that the absolute idea gives itself for its self-realization and self-appropriation as free subjectivity in a syllogism. While for human beings the world is found and not produced and is at first a presupposition, in itself or in truth it is rather thought that makes itself finite in externality. This is the Hegelian version of the logical and ontological priority of the active over the potential intellect in *De anima*. The self-conscious intellect as the "absolute *prius*" of nature (*ENZ* §381) makes itself finite in history and objectivity (see *VGPh* 2, 148–49, 413–14).

Here are my conclusions. If thought becomes unconscious when it forgets its primacy, and science (i.e., speculative logic, philosophy) must illustrate the derivation and genesis of each determination by reminding us that it is thought that gives itself reality in each concretion, then we must proceed to investigate how the concept becomes representation. *Larvatus prodeo*, "I advance concealed," Descartes wrote down, not without concerns and paranoid suspicions at the time of his debut in a dangerous and conservative world. The concept always appears clothed, Hegel says to a world that has meanwhile known the Enlightenment; and philosophy has to strip it bare.

This will constitute the object of the next chapter. Before that, however, we need to dwell on one last question, to which the following section is devoted: the productivity of thinking.

Productive Thought

Gallons of ink have been spilled to understand in what sense the Aristotelian *nous* can be productive if *poiêsis* has the features of a transitive process that is seemingly alternative to both the activity of shedding light (*De anima* III 5) and the activation of an intellectual potentiality. It is not an exaggeration to say that the discussion of this conundrum has dominated and guided philosophy throughout late antiquity and the Middle Ages. Perhaps it is only because we have forgotten it that we no longer appreciate the relevance of one of the most fundamental problems inherited from the tradition of the commentaries on the intellect: Averroism, and the problematic coexistence of personal and universal intellect. The

THE MOVEMENT OF THOUGHT

Kantian productive imagination is also among the most debated topics. It is hard to understand what imagination can produce if it is described as a synthesis unifying modes of appearance in intuition.

Hegel does not rule out the production of external objects from the variety of reason's activities; quite the opposite. He assimilates production to practice and theory precisely because they are equally forms of reason's self-realization. Yet we have seen that the fundamental activity of reason does not coincide with the exercise of that external and transitive causality over material objects to be molded and shaped which is what we usually mean by production. When we say that reason reifies itself in several determinations and that, as in the Gospels, it knows itself from its products, its is an immanent causality.

In the Preliminary Conception to the *Encyclopaedia* Logic, Hegel writes that the true nature of the object is exhibited in thought (§22). He continues in §23: "Since in thinking things over their true nature emerges and since this thinking is just as much *my* activity, that true nature is equally the *product* [*Erzeugnis*] of *my* spirit insofar as the latter is a thinking subject. It is mine in accordance with my simple universality, i.e., as an I that is entirely *with itself*—it is the product of my *freedom*." These words lead back to the difficulty we have seen: if determinations belong to the thing and are not imposed by me (they are "an explication of what is already in the object," *W* 2, 503, *SL* 701), how can they also be "equally the product of my spirit"? Have we not insisted on objective thought in order to show that it is the concept that produces itself and that the logical element has its own life? If it is up to us to produce the logos, how can reality be rational, and why should we speak of the truth's or idea's self-production? To what extent is self-determining thought not only recognized but also promoted and made possible by human thinking? What exactly do we produce? I would like to answer these questions by giving voice to three different interpretations: respectively, metaphysical realism, transcendentalism, and what I believe is the Hegelian position.

1. Speaking of production cannot be but sloppy language. If we take seriously the priority of the idea, then all production on my part cannot be but an appearance. The logic is similar to the *Phenomenology* in that it must fill the gap between appearance and truth. This gap is subjective spirit's discovery of the self-production of the idea. Yet to retrace and know the idea means to *discover* the forms of its actualization, not to *produce* them.

We must object to this interpretation. When Hegel glorifies the Aristotelian intellect, he explains that Aristotle's flaw is taking the absolute to be exemplary for the finite. The absolute is thus not its own

CHAPTER 3

self-realization in history and objectivity. Without the Christian and modern principle of infinite subjectivity, we *partake* in the life of an active intellect but cannot *identify* ourselves with the divine, sustain its self-realization, or make it our own. The result of the realist interpretation is the elimination of subjective thinking from thought as well as the elimination of life and instinct—of all becoming, that is—from logos, understood as the transcendent a priori foundation we have seen. It is true that, as the Latin adage goes, *spiritus durissima coquit* (spirit cooks the hardest things), but one thing that spirit cannot digest is a transcendent principle. At most spirit can recognize and borrow it, not make it its own.

2. If that was the core of the realist interpretation, the transcendentalist reading argues that we produce the idea. The priority of the idea is an exaggeration; the truth is that the idea is actually a result and conclusion. If the idea is a result, then it is also necessarily a historical product.

This reading must obviously undertake the translation and recasting of a large part of Hegel's vocabulary that it typically blames on a metaphysical tradition from which we must free ourselves as from a yoke and a baggage that is meanwhile acknowledged and denounced as an impediment to our philosophical life. However, this reading is unable to recognize the eternity and autonomy of the logical element or, more importantly, the objectivity of thought. Hegel's concept of history as the manifestation of truth and the idea is not the same as the truth and idea that manifest themselves in it. Without acknowledging this difference, history is all we are left with. By exalting the meaning of production in Hegel, this interpretation confuses, as did the Hegelian Left before it, Hegel's concept of history as the manifestation of truth with another notion of history we find in Hegel, history as the "positive" science wherein "it is not the concept but only reasons that can be appealed to" (*ENZ* §16 A). It comes as no surprise that this reading is one of the most favored ones today insofar as it appeals to our post-metaphysical taste in its neo-pragmatist, analytic, and hermeneutic variations.

3. The realist interpretation does not take seriously the notion of production at work in the thought that thinks itself; the transcendentalist option does not take seriously objective thought. For Hegel, the idea knows itself only in finite spirit while remaining irreducible to it. The self-production of the idea coincides with our production. We are all in our "ordinary life" driven by "the firm belief in thought's agreement with the basic matter" (*ENZ* §22 Z), and for Hegel philosophy consists in putting to the test precisely this trust. But are we not playing with words? If the meaning of production is to bring to existence something that did

THE MOVEMENT OF THOUGHT

not exist before, what could the meaning of producing something that somehow has been already produced possibly amount to?

I believe that this concept of production in thought is used to counter the illusion that it is possible to restitute the in-itself, the given, without transforming it in thought. The given does not remain unaltered when we think it. We transform it into a concept: we idealize it, that is to say, we raise it from the space and time in which it exists and make it a concept, a universal: "it is only *by means of* an alteration that the true nature of the object emerges in consciousness" (*ENZ* §22).

The reflection at work in this transformation can be the idealization of the given from which experience begins, or that form of philosophy which has pure thoughts as its object. In this second case, the result of its work has as its object abstract thoughts which it organizes systematically in their purity. Yet this is precisely a work, a work which acknowledges that thought comes down to transforming.

As we can see, the concept of production, too, is said in many ways and goes through a redefinition in speculative language.

Kant's merit is having shown that to think means to transform, even though, by holding on to the thing in itself as the truth that it is not possible to grasp except in its appearance, one can say that "according to Kant, what we think is false because we think it" (*ENZ* §60 Z). By contrast, empiricism does not realize that those objects it believes it leaves untouched in its analysis consist in the transformation of concrete reality into an abstract form that brings singularity back to its universality. Empiricism is unaware of the contradictory character of its pretension to take things as they are. Every analysis, which is the model of knowledge favored by empiricism, alters the datum with which it begins in that it separates singularity and universality, the contingent and the essential, just like the chemist who tortures a piece of meat in order to conclude that he or she has found nitrogen, hydrogen, and carbon (*ENZ* §227 Z). For the analytic method, distinctions, abstraction, and various determinate concepts count as fixed elements that are necessary to understand the object.[26] We must therefore invert the Kantian thesis as we understand its truth and bring it to its proper result: we grasp things in truth *because* we think them (*Logik 1831*, 16–17, *LL* 12–13).[27]

By way of concluding this chapter, I would like to address the problem of the duality of thought: the duality between spontaneity and reification, thinking and thought, activity and passivity. And Kant is precisely the one who could raise it: indeed, the thinking subject does not objectify itself as thinking but always as thought. Determination and determinability fall in two distinct sides: I-think or original synthetic unity of apperception vs. empirical consciousness (*KrV* B 132–33), objective vs. subjective unity of self-consciousness (*KrV* B 140), and the subject of categories vs. the object of categories (*KrV* B 422). One could hold that the active and passive sides of thinking, though belonging to the same subject, differ as markedly as the two sides of thought as it animates the world and conceives of itself. If unconscious thought differs from self-knowing thought, Hegel has eventually to acknowledge a disparity between thought as subject and as object, between thinking and thought. As can be gleaned from a literal point of view from the concept of reflection as *Nachdenken*,[28] this disparity can be translated even into a temporal gap between the logical element animating the world and the absolute idea or spirit that retrospectively trace back their own path and make time come true by annulling succession. This gap occurs between a present thought, which knows itself, and a thought which, as the object of its own reification, is like a past we reflectively retrace in an atemporal present. Just as the owl takes flight at dusk, that is, reconsiders the world at the end of the day, so is thought doomed to a form of *posteriority*.[29]

I think that Hegel would reply that what appears as a disparity and a form of temporal divisibility between thinking and thought is internal to one and the same thought. The difference is internal to unity. In fact, unity needs difference because an undivided unity would be immediate, without plurality or becoming. There is indeed an asymmetry in the Hegelian view. Thinking thinks itself and also the necessity of reification, whereas thought unconsciously animating the world does not think or know itself. This leads us to distinguish between thinking and knowing, but not to separate activity from passivity in two mutually exclusive sides. We can say that knowing is a form of thinking, so that we must reconfigure the Hegelian identification between thinking and knowing in speculative logic into, once more, a progression of degrees.

Again we obtain an unusual vocabulary that is finally articulated in a systematic way. I have already discussed the different senses of thought. When Hegel speaks of the concept's or the idea's self-consciousness,[30] he uses the term differently from the ordinary sense. For us, self-consciousness is the awareness of one's own states from the first-person point of view. While this is a form of knowledge, it is however original and underived, that is, not based on any inference or obtained as a result.[31] For Hegel, instead, self-consciousness amounts to a completely developed form of self-knowledge. It differs from the I's self-consciousness in that the latter is both one particular form of it and an individual whole in which opaque and implicit aspects subsist. In other words, Hegel questions the view according to which self-consciousness is the self-transparency of a cogito.

But if the process through which the idea retraces its own moments is intrinsically *finite*, Hegel also questions the supposed absolute self-transparency of the idea. For, what kind of knowledge is that of the absolute idea or absolute spirit? It is its certainty of being all that is; it is such certainty because it is knowledge; and yet the totality of determinations is not known intuitively at a glance but is thought.[32] And, if thinking gives itself an object and gains insight into it, this is determinate, finite, itself and not another object. Mediation—the discursivity and finitude of thought—implies that each identity between thinking and thought is pointlike and discrete, namely, it excludes everything that that identity is not. The way in which thinking thinks the whole cannot be the same as the way it thinks the determinate objects that together form the whole. In Kant's words, the whole is an architectonic unity and not an aggregate, and yet thinking cannot take the whole at once as *totum simul* (a simultaneous whole), but only discursively as *totum aggregatum* (an aggregate). To Kant's question concerning how reason thinks the unconditioned, Jacobi replies that the understanding runs through the series of conditions, while reason can think the unconditioned only in an intuition. Jacobi's reply cannot satisfy Hegel's need for mediation. Hegel's absolute is both unconditioned and a totality; it follows that the totality must be retraced discursively, step by step, sequentially. The Hegelian temptation to take the Jacobian way, albeit betrayed by some passages,[33] would not work.

For Hegel knowledge generally is a relation, and as such it is *traversed by difference*: the difference between truth and certainty, between subjective form and content. When he speaks of the simplicity of knowledge, simplicity does not amount to undividedness. And once we move about in the simplicity of knowledge, that is, within an element in which the relation is no longer between two different things and we obtain precisely the duality of active and objectified thought we have seen, then we are able to know—whereby knowing is a completely developed cognition (*Erkennen* is actually a privileged form and the culmination of *Wissen*).[34] But a developed cognition is not the identity without residue between thinking and thought. The only identity of this kind is the intuition to which immediate knowledge aspires, the instantaneous (*Augenblick*) and simultaneous grasp of a universe of determinations.[35] Cognition cannot be an undivided coincidence; in fact, it must exhibit a difference between thinking and thought because it consists in retracing its own determinations one after the other (and hence in a discursive, finite, and mediated way). And these determinations all fall equally in the same process. Knowledge of the whole is marked by disparity throughout. The whole cannot be intuited. There is always going to

CHAPTER 3

be a gap in thought. If you take the absolute idea seriously, it is impossible to expect an instantaneous grasp of the oneness of the whole and its parts.

Heracleitus's *to hen diapheron heautôi* (the self-differentiating One), not a mystical union at the expense of difference, is Hegel's answer. Once again, Hegel acknowledges the disparity in thought by seeing it as immanent in its determinations.

4

On Transforming Representations into Concepts

Mia madre l'ho chiamata sasso,
perché fosse duratura sì, ma non viva.

I called my mother stone so that
she was long-lasting indeed, but not alive.
—C. Lolli, *Analfabetizzazione*

Representation

We have seen that reification is said in many ways. Every time thought has to do with its own products, which it treats as presuppositions and starting points—and in cognition the idea presupposes itself as an external universe, we read in *ENZ* §223—we have the same movement: being is a self-making, which hands itself over to an external medium at first found as given in order later to understand itself as a product, indeed as a self-production.

In my view, the clearest illustration of this movement is the notion of representation (*Vorstellung*), which I intend to explore in this chapter. In the *Encyclopaedia*, Hegel discusses the way in which thought appears initially as representation and then understands itself as the first.[1] In particular, the introduction and the Philosophy of Subjective Spirit show distinctly that the same movement of spontaneity and reification at work in the logic reproduces itself in language (and "language is the product [*das Werk*] of thought," *ENZ* §20).

The introduction to the *Encyclopaedia* is largely devoted to what Hegel calls the transformation of representations into concepts. Philosophy presupposes a certain familiarity with its objects and an interest in them (*ENZ* §1). We are immersed in a world that presents itself to us in its richness, unpredictability, and foreignness. In relation to this world, we have feelings, intuitions, inclinations, in sum, representations. Philosophy

CHAPTER 4

must begin with representations in order to invert the ordinary view and become aware of the primacy of the concept. "Chronologically speaking consciousness produces for itself *representations* of objects prior to generating *concepts* of them. What is more, only by passing *through* the process of representing and by turning *towards* it, does *thinking* spirit progress to knowing by way of thinking and to comprehending" (§1).

Philosophy will then be a specific form of reflection (*Nachdenken*, "the *thoughtful examination* of things," *ENZ* §2). It is *one* particular form of thought among others, and above all it is different from that thought which is unconsciously operative and pervades my every representation ("there is a difference between having such feelings and representations that are *determined* and *permeated* by thought, and *having thoughts* about them," §2 A). The ambition of philosophy to be more than one form of thought among others is not due to its arrogance or status, but rather to its object, thinking, which cannot tolerate being divided into reciprocally unrelated particulars but demands unity and articulation.

In all this, the content that is the object of each representation and thought is the same: truth, God,[2] actuality.[3] Whatever object, field, or interest I have, it is always the whole from one particular perspective. If the content is ever the same, the difference is all in the form in which the content appears and is known. Representation and thought are family names for these two different forms. Each of them finds the other faulty. From the point of view of philosophy, "representations may generally be regarded as *metaphors* of thoughts and concepts. . . . In our ordinary consciousness, thoughts are clothed in and combined with familiar sensuous and spiritual material" (*ENZ* §3 A). From the point of view of representation, in turn, the concept may appear as empty and abstract. We do not know what to think in order to fill the concept with meaning, examples, and illustrations allowing us to grasp it.

Though symmetrical, the two points of view are not on a par, however. We must say that representation is not aware of its weakness when it complains about the unintelligibility of abstract forms. Representation cannot hold fast to the concept, and for each abstract form representation seeks something familiar to bring it back to.[4] In this case representation acts like *doxa* in the Platonic dialogues: it does not know itself, it does not know its own limits and presuppositions. It recognizes only the obvious, to which it is ever impatient to go back in order to lean and rest on it as on a comfortable, reassuring bed of certainties. Philosophy, too, is driven by a type of need (§4), but a need that is known as such: the need is reason's instinct which seeks to ground its way of knowing.

Nachdenken is reflective in different ways. It is noteworthy that, while *Nachdenken* looks to the thing, it keeps in mind at the same time itself, its own course, independence, and status. While representation looks to the object, philosophy in its consideration of the object considers it as well as itself. Representation aims at the content, but does not think of the form it shapes it in. Philosophical reflection instead thinks the content in relation to its form. Philosophy's goal is to reduce the differences between content and form to the point of identifying them. This is eventually obtained when philosophy, while aiming at the content, takes its own thought as an object.

Two examples will facilitate, I hope, the understanding of this relationship between form and content. If I think of the color red, I have a sensible content that falls outside representation, and representation aims at grasping it. It must turn the given content into an abstract form; representation, though aiming at the sensible content, works with universals. This is to say that thought is unconsciously at work in representation, behind its back, as it were. But if representation is unconscious reason, it suffices to say "red" in order to have to admit that logos is actual. The sensible content matters only as thought.

If, instead, I think of God, I move on a different level. The content is already a product of thought and involves nothing sensible. I can intend God as an unfathomable mystery or as that absolutely transcendent personality that makes consciousness unhappy, or I can even think of God as clothed in the garments Michelangelo paints Him in in the Sistine Chapel: as a beyond, a transcendence that spirit considers from without. Alternatively, the divine is for me like pure thought in its absolute form wherein the relation between thinking and thought is no longer external, and content and form coincide.

This is the sense in which philosophy takes contents from representations and turns them into thoughts (*ENZ* §20 A). Yet, as we can see, it is necessary that representation preliminarily transform the sensible content into a universal. Here representation appears as the unconscious way in which the concept operates. It is the logical element at work underground like a mole in spirit which is still concentrated on the sensible given and has not yet understood itself as all truth. Thought grasps itself in a particular determination in intuition, images, signs, recollection, and language. Representation, the collective name of all these forms, is how thought gives itself a finite existence in them.

The contents of experience and the sciences are acknowledged by philosophical reflection, taken up and transformed into thought "that *generates* and provides *its own object for itself*" (*ENZ* §17). We have seen that this transformation of one form into another, now necessary, is identified with philosophical reflection, and that each concept is a production (§§22 and 23). However, in each production brought about by intelligence, spirit infects with its spirituality all things with which it comes into contact. Spirit produces in its objectifications a second-order world that is higher than the sensible world, a world in the form of representation. Spirit transforms the sensible into language, culture, institutions, practices. Thus, intelligence is able to recognize itself in its diverse products. While these are indeed the forms by means of which we aim to grasp the given, they are also the property and product of spirit, which is aware of being their maker.

The Philosophy of Subjective Spirit investigates in what way full-fledged rationality, which has been demonstrated in the logic, becomes real—acquires validity, confirmation, and truth—for spirit.[5] Spirit, which finds itself initially immersed in nature, gradually appropriates externality. It internalizes the given and makes it its own product. The color red no longer counts as this red and is (has value and being) for me as intuition, symbol, recollection, word, and more generally as color, quality, a determination I relate to other qualities and distinguish and exclude from other concepts, and so on. If the content is initially alien to me, the form in which it is assimilated comes to be understood progressively as the form the content has for intelligence. In the Psychology, spirit is the movement that adequates form and content to one another and knows itself while knowing objects:

> Intelligence *finds* itself *determined*; this is its semblance from which in its immediacy it sets out; but as *knowledge*, intelligence consists in positing what is found as its own. Its activity deals with the empty form of *finding* reason, and its aim is that its concept should be *for the intelligence*, i.e., to be reason *for itself*, whereby the *content* also becomes rational for the intelligence. This activity is *cognition*. (*ENZ* §445)

But what exactly is representation? Representation, which was considered in the *Encyclopaedia*'s introduction as a ready-made product as opposed to the concept, is actually the result of a complex elaboration explained in the Psychology (the third part of the Philosophy of Subjective Spirit after Anthropology and Phenomenology). Representation emerges from intuition, which is knowledge of a single sensible datum but not yet objective thought. Representation is the overcoming and negation of intuition in that it is an internalized intuition, in which the being of the given object is immediately seen as mine ("red" is my own image of redness). But the content is determined by the form in which I experience it (the red as perceived is different from the recollected red). And the movement of the Philosophy of Subjective Spirit, and particularly of the Psychology, is the progressive reduction of each content to the form in which we experience it (red *is* the image of redness, the recollection of red, the word "red"). In this way, spirit progressively reduces the difference between content and form until in thought we attain to their identity. Representation is the central mediation of this process: it negates the externality of being and transforms the immediate into an abstract possibility for intelligence, as an image or sign in which the thing is stored as a property of spirit that has assimilated and internalized it. From now on intelligence relates to things as to itself through its own representations.

"Representation is the recollected intuition and, as such, is the mean between intelligence's immediate finding-itself-determined and intelligence in its freedom, thinking" (*ENZ* §451). In internalizing the datum, intelligence recollects itself and relates to its products in recollection. But recollection is not the same as memory: the role of *Erinnerung*, which is even more fundamental here than elsewhere, consists in suspending the relevance of the given. In each new experience, I relate more and more to myself and to those contents that are already mine.

In an 1827–28 lecture, Hegel says that in representation "intelligence makes the perishable imperishable, it makes a mummy out of the past and preserves it. This event is in the intelligence imperishable, preserved in the time of the intelligence" (*Erdmann* 216). Having removed contents from external time and space and transposed them into its own virtual space and time, spirit has them at its disposal without having to look for them in externality. As we can see, spirit is the activity of addressing the given, appropriating and preserving it. Thus spirit removes contingency and transforms givenness into its conceptual organization by turning being into an ideal property. This is a progressive liberation from the sensible.[6] When spirit makes the sensible content an isolated though mummified determination (now an ideal and available determination, and thereby a lasting universal), its capillary penetration of the world begins.[7]

If, however, representation were limited to this, it would be nothing more than the elaboration of the moment of assimilation of experience that it shares with its historical empiricist and rationalist antecedents. In truth, at this point of the Psychology we witness an inversion. Up to this moment the movement progressed from outer to inner, but now the inner aims to become being. As imagination, representation externalizes itself and "makes itself *be*, makes itself the *thing*."[8] It transposes its contents into the objective signs in which it gives itself a figurative existence (*ein bildliches Dasein*). It acquires a historical-cultural reality, a permanence and temporal thickness. Indeed, an internalized image "needs, for its reality, a real intuition [*daseienden*]" (*ENZ* §454). As we have seen

CHAPTER 4

repeatedly, the concept must be able to intuit itself in an external existence. Intuition, which initially appeared as a given content, is now spirit's production. Indeed, intuition forms the basis for spirit's self-knowledge, since spirit can now intuit itself objectively in an external being, in productions it has itself posited. While so far spirit has internalized the given, it now reifies the rational.

Signs, and above all names and their system, language, are the being that intelligence gives itself to intuit itself outside itself. Taken in isolation, however, a name is a singular production, while it does not exist save in a language, and we need a permanent bond. In order to talk about the process of internalization, Hegel employs the metaphor of intelligence as an unconscious pit in which everything is stored; now he refers to memory as a permanent connection, an inadvertent system of names. Even memory does not have the usual meaning accepted by the ordinary conception. Memory is no longer a personal deposit of images and experiences that we can recollect. Rather, it is the unwitting possession of signs by means of which spirit freely moves. And spirit is now free because it need not focus on differences and particular determinations of meaning. In fact, memory overcomes precisely meaning understood as reference to something external and sensible. Now thought shows it has no more need for an external reference in order to work or activate itself, because it has only itself as object. We think in names ("Es ist in Namen, daß wir *denken*," *ENZ* §462 A). That is, we do not need to associate a name with an image or meaning in order to understand it. The name has sublated, that is, stored and lowered in itself, all reference to the thing. It can be used by mechanical memory which is the "supreme self-externalization of intelligence, in which it posits itself as the *being*, as the universal space of names as such, i.e., of senseless word" (§463). If memory is understood as this indifference, a mechanism in which intelligence has alienated itself, how can it be the direct premise for thought?

Memory can make itself thought (which "has no *meaning* any more," *ENZ* §464, i.e., it has only itself as object) because it is an arbitrary connection that has become permanent. In memory intelligence understands its autarchy, so that the essence (the true content and value) of mechanical memory coincides with intelligence itself in its self-sufficiency. Intelligence is at home in its highest self-externality. Intelligence is now certain that it does not lose itself in senseless signs. Likewise for thought: having overcome the reference to anything external, thought finally understands itself as "the thing; simple identity of the subjective and objective" (§465).

Second Nature

This mechanical form of operation on the part of thought in memory is not a novelty brought about by representation. We encountered an analogous turning point in the case of habit in the Anthropology. Habit allowed the soul to master its corporeality and turn given qualities into its own conscious dispositions (which are themselves the premise for those determinations that consciousness further isolates voluntarily and consciously in the Phenomenology, which is the stage of consciousness's opposition). Before considering habit, though, I would like to stress that the theme of second nature is not limited to these functions of subjective spirit, but represents one of the most fundamental ways of acting of both the concept and spirit. Here, too, representation embodies one of the forms in which the concept manifests itself and spirit operates: spirit lives in a world of its own—no longer in nature, but in a *second nature*.[9]

The concept of second nature is pivotal for Hegel. Spirit intuits itself in the world because it has given itself an external existence there. In it, each form of indifference, from habit to mechanical memory and ethical life, is an inadvertent possession in which spirit freely and confidently moves. Each of these forms is permeated by the self-knowledge of spirit, which is trust in the rationality of a world that no longer appears as alien, but rather as the work of each and everyone.[10]

In the various critiques of reification, particularly in Marxism, the thing reified is often seen in light of a repression that must be brought back to consciousness. This holds for Marx, for whom in commodity fetishism the product of work becomes a value suppressing the consciousness of the human activity that went into its fabrication. It also holds for Adorno and Horkheimer, according to whom reason seeks to dominate nature and yet forgets that it is part and parcel of it.[11] There is fraud, bad faith, deceit in reification, and the task is to tear the veil and unmask it. However, even in the absence of fraud and without necessarily identifying reification with alienation, from a conceptual point of view reification is an error; and philosophy is seen as the anamnesis that corrects it.

Far from being an error or a loss of freedom, in Hegel second nature is the objectivity of freedom. It is that medium in which shared life is known as such and provides satisfaction. In ethical life, the *"concept of freedom which has become the existing world and the nature of self-consciousness"* (*GPR* §142), ethos is the second nature of freely chosen practices and duties that weave together a shared life.[12] "The goal of world history is precisely this, that spirit should take shape in a nature, in a world fitting to it, so that the subject may find its own concept of spirit in this *second nature*, in this reality produced by virtue of the concept of spirit, and in this objectivity become aware of its freedom and subjective rationality" (*VPhG* Lasson I, 246).[13]

Objective spirit, habit, and mechanical memory, like all reification, can appear to the individual as an alien power with the sinister, threatening, and overwhelming features of thwarting constraints or a quasi-natural determinism. Hegel has to show that ethical life is knowledge and a system of customs and shared practices. Otherwise, since it is possible to experience them as alienating rather than feeling at home in them, the difference between particular will and the substance of individuals acknowledged as the result of everyone's work cannot come to the fore. In other words, it is possible to see in the limitation of my freedom a crucial threat and damage, or alternatively, considering that my freedom must be in harmony with that of others, as the incarnation of the living good (*lebendige Gute*). Just as the logical element could be considered as the soul of things or, alternatively, as an ossified collection of empty abstractions, likewise, the same content can be understood in opposite senses. Once again, it is important to consider all objectification as the particular—unwitting, unconscious—way in which something we must begin again to consider as living takes shape. And philosophy (in agreement with the Marxist notion of critique) must bring to consciousness what has been reified and become unconscious in second nature.

This is particularly evident in the case of habit. Habit is often depicted as the externality and passivity that reduces the space for the active exercise of freedom. For example, in Kant's *Anthropology from a Pragmatic Point of View*, habit is usually reproachable (*Ak* 7, §12, 149; English trans., 261) because it is the weakening of attention which jeopardizes the alert consciousness that is required to understand duty.[14] For Hegel, instead, habit is a fundamental mediation in the objectification of freedom precisely insofar as consciousness is faint.

In the Anthropology of the *Encyclopaedia*, habit is investigated in terms of bodily training. We are immersed in nature and all manifestations are psychophysical (feelings, sensations, dreams, ages of life, sleep and wakefulness, bodily responses to stimuli, etc.). The soul appears more and more clearly as the subject of these manifestations and as ideal self-relation. It tends to detach itself from the body and shape it. The body's limbs gradually become the soul's possession. The soul is no longer in immediate identity with the body but, by distancing itself from it, begins to discover itself as at once identical with and different from the body. The soul makes the body something ideal in the sense explained above:

it is a moment of the soul's existence, available as such, lowered to an un-perceived possession. The soul is free from the determinations in which it has left its imprint through exercise and repetition. For the soul these are inadvertent (while playing the violin I need not pay attention to the callus on my finger or the background noise).

This is why habit is "an acting without opposition" (*VPhG* Lasson I, 46), in which consciousness numbs its own sensibility. "Habit has rightly been called a second nature: *nature*, because it is an immediate being of the soul, a *second* nature, because it is an immediacy *posited* by the soul, incorporating and molding the bodilyness that pertains to the determina-tions of feeling as such and to the determinacies of representation and of the will in so far as they are embodied" (*ENZ* §410 A).

Habit is not an extension of nature, as in Hume, but the beginning of the detachment from it. In habit individuals begin to be free: they can pursue their goals without being distracted from without; they do not need to focus on or concern themselves constantly with the sensible. In fact, the sensible is now posited as indifferent, so that we depend on it less and less. For example, developing inurement to cold, tiredness, or misfortunes is a strength. The body, permeated by the will and by now the sign of the soul, becomes a particular possibility for voluntarily chosen goals: a tool (ibid.).

By means of habit we emancipate ourselves from nature. From the point of view of spirit, however, nature is used for its self-affirmation. Nature is not suppressed, but rather redeemed and valued for determi-nate purposes. And spirit does not demand a disembodied existence, but seeks to make itself real through the body. The body turns "into its own property, into its serviceable instrument" (ibid.).

Habit produces a seemingly natural immediacy through spiritual mediation. It produces automatisms that make thought's application to and appropriation of the thing quick, effortless, and confident. Habit is spontaneity that produces itself in receptivity, reason that has become a world in the body. Hegel's examples (upright posture, writing) reveal that the dispositions acquired through exercise and repetition are convenient tools at our disposal precisely because we have forgotten the strenuous labor they cost us and only the result, the specific skill, matters to us.

If "habit is a form that embraces all kinds and stages of spirit's activ-ity" and "habit is the mechanism of self-feeling, as memory is the mecha-nism of intelligence" (ibid.), then in the mechanical character of habit and second nature in general an exoneration and relief of intelligence from sensibility are at work. Insofar as a form of naturalness is main-tained, in habit and mechanism something objective and natural can retroact on the individual, yet the individual must be aware (he or she must remember, because he or she has forgotten) that second nature is a product, not an original given.

Habit works to the extent that I blunt my consciousness of those particular differences I have reduced to moments. At the same time, habit works because I have posited my will in nature and made it a second nature. The contradictory character of habit concerns consciousness, which I silence in the first case, and bring back to light in the second. But this is the same contradictoriness that characterizes the movement of thought in general. Since reason has left its imprint on the body, on external existence, it can move about imperceptibly trusting the rationality of the world. As the logical element has stored and forgotten itself in language and history, it can know itself as pervasive of actuality. Since the logos has made itself concrete and become unconscious to itself, it can recognize everywhere its imprints.

The Logic of Representation

Initially for us, all contents are but representations: God, world, spirit, and truth are simple universals clothed in concrete meaning. If we now go back to the transformation of representation into concept discussed in the *Encyclopaedia*'s introduction, we acknowledge that representation is as important for philosophy as is the understanding. In fact, representation and the understanding share a well-defined ground, a specific logic. But the logic that is partly common to representation and understanding is less developed than the logic of the concept which must include it within itself.

We have seen that representation, as internalized intuition, behaves negatively toward the sensible. It can be an image, a symbol, a sign, a word, whereby in all these examples what changes is the relation between figurative illustration and meaning. However, whether it is a sensible or an abstract figuration, whether it concerns a sensible or an already conceptual content, representation marks an essential difference between itself and its object. The object falls outside representation.

Representation, however, turns the sensible content into a simple universal "posited in the determination of being *mine*."[15] In being known as mine, the content is simplified, reduced, impoverished. Unlike sensible intuition, which is directed to the sensible material and fears losing its richness, representation begins to see the benefits of this simplification: the summary, the epitome (*Logik 1831*, 13, *LL* 10). The universal is an abbreviation that lends itself readily to a cognitive use. The problem of representation, however, is this: since the content of representation falls outside it, the universal and the sensible are mutually external. The former falls in representation, the latter in the thing. Thus, the universal and the sensible do not interpenetrate; the connections among determinations are not thought through; the object, instead of being known as a relation of different determinations, is actually held off as an opposite.

We have seen that the experimental sciences tend to break apart the form in which their content presents itself (*ENZ* §12). Starting with experience, the sciences find their content as a given, but they seek to minimize its contingency and raise it to some kind of necessity by treating it with rigor and method. Above all, they try to avoid the consideration of the given in the form of juxtaposed, side-by-side determinations that representation is naturally inclined to adopt. For representation does produce the universal, but it reproduces universal connections as it first finds them: in the form of juxtaposition, as being united by the mere "and" and "also" (§20 A). The thing is one, and red, and salty; God is good, but also fair and almighty. "In representation all [determinations] quietly have their seat, side by side. . . . In thought they are related to one another, and in this way contradiction appears" (*VPhR* 117).

In representation the universal does have worth, but it remains isolated in its independence and simplicity. "Representation here meets with the understanding" (*ENZ* §20 A). The relational character of determinations is understood only by thought. What escapes both representation and the understanding is "the activity of the universal" ("die Tätigkeit des Allgemeinen," *Logik 1831*, 15, *LL* 12), the view of the universal as promoting itself to particularity and in relation to other determinations: the conception of thought as movement.

We have two different logics: the paratactic logic of representation and the hierarchical and architectonic logic of the concept. In the former, determinations subsist quietly next to each other; in the latter, each moment of the whole that is the concept is the whole in a finite way, and the universal traverses each particular.

Besides two different logics, we also have—as Hegel writes in the preface to the second edition of the *Encyclopaedia* and in the review of Göschel—two different languages. Hegel compares this to when Homer gives constellations different names for immortal gods and for men (*ENZ, W* 8, 24; Eng. trans. 15; *W* 11, 378) in two languages that can communicate with each other.[16] Yet even here the relata are not on a par. One thing is pure thought, another is clothed thought, a metaphor of the concept: not because representation stays away from the sight of naked thought out of modesty, but because representation is all the more satisfied the more colorful, ornate, and rich the clothing appears. Representation is disoriented without an intuitive fulfilment. In fact, we can say that representation is not even able to understand philosophy's demand of purity because it cannot detach itself thoroughly from sensibility, from which it has nonetheless begun to emancipate itself. Representation is shy; it leaves its job unfinished for fear of losing the sensible. It is as if representation could not take seriously to the end its work of transformation of the given, which is essentially what representation is about, and the concept of production we have seen in chapter 3.

This notion of transforming representations into concepts retains a certain obscurity, and we need to dwell on it. First of all, the fact that representation is a metaphor for thought can be taken in two opposite senses. From the point of view of representation, a strong thesis seems to operate implicitly: the complete translation of metaphor in terms of thought, and with it a theory of language that may be charged with not acknowledging the superabundance of sense and the gap between metaphor and denomination that persists in the metaphorical process.[17]

Conversely, a different principle of translation is at stake in the thesis that philosophy consists in transforming representations into thoughts (*ENZ* §20 A). It can be understood as if representations gave us the starting point and the guide for philosophical reflection and it were simply a matter of explicating and formulating them in a different language. But the translation of form should not be intended in this way. We do begin with representation and the sensible, but this does not determine either the theme or the orientation of thinking. In turning to representations, thinking seeks in them the conceptual determinations it deems essential, but the necessity of thought is independent of the representations to which it turns and in which it seeks itself.

We have seen that philosophy acknowledges the work of the sciences as it appropriates their laws and genera because the categories elaborated by them are useful to the concept's self-knowledge. Representations play a similar role of vehicle. We all begin to reflect starting with representation, but it is necessary to distinguish between beginning and truth and infer that philosophy owes much to representation, but not the necessity of its development.[18]

In order to avoid the inverse misunderstanding—that is, the translation of representation, as if it were a nonconceptual element, into the concept—it must be reiterated that representation is thought that initially does not appear in the form of thought. Indeed, when I say that representation has become the concept, I am not supposing a given starting point that is recalcitrant to rationality and has to be made rational. Representation is already *in itself thought,* it is already the result of the work of universalization we have seen. Without thought, there would be no representation. It is only the form of such thought that must be articulated according to necessity, and this is the task of philosophy.

When we say that the content stays the same but the form changes, we must not conclude that the content is altogether independent of the form or is given without any form whatsoever (*ENZ* §133). Content and form are intimately intertwined. In the case at hand, this means that the problem of form and content must be reconsidered in light of the difference between philosophical reflection and scientific-representational knowledge. In the latter, thought is a formal activity that receives its content from without. Form and content do not interpenetrate (§133 Z). Properly speaking, philosophy is the way in which the separation of form and content collapses and thinking knows itself.

Here it can be seen that the supposed disadvantage of philosophy (it does not presuppose either existing and familiar objects or a method for their treatment), with which the introductions to both the *Science of Logic* and the *Encyclopaedia* begin, is actually the mark of its superior dignity. In philosophy the concept is everything. It is "the thing, substance, like the seed from which the whole tree unfolds. The seed contains all of its determinations, the whole nature of the tree," we read in the *Lectures on the Philosophy of Religion* (*VPhR* 63). "In philosophy reason is for reason" (*VPhR* 58). Even when philosophy has representation as a content and changes it into the form of the concept, philosophy has the movement of thought as its only object. In sum, only philosophy recognizes that the content of philosophy and religion is the same; only the concept can recognize that the content of concept and of representation is the same. However, only the concept recognizes its affinity with representation *because* it is the infinite form, not limited from without, in which the content has made itself form. When we speak of different forms of the same content, we are led back to the relation between finite and infinite.

Still, the most important aspect, so far in the background, for understanding the transformation of representations into concepts is the negativity of thought. When Hegel says that thought elaborates the categories of the sciences, he means that thought does not leave them untouched, but changes them from within. This is to say that when thought turns *toward* representation, it turns *against* it. Thought is critical of the presuppositions of representation and of its whole way of knowing.

Thought cannot let any presuppositions and assertions sneak in (*ENZ* §1). When we say that representation does not care about its necessity, we mean that familiarity represents for it a goal. Representation settles and rests content in the universals it establishes. They define its reassuring horizon of familiarity. The obvious and well-known is not called into question. The unconscious logos has in common with the familiarity in which representation moves the fact that both are equally pervaded by thought but do not know it as such.

One of the most famous passages in the preface to the *Phenomenology* reads: "The familiar, just because it is familiar, is not cognitively understood" (*W* 3, 35, *PhS* 18). To presuppose something as familiar means to be under the illusion that we possess it. Immersed in the familiar, representation's way of thinking "is finished and done" (*W* 3, 34, *PhS* 18). It has no interest in penetrating it, for it believes it can keep it at bay when in fact it only scratches the surface. In the familiar, we appease the restlessness of thought, stop asking questions, content ourselves. We assign to shared and known representations the safe value of fixed foundations, and even of guides for philosophical knowledge. Familiarity blocks the movement of thought. Familiarity numbs us and makes us lazy. It dulls and blunts the sharpness of thought's blade.

In these pages of the preface, which are run through by strong Socratic overtones (we could say that the stingray removes numbness), this sharp blade is in the understanding's hands. Unlike the *Encyclopaedia*, which stresses the continuity between representation and the understanding, in the preface representation is opposed to the understanding, which is here the absolute power of analysis looking the negative in the eyes that representation tries to placate. The understanding revolts against familiarity and the representation that sustains it. It is the removal of the familiar; but, as we know, it in turn cannot help but determine thought in fixed and isolated abstractions which philosophy must fluidify.

For a number of reasons (from the renewed attention to representational knowing par excellence, religion, to the final awareness of the logic common to understanding and representation, up to the detailed elaboration of the moments of representation as the middle term between intuition and concept in the Psychology), in the *Encyclopaedia* the role of representation changes compared to 1807. What does not change is the intention to know familiar contents by turning to representation. Hegel himself explicitly recalls the passage from the preface later on. In the *Encyclopaedia* philosophical reflection, though it takes as objects not things but their representation, is wary of "the yearning for some *familiar, current representation*" (*ENZ* §3 A). In the *Science of Logic*, we know the familiar when scientific thinking takes "natural thought" as its object.[19]

As habit allows wakeful consciousness to exonerate stimuli, so is unconscious logic inadvertently at work. Like familiarity relative to the

ON TRANSFORMING REPRESENTATIONS INTO CONCEPTS

understanding's blade, unconscious logic is literally dull. Nevertheless, it is not blind and irrational. In fact, it is that which has been transformed into an apparently inert passivity, but in which pulses a life that active thought must bring back to light.

Representation and Language

When thought hands itself over to an objective medium, it must come to terms with the type of medium: its specific constraints and limits. The medium does consist in the objectification of thought, but it is hardly ever its docile tool. It can prevent the development of thought, divert it from its goals, and be an impediment as much as it is indispensable for its expression. The medium posits restrictions to thought's freedom. While the idea that thinking amounts to controlling what we do is naive, the idea that by focusing on the products of thoughts we can presume to have them readily available is fiercely criticized by Hegel. Often thought finds it difficult to recognize itself in its existence. Counter-finality, preterintentionality, or heterogenesis of ends can take place. We intend something but obtain an altogether different, if not opposite, effect. It may happen that a law aimed at preventing corruption multiplies opportunities for illegality, or that an action chosen with the best intentions has the most noxious effects, or that something we say turns out to be the opposite of what we meant.

Language seems the ideal touchstone for Hegel's notion of thought as spontaneity and reification. It seems to have a life of its own, as Hegel had shown ever since the well-known dialectic of sense-certainty in the *Phenomenology*. We mean a "this" in its singularity, but each thing is "this." We say "now," but "now" is an abstract term for every instant in which we utter it. We say "I," but we are all "I's." We want something singular, and we end up getting a universal. In the same way in which we believed that thought could be ours and discovered that it is we who are in thought's possession instead, similarly, the universality of language possesses the I that demands to control it.

But this is only an example. Every natural language is a historical product with sedimentations that elude us. Languages present themselves to us in their fixed givenness as something alien. The I finds language as a ready-made product and must strive to make it its own. Homonymy, plurivocity, analogy, metaphor, and in short all that cannot be reduced to apophantic predication presuming to be self-transparent is enough to persuade us that language reveals as much as conceals what it says. By so doing it opposes a surd, voiceless indifference to our manifest intention. However, since both language and thought stand over the individual I, the problem is their mutual relation: can the life of language be resolved into the life of logos?

One of the most important challenges for Hegel consists in thinking critically about language in the same way that we call into question the familiar. Representation has encrusted language and the familiar for the simple reason that language is set in words that are repeated daily to the point of becoming spent and emptied of sense. How can truth, which is self-development, how can the concept, which is restlessness and labor, and how can the negative, which does not tolerate fixity, find an adequate expression in language, in worn-out words, in a finite syntax? This question is not rhetorical, that is, it does not intend to back the thesis that thought can be given outside language: we have seen that thought can be only in its exposition. This question actually lays bare an authentic dilemma for thought, an unsolved tension: thought determines itself in language, and yet it is not clear whether language contributes to determining the very thought that exposes itself in it.

According to Gadamer, it does. Thinking through the familiar for Hegel should amount to thought's liberation from the clothes it wears. But this is a vain effort, for language is not a shell or a provisional cover that one can simply dismiss. The natural logic of language is not a "prefiguration of philosophic logic."[20] The logic of the concept points beyond itself, to the natural logic of language. If speculative dialectic "were to include full acknowledgment of its relationship to the natural logic," it should "retrieve itself in hermeneutics."[21]

It seems to me that this position is vitiated by two fallacious presuppositions. Gadamer reduces the logical element that is unconsciously at work in everything to the logical instinct of language. When Gadamer makes language an unalterable power of concealment and a horizon that cannot be transcended, he does not realize he is depicting natural logic not as a second nature, but with those brushstrokes that for Hegel characterize nature itself: an unsolved contradiction between essence and manifestation, a being to which we remain external. Language becomes that living domain with regard to which thought should concede its foreignness and powerlessness, acknowledging the aporia (here in the literal sense of a nonviable path) of speculative logic. It is even more important to note that when Gadamer explains the natural logic stored in language, he describes it as if thought investigated an object that it does not change at all. Gadamer does not understand that the concept's work of translating forms is a critical work. When critique turns toward language, it does not leave it unaltered.

Hegel's prose has never ceased being a problem for his readers. It strikes us by its sometimes impenetrable obscurity. To be sure, denouncing it as a windy mystification, as neo-positivists used to do, does not help us to understand it or to appreciate the fact that Hegel's language can even be illuminating and, like a lightning bolt in an overcast sky, can offer "an impetuous clarity over the whole landscape."[22] Still, the effect of fatigue and heaviness can hardly be shaken off. To his contemporaries, and even his fondest students, Hegel's exposition sounded tormented, as if language were an opponent he was bound to fight continuously.[23] Rosenkranz quotes an eloquent note from Sietze: "I might explain Hegel's manifest difficulty of expression by assuming that he used to think to a certain extent in nouns. In the consideration of an object, relations appeared to him more or less like shapes that acted upon one another, so that he then translated these actions into words. . . . He first had to *translate* the content of his thoughts *such that every language was for him to some extent a foreign language.*"[24]

We can agree with much of this comment. The description of the shapes acting on one another to be expressed in words is apt; the feeling of not being at home in one's own language is certainly a phenomenon with which everybody is familiar.[25] And yet it is hard not to feel sympathy and even a certain compassion at the sight of a mind that, facing the resistance of language, must translate each thought into an acquired and foreign idiom.

By contrast, the idea that Hegel thought in nouns is a peculiar expression. In part it is almost obvious, given what we have seen regarding the nominalization of predicates (the true, the logical, the absolute, the familiar, etc.), and even verbs (being, becoming, thinking, etc.). In part, however, it is a point that calls for more careful consideration, because speculative language should speak differently than representation, and we have seen that it is in regard to representation that Hegel concludes that we think in names (*ENZ* §462 A). It is ordinary language that reifies thought into words. It is the understanding that arrests the fluidity of thought into independent, isolated, and reciprocally external objects.

It is representation that speaks of God. In this regard, speculative logic prefers to speak of "the divine" because, let us recall, philosophy considers thought-determinations for themselves, "free of those substrata which are the subjects of *representation*" (*WL* I, 62, *SL* 42). Certainly, however, we cannot imagine that a language, in order to conform to the movement of thought, should be articulated in verbs in active and passive modes rather than in nouns and adjectives. The question of speculative language must be raised urgently, but it must be understood that language presupposes a tendency to reification that is instrumental to the ontology of representation and the understanding. Such an ontology is made up of real and reciprocally separate objects.

The ordinary conception of knowledge according to which thought is a property of an I reduces language to judgments on things. In a judgment, subject and predicate are connected; the subject is a real, fixed object of which we predicate a property. We take for granted that the subject has different predicates over and above those we focus on, and the predicate can be said of other subjects. In inherence, subsumption, and predication in general, judgment moves among determinations which, though assumed as different, are unified by the statement.

The ordinary view, as we can see, needs to assume a consciousness, and also an actual object whose properties it predicates. Kant expresses this position best: the connection falls in the I, and for this reason—as the I-think speaks of things and not just of subjective representations—the task is to show the reality and objective validity of judgment. However it is understood logically, the copula is the I-think's function of objectification.

Consciousness believes that this form of expression by means of judgments is inevitable, but it is led to reflecting on its own twofold activity of separation and connection: it keeps distinct the moments that it at the same time connects. The *Phenomenology* is the exposition of the discovery on the part of consciousness that this twofold activity of identity and difference is the concept at work in the various forms of judgment, the original whole at the foundation of its division, behind the back of judgments. Consciousness is thus led beyond the opposition it takes for granted toward the logic, the investigation of the concept as it determines itself.[26] Since the concept is dialectical in nature, that is, truth must be exposed as the subject's progressive self-realization, as an identity in becoming and not as an identity between different elements, the problem is: In what language can dialectic be best expressed?[27] However, it turns out that a dialectical syntax that is an alternative to the ordinary one does not exist. Philosophy can avail itself only of judgments. Thus, the only way in which philosophy can show truth is the very calling into question of judgment, the predicative way of expressing the concept that consciousness assumes to be necessary.[28] Philosophy must set in motion language, its grammatical forms and the identity of the meaning of its words.

The defective nature of judgment for speculative logic is repeatedly pointed out by Hegel in the *Science of Logic*. Identity is expressed in the form of a judgment, but identity *must* turn into difference. To the questions "What is a plant?" and "What is God?" one would expect a different determination than what is expressed by the subject, an additional determination (a plant is—; God is—). Identity consists in going past

ON TRANSFORMING REPRESENTATIONS INTO CONCEPTS

itself; it cannot be analytic. "*More* is entailed, therefore, in the *form of the proposition* expressing identity than simple, abstract identity; entailed by it is this pure movement of reflection. . . . The propositional form can be regarded as the hidden necessity of adding to abstract identity the extra factor of that movement" (*WL* II, 44, *SL* 360).

Identity and difference must be conceived together, but in the object, not in an external reflection. The different forms of judgment (judgment of quality, reflection, necessity, the concept) are exposed according to a progressive internalization. The relation between subject and predicate moves progressively from externality to internality toward a growing identification. The objective validity of the judgment is not exposed in a Transcendental Deduction grounding a subjective operation of connection (*WL* II, 345, *SL* 582). It consists in the inner self-articulation of the concept. In the concept, the copula expresses an already existing relation—not one imposed by reflection—between the individual and the universal. The individual is "raised to universality," and conversely the universal "exists for itself" (*WL* II, 307, *SL* 554). In speculative logic, the judgment is "a movement" whose aim is the explicit position of the identity of the concept (*WL* II, 309, *SL* 556).

"The subject matter, as it is apart from thought and conceptualization, is a representation or also a name" (*WL* II, 560, *SL* 743). "This kind of external and fixed subject of representation and understanding, and also these abstract determinations" (ibid.) are assumed as separate. "If a consideration that avoids the concept stops short at their external relation, isolates them and leaves them as fixed presuppositions, it is the concept that, on the contrary, will fix its sight on them, move them as their soul and bring out their dialectic" (*WL* II, 560–61, *SL* 744).

Judgment is unfit to express speculative truth because it is an identical relation between subject and predicate that leaves aside their nonidentity (*WL* I, 93, *SL* 67). Thus, truth is not a function of judgment, but rather of the complete movement of all judgments. It is the dissolution of the static structure of the sentence. What the ordinary conception calls truth is the correctness of a statement that reflects a state of affairs properly. But "whoever calls *truth the correctness* of an *intuition* or a *perception,* the agreement of *representation* with the subject matter, has for a minimum no expression left for that which is the subject matter and the aim of philosophy" (*WL* II, 318, *SL* 562).

It is worth stressing that not every proposition is a judgment for Hegel. Empirical and positive propositions have facts as contents and therefore have no internal relation to form. This is why they are not philosophical.[29] In this sense, an empirical proposition is like the zero degree of representation, is still absorbed only in an external content, and is

CHAPTER 4

totally unaware of the problem regarding its form. By contrast, we can consider the judgment as the form of expression of representation, which has meanwhile become subjective universality and behaves as understanding: it takes the subject as a passive pole of attribution and the copula as the external link between two independent terms (*ENZ* §§168–71; *WL* I, 92–93, *SL* 66–67). To put it differently, at stake is the truth of the content, not the correctness of our knowledge. Insofar as I represent an empirical content, for example, the house or the red as existing outside myself, I am a consciousness that turns toward something external. I have not understood yet that the "I" is one with its content because it has produced the concept. In the philosophical proposition, a relation between content and form—whatever it turns out to be—is thematic.

Hegel gives us two excellent illustrations of all this in the *Science of Logic*. About the identity of being and nothing, he writes:

> As expressed in the proposition *"being and nothing are one and the same,"* the result of considering being and nothing is incomplete. The accent falls primarily on the *being-one-and-the-same*, as is the case in judgment generally, where the predicate says what the subject is. Consequently, the sense seems to be that the distinction is denied which yet patently occurs in the proposition at the same time; for the proposition says *both* determinations, being and nothing, and contains them as distinguished. (*WL* I, 93, *SL* 66).

The proposition contains the result; it is in itself the result; but this is not expressed by the proposition (*WL* I, 93, *SL* 67). We can remedy this flaw by adding the opposite conclusion (being and nothing are not the same), "but another defect then crops up, for these propositions are disconnected and therefore present their content only in an antinomy" (ibid.). It is further possible to speak of a unity between identity and nonidentity, but this is also an unfortunate expression: again, a subjective reflection. "It would therefore be better to say simply *unseparatedness* and *inseparability*; but then the *affirmative* aspect of the connection of the whole would not be expressed" (*WL* I, 94, *SL* 68).

Every judgment expresses a one-sided truth (and "the commonest injustice done to a speculative content is to render it one-sided," *WL* I, 94, *SL* 67). Hence, if we consider being and nothing in speculative terms as inseparable, the proposition "turns out to vanish spontaneously" (*WL* I, 93, *SL* 67). Their result, namely becoming, "consists rather in this movement, that pure being is immediate and simple and for that very reason is just as much pure nothing; that the distinction between them *is*, but equally *sublates itself and is not*" (*WL* I, 94, *SL* 68). We cannot say that the

ON TRANSFORMING REPRESENTATIONS INTO CONCEPTS

difference is in a third element, in our consideration, for we would again have "a form of subjectivity, and subjectivity does not belong to the present order of exposition" (*WL* I, 95, *SL* 68). What is left of this dialectic? The third in which the difference is resolved is "presented" in becoming (*WL* I, 95, *SL* 68), wherein the identity of identity and nonidentity is "*present* and *posited*" (*ENZ* §66 A). Becoming is like arresting the dialectic in a determinate form that cannot, however, be exhibited by judgment. It appears, then, that language is unable to say the truth—or at least, it is unable to do so in a determinate, fixed, and isolated form. Only as system, syllogism, and self-mediation can truth be expressed.

The second illustration can be found in the concept of sublation (*aufheben*). "To sublate" means both to preserve and to put an end (*WL* I, 114, *SL* 81–82). However, the identity and simultaneity of these two meanings is from the linguistic and lexical points of view the unity of two different moments. What language cannot exhibit is the "vanishing" of determinations in a result that is by now something else (*WL* I, 115, *SL* 82).

Language fixates its objects, whereas speculative logic must be able to show their contradictoriness, their becoming, their dialectical movement, their fluidity. The 1817 Heidelberg *Encyclopaedia* says that the object of logical thought is the sublation of determinations through "successive meanings" (§40 A, with regard to being and nothing), which provide ever more fitting characterizations of the thing and ever truer definitions of the absolute.

A Speculative Sentence?

These two illustrations are eloquent, but they remain negative in that they are two examples of something wrong: a practice for which we do not yet have a full-fledged theory. To find a compelling discussion of dialectic in language, we need to go back to the pages on the speculative sentence in the preface to the *Phenomenology*.[30] But here, too, if we were expecting a solution of the problem and a detailed account of an alternative syntax, like the outlines of a special language for speculative philosophy, we would be disappointed. Once again, all we find is a critique of the language of representation and of the understanding. And even here, as in the case of Sense-Certainty which did not concern language but rather the proof of the nullity of sensible singularity, Hegel does not sketch a philosophy of language. What interests him is the speculative truth that struggles to acquire a figuration. Still, all clothing is inadequate not because speculative truth does not like it, but rather because no particular clothing can be good for all seasons, that is, can halt and constrain the movement of thinking. Thought is infinity that gives itself finite existences and recognizes itself in them, but as in one-sided determinations, moments of a whole. The infinite lives only in the finite, but cannot bear being reduced to something finite.

Each proposition is intrinsically finite. For this reason, Hegel writes that "as a proposition, the speculative is only the *internal* inhibition" (*W* 3, 61, *PhS* 40). A speculative proposition with a structure or form that is an alternative to ordinary grammar simply does not exist. We have a speculative proposition when we intend speculatively a philosophical proposition, but each philosophical proposition is intrinsically one-sided. A speculative proposition is a way to interpret the relation between subject and predicate that pushes us to rephrase the terms at stake by turning them inside out. Despite the fact that the topic of the speculative sentence is treated only in the *Phenomenology*, the problem is the same as that of the whole logic and philosophy: the new conception of substance as subject. In my view, these pages contain the best exposition of the concept of dialectic and of the critique of the ordinary view of thinking, as well as the purest version of the movement of thought.

This theme can be found in the fourth part of the preface, which significantly does not begin with considerations on language, but with the notion of scientific investigation which must take upon itself the strenuous effort of the concept (*W* 3, 56, *PhS* 35). "The habit of representation" and "formalistic thinking" can hardly tolerate the concept. They experience it as an intrusion, as an inconvenience: the concept disrupts representation, which demands to stay focused on its object, holding fast to its distinctions. "That habit should be called material thinking, a contingent consciousness that is absorbed only in material stuff, and therefore finds it hard work to lift the self clear of such matter, and to be at one with itself" (ibid.).

For representation, demonstration and dialectic fall asunder. Representation and the understanding cannot see that the concept is a self, a movement to which negativity immanently belongs; the concept is the becoming of the object. Since representation endorses an ontology made up of distinct and separate entities, it believes instead that it must avoid all movement. It presupposes as given and fixed the self-identical subject of the proposition, the name as "an empty unity without thought-content" (*W* 3, 62, *PhS* 40). However, representation, too, is a movement; only a movement of a different kind, "the vain hovering" over the thing (*W* 3, 56, *PhS* 36) that is unable to follow through the inner necessity of the content. "This Subject constitutes the basis to which the content is attached, and upon which the movement runs back and forth" (*W* 3, 57, *PhS* 37).

ON TRANSFORMING REPRESENTATIONS INTO CONCEPTS

There is indeed movement therefore, but this is only external, the hovering as the reiterated transition from the subject to the predicate and vice versa. And this transition is unknown to consciousness. As it thinks of the content of its statement, representation realizes that the grammatical subject does not express it. Representation moves then to the predicate in order to know what the content is. However, the predicate is something accidental and one has to move past it. But it is not possible to move past it once we discover that it is the truth of the subject, its substantiality. Representation believes *it* must find the truth now in the subject, now in the predicate, namely in the distinct elements it has itself reified into opposites.

From Hegel's exposition (at *W*3, 58, *PhS* 38), we gather that representation must become understanding. When representation moves back and forth between subject and predicate, it understands that predicates are a variety that requires an objective bond, and this cannot be but the subject that sustains them. Thus, the object isolated by representation as a grammatical subject becomes subject in an altogether different sense: the I that knows and supports predicates in their mutual relation. Inversely, it can be said that the I finds itself in the object expressed by the grammatical subject. This is the understanding that representation must raise itself to, and this is why Hegel believes that Kant has given philosophical dignity to common sense.

In both forms, however, the movement of representation is subjected to an inhibition and a recoil. For representation, reading a philosophical text constitutes a hindrance to its freedom. Something weighs on the movement allowing representation to live as a free bouncing back and forth between one point of view and another, and drags down its unreflected association of opinions. By contrast, for philosophy this is no baggage, but the sign of the cogency and necessity of the content. That which representation misunderstands as a constraint and a hindrance depends on the fact that the subject remains external to the immanent movement of the content. Representation does not realize that it is constantly led back to "the self of the content" (ibid.).

The confusion into which representational thinking is thrown is salutary. In being relentlessly led to reconsidering the thing, representation can now realize that the movement of the thing must replace its own subjective reflection. Representation can now understand that the self-identical structure of the sentence is not left untouched by the corrosive force of thought, by the restlessness of the concept.

We have seen that a speculative proposition as such has no inner properties distinguishing it from ordinary syntax. It is possible to understand a philosophical proposition speculatively when, rather than taking the judgment as a juxtaposition of different terms, we follow out its movement. Whether a proposition can be considered speculative depends on how we intend it. "The general nature of the judgement or proposition, which involves the distinction of Subject and Predicate, is destroyed by the speculative proposition. . . . In the philosophical proposition the identification of Subject and Predicate is not meant to destroy the difference between them, which the form of the proposition expresses; their unity, rather, is meant to emerge as a harmony" (*W* 3, 58–59, *PhS* 38). Hegel provides an example: in "God is being," the predicate is not accidental but is the essence to be expressed. It has a substantial meaning in which the subject is resolved; God stops being a fixed subject; but in this way the subject is lost, and thought, "missing it, is thrown back on to the thought of the Subject" (*W* 3, 59, *PhS* 38). Thought thinking together subject and predicate is immersed in the content. It is one with it.

It is precisely here that the impression of the unintelligibility of philosophical writings arises: the opinion that representation expected to see confirmed is destroyed. Representation is unsettled, and this "compels our knowing to go back to the proposition, and understand it in some other way" (*W* 3, 60, *PhS* §63, 39). When Hegel recalls this point at the beginning of the introduction to the *Encyclopaedia*, he adds that the incomprehensibility of philosophy is due to a "*lack of training* to think abstractly, i.e., to hold on to pure thoughts and to move among them" (*ENZ* §3 A). Representation seeks to fill concepts with intuitive contents, to bring them back to its familiar horizon.

Thinking wreaks havoc in representation and educates it philosophically. But its effect is only indirectly pedagogical: its main task is the exposition of the logical element. Therefore, thinking must not only represent an inhibition for representation; in addition, "this opposite movement must find explicit expression. . . . The return of the Notion into itself must be *set forth*. . . . The *proposition* should express *what* the True is; but essentially the True is Subject. As such it is merely the dialectical movement, this course that generates itself, going forth from, and returning to, itself" (*W* 3, 61, *PhS* 39–40).

If philosophy must acknowledge and express substance as subject; if the subject must be as much substrate as an activity of self-realization and the goal of its own movement, then it seems necessary to conclude that this critique of representation, this negative dialectic of the ordinary conception of thinking, has to address the traditional notion of subject in the first place.

> Since the Notion is the object's own self, which presents itself as the *coming-to-be of the object*, it is not a passive Subject inertly supporting the

> Accidents; it is, on the contrary, the self-moving Notion which takes its determinations back into itself. In this movement the passive Subject itself perishes; it enters into the differences and the content, and constitutes the determinateness, i.e., the differentiated content and its movement, instead of remaining inertly over against it. The solid ground which argumentation has in the passive Subject is therefore shaken, and only this movement itself becomes the object. (*W* 3, 57–58, *PhS* 37)

Unlike representation, the concept is the subject of its becoming that makes itself determinate and retrieves determinations in its movement. In addition to the subject the copula, too, changes in this process, as it takes on different functions in proposition: predication and the identification of nonidentical terms, and even the partial identity that coexists with nonidentity.[31]

Thanks to such plasticity, dialectical thinking exploits language for its own purposes. But this does not mean that thought suppresses the need for meaning.[32] Nor does thought believe that the reification and finitization of language into grammatical functions is an "error." Reification is necessary so that the understanding can dwell on fixed determinations; but it is no less necessary that reason disrupt such fixity. Philosophical critique allows us to understand that the subject must be understood differently. It is recast as self, and such nominalization of the reflexive pronoun means that the subject is no longer the external substrate that is external to judgment or the individual I, but that it is subject as thought which can make itself into self-consciousness: substance that becomes subject.[33]

I would like to conclude with three theses:

1. We can say that representation and concept are continuous from the point of view of the individual who reflects, but they are incompatible for philosophy ("the one method interferes with the other," *W* 3, 60, *PhS* 39).

2. The speculative proposition is not a thesis about language, but the demonstration of the limits of language starting from a reflection that is internal to language. While thought can only express itself in propositional syntax, it is other than that. There is a nonidentity between thought and language.

3. The subject matter of the speculative proposition is truth as subject, the ideality of the finite, the self-development of the concept. In this self, identity is not at the expense of difference: identity is not a fixed and defined pole, the I with its faculties or the soul as the inert substrate of its processes, but spirit that reclaims itself from its manifestations. This is why there is a deep thematic affinity underneath the speculative sentence, the self of the concept, and the philosophy of spirit as it is developed

CHAPTER 4

in the *Encyclopaedia* starting with the critique of interpretations that break up spirit (from pneumatology in §§26–36 up to all theory of spirit as agglomeration or aggregate in §445 A and *W* 20, 520).

The speculative proposition is the critique of the ready-made truths of representation, which finds it idle to reexamine them and "believes it is entitled to assert them, as well as to judge and pass sentence by appealing to them" (*W* 3, 62, *PhS* 41). The speculative element is the revolution that dialectical reason brings to the familiar, the corrosive bath in which it melts it.

The speculative proposition best explains a point that has occurred several times: each term is more fluid than it seems, more than the understanding, which needs a stable and univocal world, would like it. A fixed meaning is handy and convenient; but for philosophy it is a pretense to be undermined. A world without stakes can give us dizzy spells; but it is not without order, and from this disorientation we can recover, entering a different horizon of meaning.

Philosophy disorients us, so as to reorient us. Philosophy proceeds to a radical critique of ordinary views like an analphabetization that takes the familiar off its hinges, so as to educate us in a different alphabet and literacy. Philosophy provides us with a new speculative vocabulary.

5

Kant's and Hegel's Reason

> This kind of thinking, called *reason* here, is stripped of all *authority* by being robbed of every determination.
> —*ENZ* §60 A

A Radicalization of Kant?

In this final chapter, I intend to bring into reciprocal relation Kant and Hegel on the topics we have discussed in this book, and particularly on reason and the I. In order to proceed to a comparison worthy of this name, it is necessary to put in question the tenets of Hegel's interpretation of Kant, which is often dismissive, schematic, and instrumental to the overcoming of Kant. The goal is not to oppose a different picture of Kant to Hegel's, but to understand the distortions and assumptions of Hegel's interpretation, which is possible only by comparing it with Kant's writings.[1]

This chapter begins by asking what it means to read Hegel in light of the results of Kant's philosophy (in the first section). It then moves to an examination of Hegel's interpretation of Kant (second section), discusses the relation between reason and the I in Kant and Hegel (third section), and brings to light some tacit assumptions that are inherent in Hegel's reading (fourth section). My objective is not to defend Kant from Hegel, not even in the fifth section, where I dwell on the problem of a priori synthesis and reason's self-determination in Kant. My intention is to explain why certain Hegelian simplifications are more problematic than they appear, and to prepare the ground for the sixth section, where I show the novelty of Hegel's reason compared to Kant's. In my view, Kant and Hegel share more than those who profess themselves to be Kantians or Hegelians would care to concede. But I also want to show that, even if they start from common premises, the outcomes will be quite distant, so different in fact as to configure themselves eventually as neat alternatives. And this also applies to the becoming of reason of which both Kant and Hegel speak (seventh section).

Contemporary philosophical historiography assumes as established that Hegel's philosophy is a compelling discussion of criticism. Kant's philosophy, so says the widespread assumption, is the unavoidable starting point of Hegel's philosophy. To be sure, we cannot ignore the numerous claims made to this effect by Hegel himself, who is rarely so unambiguous. Regardless of how many reservations we may have about Kant's philosophy, it is on its grounds that we build up the new philosophy, and there cannot be any hesitations on such a breakthrough.[2]

But what does it mean for Hegel to share Kant's principle? To begin to answer this question, we can provisionally take into account what Hegel's introduction to the *Science of Logic* considers the great step forward of Kant's Transcendental Analytic. It has turned metaphysics into logic, and the question of being into that of categories (*WL* I, 45, *SL* 30). Since experience cannot ground itself, it is only categorial thought that can bestow universality and necessity upon our knowledge. The principles ruling the use of our understanding are the same principles at work in the experience of nature.

If we ask about the meaning of Hegel's supposed endorsement of Kant's novelty, it is worth pointing out that Hegel does not intend to claim that Kant has "influenced" him more than have other philosophers. The notion of influence, as an external action upon a passive subject, has no business in a history of philosophy that takes seriously the freedom of thinking. We let ourselves be influenced only by that which we are already aiming at and which is struggling to take shape in our thought. Hegel often repeats that the category of causality does not apply in the realm of spirit or life. In fact, already in the organism "nothing whatever could have a positive relation to living being, if living being in and for itself did not constitute the possibility of this relation" (*ENZ* §359; compare *WL* II, 228–29 and 482, *SL* 497–98 and 685).

If Kant did not influence Hegel, even though Hegel admittedly adopted his principle and saw it as a breakthrough, we should wonder whether this warrants theses that are widely accepted today and repeated uncritically by many authoritative interpreters. It is precisely the point on which most agree that seems to me particularly questionable: one adopts a certain picture of Kant (as an epigone of Hume interested in giving a solution to the problem of skepticism) in order to find then in Hegel a transcendental development of categorial thought, purified of its more empiricist and subjectivist implications. I find it surprisingly naive to claim that, since Kant had subjected Scholastic metaphysics to a radical critique, Hegel could not help but share its anti-metaphysical outcomes. Actually, the critique of pure reason aims to build metaphysics as a science; and Hegel, who sees in pre-Kantian Scholastic metaphysics the triumph of the understanding's separate and isolated abstractions, finds also that Plato's and Aristotle's metaphysics, to which the *Science of Logic* as well as the *Encyclopaedia* refer at crucial junctures, are in truth the work of speculative concept (*ENZ* §36 Z).

But above all, we must beware of an arrogance that goes strangely unnoticed. More and more often we read that Hegel proposes a "continuation of the Kantian project" or a "radicalization of Kant's philosophy" (McDowell among others expresses himself in these terms). The problem with expressions like these is that they lend themselves easily to the building of houses of cards which are all the more fragile the more they rest on a psychological hypothesis. Interpreters take for granted that they already know what Kant aimed to do; are in a position to identify the limits of what Kant had introduced without being able to defend it thoroughly due to the insurmountable inner flaws substantially jeopardizing and blocking his philosophy; and, lastly, with the necessary resoluteness, Hegel has finally brought to the extreme consequences what Kant had treated with unfortunate timidity, prudence, and a soft spot in his heart (*Zärtlichkeit*) for things of the world.

Notice that in order to develop these arguments, what the interpreter identifies as the core element of Kant's philosophy is only secondary. It could be a critique of reason, thinking, and categories left half-baked; a philosophy of reflection or a transcendental idealism whose finitude or subjectivism we must overcome; an architectonic articulation of reason in its constitutive moments; or the defense of the autonomy of reason as legislation for the different fields it aims to rule.

Naturally, the first one who (well before his followers today) believed that Kant had left his revolution halfway through was Hegel himself. He wanted a critical attitude that is more consequential than Kant's, wherein "critical" means the rigor of objective thought and the absence of presuppositions that we have seen in the previous chapters. My mention of the more specific notion of philosophical critique calls for immediate qualifications. My denouncing as arrogant a particular interpretative stance does not mean that I complain about an alleged slight against civil manners. In fact, I believe that Hegel has raised a powerful criticism of Kant. It does not leave any point untouched and represents one of the highest moments of any philosophical encounter between two giants of thought, even if it is one-sided and often unduly harsh (not to say based on fundamental or occasional misunderstandings that I shall address in the fourth section). I am convinced of this because I am convinced of the goodness of Hegel's teaching: free thought must examine the ground of its own possibilities and the modes of its realization. Hegel puts this into practice, and we must be grateful to him for this: the notion of the spontaneity of thinking must be investigated internally. Autonomous reason must be examined in light of its capacity to sustain itself.

On the one hand, however, I believe that we should not accept uncritically the historiographical presuppositions of interpreters who, as I said, assume they know and, above all, possess the required audacity that Kant would have lacked. On the other hand, the so-called overcoming of Kant on Hegel's part should not be accepted uncritically and wholesale. Obviously, I am not interested in salvaging the *Critique of Pure Reason* from Hegel or acknowledging in detail the extent of the supposed Hegelian indebtedness toward Kant (if anything, I believe a contextualization is rather what is called for). What I mean and intend to discuss in this chapter is that it is worth considering how things between Kant and Hegel could have gone otherwise. A counterfactual imagination can be illuminating, especially in quarrels we are asked not to adjudicate rashly.

I believe that with regard to certain topics Hegel could have shown more appreciation of Kant's philosophy and also learned more from Kant, if only his critique had been at times less hasty and summary, or more open and receptive. Besides, in the history of philosophy, the richness of a comparison is often cut short by those who, coming later, translate all points at stake into their own conceptual terms and easily turn everything in their favor. The hands-down victory of those who come later is the positivism of time. It seems to me that we do not sufficiently regret that, instead of considering merits and contents in the light of potential alternatives, we are too early called to take a stance, almost invariably favoring the winners. But philosophers are not compelled to answer the draft to arms. Not because they wash their hands, but because conscription silences criticism, which is all philosophy is about. Becoming partisans of either camp, construing the other as defiant and antagonistic, is not an inevitable doom.

Perhaps it is not surprising that in the secondary literature we end up witnessing a dialogue between the deaf. Kantians have little interest in the problems raised by Hegelians who are insensitive to absolute idealism's possible misunderstandings or sweeping claims and are not keen on philosophical reconsideration. But Hegelians seem even less interested in listening to those who they surmise from the outset are siding with the reasons of finite consciousness and givenness. Actually, in the rich bibliography devoted to the comparison between Kant and Hegel, I am not familiar with many essays addressing *philosophically* those readers who are not already convinced of the necessity of choosing either of them.

Sometimes what passes as Hegel's solution to an unsolved Kantian problem simplifies what to a Kant scholar is a fluid reality that could have taken on other configurations; or the problem was actually solved by Kant in different ways and in other writings and contexts, that is, not as Hegel construes it; or, finally, the problem could not be reduced to unity because its sides belonged to irreconcilable fields, so that isolating a core foundation in order to denounce its defective use, as Hegel often does brilliantly, is not possible. I take Hegel's reductions and simplifications, rather than being the result of an arbitrary or fanciful reading, as the one-sided solution to a basic ambivalence regarding pure reason's powers on Kant's part. Ambivalence must be acknowledged as such, lest shortcuts and simplifications become the rule. Different possibilities must be weighed and valued in their *promise* before they are dismissed.

Let there be no doubt that it is impossible to leave untouched by the corrosive power of critique any thought, even Kant's. Celebrating Kant today and reproducing after two and a half centuries of substantial criticisms his philosophy as it was is both historically and philosophically dubious. We cannot repeat a thought which we have shown is animated by a dialectic that cannot leave it alone and still, any more than we can put away an element in a cabinet and hope to preserve it untouched by time or contamination with other elements. Let us consider then Kant's greatness and limits according to Hegel.

Kant's Greatness or Kant's Limits? Hegel's Interpretation of Kant

In this section I would like to show how, for Hegel, Kant's greatness and limits are so inseparable that they constitute complementary aspects of the same thing.

Hegel begins his exposition of Kant in the *Lectures on the History of Philosophy* (*VGPh* 3, 330–31) by emphasizing that thinking for Kant is absolutely decisive; it is an intimate certainty on which nothing external has any authority. The problem with this view can be exposed no less immediately: the thought that determines itself is taken as subjective. Accordingly, the fact that thought has an a priori synthesis, namely judgments not drawn from experience, should make thought intrinsically concrete, but it instead empties thought of the power it had assigned to it (*VGPh* 3, 336). The great truth acknowledged by Kant is that all reality falls in self-consciousness. Yet Kant takes this truth in a limited and subjective sense; self-consciousness is the condition of an individual I rather than a property of the whole. At best self-consciousness is an original unity, not the return to itself and the "self-*restoring* sameness, or this reflection" in itself (*W* 3, 23, *PhS* 10) in which truth must be expressed.

Indeed, it is in this way that Hegel interprets Kant's reason since *Faith and Knowledge*: as an original bilateral unity "out of which subjective Ego and objective world first sunder themselves" (*GuW* 329, *FK* 73). In other words, reason is the identity out of which opposition is generated; the identity of subjectivity and objectivity as it appears in consciousness rather than the sublation of oppositions. In this reading Hegel fuses in one thing pure reason, the original unity of apperception, and schematizing imagination. The unity is original in that it is rational, not intellectual; and it is productive in the same way as imagination in that it manifests itself as pluralized and produced within empirical consciousness. This point returns in the *Science of Logic* (*WL* II, 254, *SL* 515). With respect to the original synthetic unity of apperception, it can be said that Hegel values particularly one term, the originality. It is the original unity that splits itself up in subject and object and is superior to, and more fundamental than, the opposition between consciousness and object that it itself generates.

Hegel's question restates faithfully Kant's, but notice how there is not one single concept in this translation that is recognizable in its context and original meaning.

> This problem expresses nothing else but the Idea that subject and predicate of the synthetic judgment are identical in the *a priori* way. That is to say, these heterogeneous elements, the subject which is the particular and in the form of being, and the predicate which is the universal and in the form of thought, are at the same time absolutely identical. It is Reason alone that is the possibility of this positing, for Reason is nothing else but the identity of heterogeneous elements of this kind. (*GuW* 326, *FK* 69)

We shall go back to this point, but for now let us note that the synthetic a priori judgment is the original division of a reason that is presupposed as identical. Difference is posited out of an undivided whole. When Hegel speaks of an original bilateral unity, he takes as a principle what for Kant is a result and the main object of investigation.

"His [Kant's] principal idea is to vindicate the categories for self-consciousness understood as the *subjective 'I'*" (*WL* I, 59–61, *SL* 40–41). In the *Phenomenology* Hegel further develops the notion expressed in *Faith and Knowledge* that the category, an original identity, must pluralize itself in many categories while still remaining the negative unity of differences.

Despite the difference between the I and categories stressed by Kant (the I is their subject, hence it is not on the same level with categories), here for Hegel the I is "pure essentiality," "simple category" (*W* 3, 181, *PhS* 142). In fact, "the category means this, that self-consciousness and being are the same essence" (*W* 3, 182, *PhS* 142). The I is the simple unity that generates difference and categorial multiplicity out of itself. We could even say that categories are the several species of the pure category that is their genus or essence (*W* 3, 182, *PhS* 142).

The same point returns later on in the *Science of Logic* and the *Encyclopaedia*. Speaking of the Kantian original synthetic unity of apperception, Hegel writes: "This proposition is all there is to the so-called transcendental deduction of the category" (*WL* II, 254, *SL* 515). Notice: "the category" in the singular. This is because for Hegel, as we read in section 20 of the *Encyclopaedia*, "the I is thinking as a subject . . . , and thought is present everywhere and permeates all these determinations as a category." Categories are forms of thought, and thinking is the activity of an I, so that the various concepts are determinations of thinking. In this sense, for Hegel, Kant overcomes the extrinsic relation between the I and the understanding. Therefore he no longer speaks of an understanding that "I have," as if it were a faculty or a property (*WL* II, 254, *SL* 515). Thinking is not a subjective activity *next* to others (*ENZ* §20).

The problem for Hegel, however, is that Kant does not say that "thought is present everywhere and permeates all these determinations as a category" (*ENZ* §20 A). And the expression Kant uses is unfortunate: according to Hegel, when he says that "the I *accompanies* all my representations" (*ENZ* §20 A), Kant does not treat the I as an active universal. For Kant, the I is simply the common thread to all representations (*Logik 1831*, 10–11, *LL* 7–8).

Note again that Hegel simplifies the modality of the Kantian I-think which "*must be able* to accompany" representations (*KrV* B 131, my italics). This particular modality, the necessity of a possibility, has in Kant the precise meaning that various representations are not analytically mine; they are mine if I make them my own and recognize them as mine. I must be able to find myself in them because I am their synthetic unity, subject and movement of subordination. Representations are not all conscious (*KrV* A 320/B 377); in fact, we often ignore that we have them (*Refl.* 1677, *Ak* 16, 79). It is difficult not to hear in this Kantian solution echoes of references to the Cartesian cogito, Locke's critique of ideas (starting with innate ideas), Leibniz's notion of the latency of ideas, and Wolff's and Meier's conception that every representation is a cognition in one way or another. On the one hand, this principle amounts to saying that I can have latent representations, but I must recognize them as mine if I want to claim them as my own. On the other hand, the principle of the I-think is introduced as a synthetic unity. Kant, that is, thinks that an act of spontaneity makes possible the identity of consciousness, and all analytic consciousness is possible thanks to a prior synthesis (*KrV* B 133–35). Also, as he shows this requisite Kant employs a prescriptive, not a descriptive, language: the issue concerns a condition, not a fact. The distinction between de facto and de jure considerations is the key premise for the argument introducing the I-think in the Transcendental Deduction. That Hegel should miss this "supreme principle in the whole of all human cognition" (*KrV* B 135) is striking.

Now, we may be provisionally charitable to Hegel and argue that this simplification on his part is not a problem in itself after all. For Hegel, active and concrete universality is such because it is the substance and unitary subject of its determinations, and therefore encompasses unconscious determinations like a pit or an in-itself wherein representations are contained unperceived. He thus does not draw any critical consequences regarding the latency of representations in the I or the possibility that the conscious I is unaware of some of its representations. Nor does he highlight the continuity between Kant and the problems of the Cartesian cogito and its ideas. The fact that the I is a category rather than their unity and source is not a problem in itself, either.

Nevertheless, it must be noted that translating the I into a category means to transform deeply the ground on which we move. The ground is now the self-movement of the categories, which are all interconnected in a system. This leads us to assess the category by its inner meaning rather than as a synthetic I. And the inner meaning of the category through which, according to Hegel, Kant thinks the I is that of commonality (*Gemeinschaft*). For all my representations share the property of being *mine*. And yet, commonality is an extrinsic relation and not the concrete universal that Hegel means. This is why in Hegel's view Kant always tends to misunderstand the original synthetic unity and associate to it the I of representation (*WL* II, 255–56, *SL* 516–17). In other words, Kant treats the I as consciousness. Far from taking the I as a productive origin, for Hegel, Kant treats the I as an empty I-think by means of which, as Kant famously says, no manifold can be given (*KrV* B 135).

It is also worth considering that Hegel takes a requisite as a description because he ascribes prescriptive value only to Kant's *practical* reason, not to theoretical reason, which is for him psychological in nature. As we shall see, this depends on the fact that the Kantian pure reason, instead of being a form of autonomous legislation in theoretical as well as practical terms, is actually for Hegel indistinguishable from Hume's notion of *human nature*.

Kant distinguishes general from transcendental logic in that the latter "does not abstract from all the content of objective cognition" and "goes to the source of our cognition" (*WL* I, 59, *SL* 40). But, Hegel goes on to argue, Kant is ambivalent with regard to such a discovery. Thinking seems to be considered in its truth, and yet if the category were a form of absolute thought, then it would not be left with "a *thing-in-itself,* something alien and external to thinking" (*WL* I, 60, *SL* 41). If, despite the difference between general and transcendental logic, knowing means combining form and matter, then truth is contrasted to something that remains outside it (*WL* I, 36, *SL* 24). Form is thus conceived as wanting, waiting to be filled with actual matter. Thinking and object remain mutually external. Transcendental idealism is undermined in its unity by transcendental realism (the thing in itself), as well as by empirical realism (matter and given sensation, which are irreducible to our concepts). This is why Hegel's final, dismissive verdict in the *Encyclopaedia* is that, Kant's crucial distinction between general and transcendental logic notwithstanding, his categories are in themselves "empty" (*ENZ* §43 and Z).

Hegel acknowledges the great novelty of Kantian reason. In particular, he repeatedly admits that Kant is the first one who thematically distinguishes between infinite thinking and finite knowledge, between understanding as the faculty of abstraction and reason as the unity of opposites (for instance, see *ENZ* §45 and Z, §467 Z). Notice, however, that quite often Hegel regards Kant's distinction between understanding and reason in the terms into which Jacobi had translated it in the *Briefe*: as a divide between finite and infinite, between the mediation supporting the series of the conditioned and the faith in, and intuition of, the unconditioned as the unity of opposites.[3] Rather than distinct modes of operating of one and the same reason, as Kant would have it, understanding and reason proper are in a neat opposition—and Hegel ascribes this view of reason to Kant himself.

In Hegel's mind, the problem in the Kantian distinction is that Kant conceives of reason and understanding as two independent faculties. However, if understanding and reason are two independent faculties and the understanding is not integrated in and subordinated to reason, then this inevitably ends up construing reason as understanding (*WL* II, 262, *SL* 520; *ENZ* §60 A). For Hegel, Kant, by distinguishing the Transcendental Analytic—regarding concepts—from the Transcendental Dialectic—regarding ideas—separates two aspects of the same rational activity and assigns to them different features and criteria of functioning. Kant separates the understanding from reason because he separates the constitutive job of pure concepts in experience from the regulative function of reason facing the problem of the unconditioned as well as of totality, and he is thus bound to treat the latter as a source of error. Indeed, according to Kant, it is because reason misunderstands itself and takes its regulative function to be constitutive of objects that it gets involved in contradictions. It is not in itself contradictory; it is the misuse of reason that must be kept under control. Thus reason has to be disciplined and confined to a meaningful use, namely to the forms of possible experience. In this picture, reason must censor its leaps and be able to contain itself within its essential limits.

Kant's greatness for Hegel consists in having rescued contradiction from the inconsistency and arbitrariness which for too long had been assigned to the field of semblance. Dialectic is no longer the logic of error, separate from the analytic, the logic of truth. Now contradiction belongs in reason. Dialectic is "*a necessary operation of reason*" (*ein notwendiges Tun der Vernunft, WL* I, 52, *SL* 35) and is therefore integral to truth. Both analytic and dialectic are actually necessary for the system of pure reason. However, for Hegel, Kant is once more disappointing, for he hastens to dissolve the contradiction by distinguishing respects and points of view and denying that an inner contradiction is actually there.[4]

Critical reason seems to have to limit its goal so as to respect the untouchable core of experience. It is clear why Hegel takes this to be a fatal timidity: reason sacrifices its highest demands in order to depend upon sensible and finite experience, which it leaves unaltered. In this way reason falls prey to a misunderstanding. It believes it must be knowledge, but thinks that knowledge must consist in presupposing an object as something given and external that it has eventually to grasp in its truth. However, since the object is in any event only an appearance, such truth is empty and barren. In doing so, reason does not investigate in their true relation knowledge (of something) and science (of itself), and in fact it confuses them. Unlike knowledge, science must not presuppose anything given because it is reason's exclusive examination of itself and its own activity.

One point on which Hegel cannot agree with Kant is this: reason is not a faculty of ideas that can be separate from them, that is, we cannot distinguish between reason's essence (or in-itself) and its use (or application). Reason is what it thinks, and this means that it is contradictory in itself, not only when it ventures beyond the boundaries within which it is allowed to move. It is not as if we had an activity on the one hand, and a misuse and transcendental illusion that reason can *later on* incur on the other.

As we have seen, for Hegel every concept expresses in itself a contradiction, not only transcendental ideas. Every concept is dialectical and antinomic in itself, as well as referring to a superior unity in which the opposition is overcome (*ENZ* §79). Every concept (just like every shape of consciousness in the *Phenomenology*) is an abstraction that demands to count as an isolated, independent, and fixed determination. As such, it must try itself and verify its own consistency, its capacity to count as true. Thus, it discovers soon that it cannot remain still and content with its distinction, for it is only in relation to something other and is negativity, dialectic, restlessness (*WL* I, 16, *SL* 9).

In all this, as we can see, dialectic is the vanishing of the finite. Rather than a final and unavoidable being, the finite finds out that it is insubstantial and null in itself. Dialectic is an inner force—objective, anonymous, impersonal—not a contribution that it is up to our free will or decision to practice or not. Critique is not my reflective activity, but the driving force of truth, the activity immanent in each concept; and each concept is the result, the product of this inner dialectic. This is why at the end of the introduction to the *Science of Logic* we read that, once they are liberated from the substrates of representation employed by ontology, concepts in the Objective Logic are their own "true critique" (*WL* I, 62, *SL* 42).

If, then, the relation between the understanding and reason must be conceived as the relation between two different aspects of the same rationality and as constitutive of every concept, then every concept is one determinate concrete instance of a fundamental conceiving. Thus it is not surprising that, as we have already seen, in Hegel "the concept" is used in the singular. Kant instead necessarily thinks the concept only in the plural. In Kant the concept is a synthesis, an act of *begreifen*, an activity of unification of a manifold. Before it is a content it is a mental act. And concepts are articulated only in judgments, which are the realization of knowledge (as Kant writes to Beck, "the white man" is only a problematic concept, whereas "the man is white" is an actual judgment in which we assert a property of a subject).[5]

By contrast, in Hegel thought does not presuppose anything external to itself—even its own plurality or inner articulation, as we have seen. It is the concept that makes itself plural, that differentiates itself in concepts and determinate universalities as well as in judgments. It is not the understanding first defined as the faculty of rules, then of concepts, and finally of judgments, that is responsible for predication. It is rather the concept that divides itself in its moments and thereby judges itself. Hegel holds that he can show the short-sightedness of the presumption to criticize the forms of reason while taking for granted the form of expression of judgment, without first examining it critically. In this way, as we saw in chapter 4, it is possible to speak of truth only in relation to what is asserted; we cannot judge the truth of the very form of asserting.

And yet it is also true that, more fundamentally, for both Kant and Hegel reason has no opposites. In Kant, reason is a supreme instance and the original source of a world of laws. Nothing, neither the sanctity of religion nor the majesty of political power, can escape the absolute tribunal that reason has now become in the age of critique (*KrV* A XI and n.). Since, as we read in the *Critique* (*KrV* A 290/B 346), no concept can divide itself save as the division of an original unity, it is one and the same reason that divides itself into different fields of application. But these, nature and freedom, are precisely two worlds of laws that descend from a unique power, that is, rational legislation. Similarly, in Hegel, reason has no opposite: "das Vernüftige hat kein Gegenteil" (*W* 2, 247). In both of them, as we will see better in the next section, thinking must articulate itself as an I or self-consciousness. In Kant, reason must articulate itself as an original synthetic unity, hence as an I-think, to exist then exclusively as embodied in a particular I. In Hegel, the I is the concept that has achieved its existence. The I is pure self-referential unity that, insofar as it abstracts from every determinateness and content, is self-identity, simple universality and individual personality (*WL* II, 253, *SL* 514). According to Hegel, contents become mine insofar as they are led back to the form of unity. The I is this unity and this leading back; its categories are the particular forms of referring the manifold to the unity on the part of the understanding (*VGPh* 3, 343–44). If the I is "pure thought in its presence" (*ENZ* §24 Z 1), it is so because it divides from itself the contents to which it nonetheless relates. The I is activity, and activity means to give oneself objectivity, overcoming the mere subjectivity of thinking to become a thing.

Even though this is a domain shared by Kant and Hegel beyond our expectations, still the way in which reason becomes an I presents differences that are much more important than the affinities we can find. Let us consider them more closely.

Reason Makes Itself I

In the Subjective Logic, Hegel no longer expresses himself as in *Faith and Knowledge*. He no longer says that reason manifests itself in its original identity in finite consciousness. Now, more faithful to Kant, Hegel distinguishes between the subjective and objective unity of apperception so as to stress that only when the content has been thought (that is, penetrated and formed) by the I does it become a determinate universal, that is, something posited and not alien as it was when considered in its sensible

KANT'S AND HEGEL'S REASON

form. In this sense the object is in and for itself, namely in truth, only when it is led back to the unity of self-consciousness. The object is true insofar as it is the I (*WL* II, 255, *SL* 516). Hegel says that it is a well-known Kantian doctrine that one needs to mention the I in order to understand what a concept is. In truth, the concept and the I are two names for the same function of essential universality and particularity (*WL* II, 255–56, *SL* 516–17).

Naturally, we have seen that this is true only if by I we mean the universal, the objective, the true, that is, nothing subjective or finite. Above all, for Hegel, the I-think cannot be one faculty among others (thinking alongside sensibility, intuition, etc.: *ENZ* §20). The I, in other words, cannot be the I of representation, such as we know it from representation. Insofar as Kant does not deduce the categories from the I but finds them lemmatically ready-made in the history of logic, he expounds the different determinations of thought empirically. The I, despite being the source of categories, is external to them (*ENZ* §42).

Kant holds on to a mere unreflective representation (devoid of concept: *begrifflose Vorstellung, WL* II, 491, *SL* 692) of the I. He wavers between giving the I sensible existence and assigning from the very beginning subjectivity to the empty I-think (*ENZ* §445 A). Kant does show that categories are pure concepts, but he does not draw the conclusion that categories must be understood as the forms of being of the understanding and the whole truth. And the I cannot be a vehicle, a self-identical pole, the owner of its own representations. Differently stated, the I cannot remain unaffected by its thoughts: the I *is* its own thoughts.

How can we then grasp this truer Kantian I without making it the subject of a finite consciousness? The I is the existence of the concept, but as infinite self-reference. The I is not an identical pole that is presupposed as independent, but is simple infinity, pure negativity that finds itself in its determinations as in its own moments. It is concrete universality, not something abstract. It maintains itself as such by rejecting from itself all the determinations to which it knows it at the same time relates (I can say: "this is my representation, I am I in it," but I must equally know "my representation is not what I am, I am also something more").

For Hegel, the I becomes finite when it conceives of itself as a consciousness standing against the world. This is why for him the problem is always the same: Kant preliminarily separates form and content. The fact that concepts should be considered in their origin in intuition is a serious flaw revealing Kant's uncertainty. Concepts, which should be the truth of things, are thus opposed to actuality as something merely formal. If the concept owes its reality to intuition, then, instead of turning externality into something posited and sublated by the I, it is subordinated to

CHAPTER 5

empirical matter. And matter has more intrinsic value than the understanding's abstraction. But philosophy, Hegel writes in the introduction to the Logic of the Concept, neither is nor must be abstractive thinking that *discards* matter. On the contrary, philosophy is the transformation of appearances, the reduction of matter to essentiality.

Confusing beginning and truth is then "a capital misunderstanding" (*WL* II, 259, *SL* 519). In these pages of the Subjective Logic, Hegel uses some tenets of his thought to criticize Kant. Recall, for example, his claim that philosophy owes its genesis to experience (introduction to the *Encyclopaedia*, §12 A), but thought behaves as ungratefully toward experience as we do toward the food we consume and to which we owe our subsistence. In sum, the starting point cannot be denied, but it cannot be mistaken for truth, either. Actually, the development consists in sublating the beginning as a principle in order to show its movement of becoming something other. Hegel turns a Kantian principle against Kant, who famously begins the introduction to the *Critique of Pure Reason* (*KrV* B 1) by claiming that, although all forms of knowledge arise with experience, not all of them derive from experience. Hegel complains that Kant regards the matter from which we begin in the development and history of the individual "as the *truth* and *conceptually the first*" (*WL* II, 259, *SL* 519). In this way, Kant describes the I in the form of a narration of what happens. Differently stated, Kant psychologizes the concept; he reduces it to its genesis. He does not see that the concept is a determinate universal because in the definition he is after, the genus requires the assumption of a specific determinacy. Kant does not realize that the concept is the activity of distinguishing and realizing itself.

And yet he could, and should, have understood active universality: not only by virtue of his concept of self-consciousness in which I find myself in my determinations, but even more so by virtue of the speculative outcomes of the third *Critique*. For Hegel here, in the discussion of the intuitive understanding and life as inner purposiveness, Kant has achieved the concept of the idea (*ENZ* §55). The beautiful and the organism reveal the actuality of the ideal. Notice that, after taking the relation between understanding and reason proper as an opposition in a Jacobian fashion, at this point Hegel construes the *Critique of the Power of Judgment* as the concrete unity of universal and sensuous in the manner of Schiller (*ENZ* §55 and A). Instead of an investigation of judgment of taste and teleology, in a treatment justifiably criticized for the glaring meaninglessness of art, Kant's third *Critique* shows for Hegel the actuality of the ideal "in the products of art and of organic nature" (*ENZ* §55). The Kantian *Zweckmässigkeit* (purposiveness) is translated by Hegel into the principle according to which the purpose is the concept at work, the self-determining universal. The living being is the activity immanent in matter, wherein we finally have a reciprocal relation between whole and parts as well as a different relation between conceptual universal and intuitive particular (*ENZ* §56). Here Kant's timidity takes over even more unfortunately than elsewhere. For it is only reflection that works in this way, the *Critique of the Power of Judgment* claims: we cannot attribute anything to the objects we talk about. Even here reason is "stripped of all *authority*" (*ENZ* §60).

In sum, it is clear that reason makes itself I, but it must not be reduced to the I of representation or finite consciousness. For Hegel, despite the great ideas regarding reason as the unity of opposites and the original apperception, Kant ends up reducing self-consciousness to a finite I. It seems to me, however, that while Hegel is right in showing that reason becomes an I, he is wrong when he assigns this reduction to Kant. He is right because reason and the I are not identical; he is wrong because he trivializes and simplifies a question that in Kant has a complexity that gets lost in Hegel's exposition. Notice that I am not saying this with the old-fashioned piety and somewhat snobbish attitude of a historicist who does not tolerate simplifications and wants to restore everything in its pristine richness. If we do not want to confine ourselves to repetition, simplifications are in fact necessary. But they must be the correct ones, and Hegel's are not.

It seems to me that the reduction of the *Critique of Pure Reason* to a theory of knowledge and the reduction of reason to the I-think and consciousness are complementary and reciprocally functional. It seems to me that behind these reductions an unexpressed syllogism is at work. Reason articulates itself as an I; but the I is a thought and not knowledge; hence, knowledge is the empirical cognition of an I made possible by a transcendental subject or self-consciousness of which we can only say *that* it is. By ascribing to Kant the view that thoughts are consciousness's properties, Hegel thinks that Kant ends up giving primacy to the I as a self-identical pole that is presupposed as independent and prior to its activity. However, the fact is that Kant has not only shown the paralogisms of those who take the I to be a soul, mistaking a function for a substance. He is not only aware of the problem that more than others worries him, the problem of the double I (the original synthetic unity of apperception as opposed to the empirical I, consciousness, and inner sense). He does not only infer the essential difference between the identity of the I in its apperceptive functions and personal identity. For him, the problem of reason that makes itself I appears on different levels and involves every aspect of reason.

Most notably, the problems of the individual I and reason must not be confused.[6] Reason, the unity of its faculties, forms (through the understanding, albeit not exclusively) an object in general, whereas consciousness, by referring each thought back to a finite I, is the reflective result of reason. Consciousness opposes itself to its objects and is therefore the division of the original act on which it rests, whereas reason is before all division and opposition. Reason is not constituted, it is unconditioned and acts upon itself, whereas consciousness is finite, in relation to the manifold of experience, and acts upon appearances (including itself as inner sense). Reason is not temporal or finite, and yet it temporalizes and finitizes itself in the form of consciousness.

The bridge that connects reason and consciousness is transcendental apperception. Like reason, apperception is a pure source, a first condition, trans-individual, existing neither in space nor in time. But it cannot know itself because it is only a function; reason instead knows itself in its principles and in a priori synthesis, whereas consciousness knows itself as an appearance in inner sense, an empirical being among others.

Reason works logically as an I but is not reducible to an I. The I-think is not an I that happens to think: it is the way in which thinking takes place, the way in which the original unity of apperception (which produces the representation I-think, *KrV* B 132) realizes itself. If the I is the existence of thought, it is not an individual and self-identical substance that owns its thoughts but a function (the conjunction of given representations *"in one consciousness," KrV* B 133). As we can see, the production of a priori knowledge and the consciousness of synthesis make possible the identity of the I, not vice versa. And Kant does not mistake reason for the I or consciousness in practical synthesis, either. In fact, even though it is clearly an individual I that universalizes maxims and accomplishes duty, action out of duty in morality never leads back to an I.

But it would be a simplification to reconstruct the relation between the active I and the I as appearance in terms of a mere duality, an alternative. If reason is an original synthesis that is not an I but always works through an I, we must distinguish between the moments internal to a unity (they are moments because they are given only within a unity and have no separate existence, yet occur at different levels): reason, its declension as I, and finally its sensible existence as embodied in an empirical I. Reason is the source of thoughts and rules through apperception; but reason and apperception transcend the individual I, which is consciousness of both itself and the rules it has not itself constituted but finds ready-made.

Finally, besides the perspectives of pure reason and practical reason, there is the perspective afforded by the third *Critique*. In the reflection on pleasure in beauty, I realize that I am free from causality and desire. Both the true and the good compel me to assent and are the motivation for speculative and practical reason in its autonomy. Unlike the true and the good, and the agreeable which tends to enslave me, in the experience of beauty I am myself in the freest sense. Here my feeling of pleasure arises from reflection; it is not the pleasure of the senses. At the same time, it is not opposed to my I, because I actually feel enlivened by the beautiful. And this self-feeling is not Schopenhauer's aesthetic contemplation which suppresses the will and opposes the annulment of the I to the enslavement of the pleasurable, because the I is not identified with my will. For Kant, aesthetic reflection is about the I in its fullest sense: in the case of the beautiful as a feeling of vitality and purposiveness that is not instrumental to either the will or sensible pleasure, and in the case of the sublime as a feeling of discrepancy referring to reason and my ultimate destination.

An analysis of anthropological and psychological themes would enrich this picture, but let me stop at this conclusion: in Kant, reason is never the property of a finite I. Naturally, reason is not a separate metaphysical entity, but lives only insofar it is realized by the several I's. It is a function that explicates itself above all in the understanding's concepts and judgments. But reducing reason to the role of the understanding in judgments is like constructing a straw man to dismiss it more easily.

This is why I believe that speaking of subject and object in Kant is the beginning of an equivocation. It is a practice that has grown habitual since Reinhold, Fichte, and the young Schelling and has become irreversibly standard for the public at large with Hegel. But Kant is the philosopher of reason, not subjectivity. Making him the philosopher of subjectivity means to buy wholesale a series of further moves: objectivity is reduced to the subject, but the subject, by holding on to the thing in itself as a *caput mortuum*, is the powerless shadow of itself (*ENZ* §41 and Z). Thus, we can say that Hegel, for whom thoughts are not only our thoughts but also objectivity (ibid.), invites us to take a step back with respect to subjective idealism, but we must add that Kant would invoke a step back with respect to such reduction of criticism to a dogmatism.

What Is Esoteric? The Three Premises of Hegel's Reading and Some Blind Spots

Kant's *Groundwork of the Metaphysics of Morals* reads: "Human reason in its weariness gladly rests upon this pillow . . . in the dream of sweet pretenses (which instead of Juno let it embrace a cloud)" (*GMS, Ak* 4, 426, Eng. trans. 77). "This pillow" refers to the hasty search in experience for motives that must only be pure. The pillow implies slackness, softness.

Kant suggests that weariness generates dreamlike illusion, but he is not so much talking about a natural reaction to fatigue as about an attitude of negligence, a lack of discipline. To counteract this tendency, we must strengthen reason ("der fest sein soll," ibid.) and keep its gaze fixed on what is pure.

The image of the pillow is unusual. It is even more curious that Hegel writes that Kant does not have to be understood as if his philosophy were "a cushion for the indolence of thought" (*WL* I, 59n., *SL* 40n.). Hegel means that what counts as a result in Kant is taken to be an immediate starting point on which one comfortably lies down to rest. We need to beware, not the natural tendency of reason to exert itself, but the slackness of a theoretical *shortcut*: the reduction of Kantian reason to the anti-metaphysical point of view that is typical of common sense or certain empiricism. In a similar way we must understand this passage from the first preface to the *Science of Logic*: "The exoteric teaching of the Kantian philosophy—that *the understanding ought not to be allowed to soar above experience . . .*—this was the justification coming from the scientific camp for renouncing speculative thought" (*WL* I, 13, *SL* 7–8).

If one side of Kant's philosophy justifies one camp's renunciation of speculative thought and yet Kant cannot be reduced to such a side, then we would expect that we can trust to find Kant's alleged esoteric side, which is obviously less accessible but certainly no less present behind the smoke screen of the censorship of reason's transcendence and the unreality of ideas. In other words, we must distinguish a deeper, less "popular" Kant from the advice not to venture beyond the limits of experience. To be sure, we presume that it takes Hegel's speculative talent to glimpse the rose in the crux of Kant's barbaric language built on sloppy, carefree narration ("unbesorgtes Erzählen," *GuW* 325), underneath the cushion on which most readers rest content, but it will be worthwhile.

Unfortunately, in his interpretation Hegel never gets to the point of revealing the esoteric side of Kantian philosophy. In fact, the cushion that makes thought lazy is laid with a certain indolence under the blankets of Hegel's reading. Metaphors aside, Hegel's temptation to make a starting point out of a result is strong. Ever since *Faith and Knowledge*, Hegel is convinced that all Kant ultimately wants is to propose another version of Locke's philosophy, that is, the discussion of the finite understanding within its limits (*GuW* 326, *FK* 68; see also *VGPh* 3, 355). In the Positions of Thought with respect to Objectivity in the *Encyclopaedia*, critical philosophy is a corollary or appendix to empiricism. They have in common "the supposition that experience is the *sole basis* of knowledge" (*ENZ* §40).

I think that in Hegel's description of empiricism there is something very important (as well as extremely original) which we should not underestimate. If in the standard view empiricism is any philosophy whose criterion is experience, for Hegel this is actually a consequence of a more fundamental need for certainty. The need for concrete contents and a firm support in which to find oneself again (*ENZ* §37, 38 A)—the need for feeling at home in the world—is the principle according to which the truth must exist in actuality and perception, and not remain an abstraction. I must know myself as present and participating in what I experience. The principle of empiricism shares with that of modernity a fundamental point: individual *freedom* must be *experienced* in every actual content (*ENZ* §§7–8). *Truths* are no longer accepted unless they are experienced as *certainties* in which we are actively involved. This is why Luther is as important as Galileo and experimental science, and for Hegel he is more representative of the spirit of empiricism than a Bacon or a Locke.

However, the relevance of this point is obscured by the speculative limits of empiricism. It simply takes up for its knowledge the logical model of intellectual analysis from the sciences and tradition. In doing so, it does not realize that it is massively using categories and a metaphysics that it assumes it can discard as irrelevant (*ENZ* §38 A).

These are the same limits to which Kant eventually succumbs, for Hegel. Kant does not go beyond Hume because, while he "*leaves the categories and the method of ordinary knowing completely unchallenged*" (*ENZ* §60 A), he presupposes that universality and necessity cannot be grasped through perception (§§40 and 47). Like Hume, Kant confuses the first in itself with the first in the individual's history. He starts with sensibility to get to thought, but in such a way that his narration, which loses sight of truth to focus on history, ends up giving up truth altogether (*WL* II, 259–60, 268, *SL* 519–20, 524–25).

In my view, it is possible to identify three premises of Hegel's reading: (1) the reduction of Kant's philosophy to a dichotomic way of proceeding, (2) the acknowledgment of experience as the only sense of knowledge, and (3) the thesis of subjective idealism.

(1) To begin with, all the various dichotomies we find in Kant can be led back to unsolved oppositions.

> In every dualistic system, and especially in the Kantian system, its basic flaw reveals itself through the inconsistency of *combining* what a moment ago has been declared to be independent and thus *incompatible*. While what had been combined was just declared to be true, so now instead it is declared to be true that the *two moments*, whose separate existence on their own has been denied to them in the combination which was to be their truth, possess truth and actuality only insofar as they exist in separation. (*ENZ* §60 A)

CHAPTER 5

Clearly, it never dawns on Hegel that there might be a difference between exposition and content. The exposition, no matter how clumsy, does proceed by oppositions, but in order to sever those that are bound to stay from those that Kant aims to show need mediation and reconciliation. In other words, Hegel never seems to surmise that, for Kant as for himself, oppositions must be understood as divisions that are internal to reason presupposed as unity—Hegel's view of reason as the source of opposites, the original unity of I and world in *Faith and Knowledge* notwithstanding.

Obviously, one could reply that Hegel is right. It is Kant who misleadingly emphasizes oppositions more than their unity. For instance, it is Kant who expounds the Transcendental Aesthetic before the Analytic, as though the former's results were quite independent of the latter. It is Kant who opposes blind intuitions to empty concepts in one of the most notorious and misunderstood phrases in the history of philosophy. Nevertheless, if one reads Kant with a less superficial and uncharitable attitude, one would notice that Kant himself revokes the oppositions he has sketched out. While he must insist on the essential distinction between the work of different faculties, he then shows with equal necessity that these must be combined in order to yield that unity of sensible and intellectual moments without which we could not understand intuitively the same object we think abstractly and thereby know it. Indeed, if we admitted the continuity of representations from the most obscure to the conceptual ones, à la Leibniz, without distinguishing between intuitive and conceptual knowledge, we would have to treat spatial relations as if they were conceptual ones and would not be able to distinguish between intelligible identity and intuitive individuation (or regions of space, incongruent triangles, etc.). In turn, without unifying intuitive and conceptual knowledge, we would not be able to explain how the perception of the reality of this table could be the basis or matter for the concept of this table: how the concept can refer to perception. In fact, we can say even more strongly in defense of Kant that those who not distinguish between these two ways of referring to the same object are not in a position to explain how concepts refer to intuitions, or how we can have intuitions that are independent of concepts. This is, after all, a very common experience, for example, when I face an object I do not know: I perceive it, but I cannot subsume it under its concept because I do not have its concept available.

An example of this exclusively dichotomic attitude is Hegel's wonder at Kant's *KrV* B 160–61 footnote on the form of intuition and formal intuition. This is a controversial and obscure note. All I would like to recall here is that the unity of space and time, which in the Transcendental Aesthetic depended on sensibility alone, turns out now to be made possible by a synthesis. "This can only be described as excellent and as one of his [Kant's] purest and most profound concepts," is Hegel's admiring expression (*GuW* 365, *FK* 122). Instead of thinking that the exposition had forced Kant into bottlenecks of oppositions that had to be subsequently removed, Hegel—like the majority of readers—makes the order of Kant's exposition dictate the conceptual contents of the first *Critique.*

(2) The second premise is the reduction of every cognition to experience and the combination of intuition and concept. Over and above the combination of concept and intuition, "knowledge" (*Erkenntnis*) is the term that Kant finds appropriate to designate, among other things, the following: analogic and symbolic knowledge (*Erkenntnis nach der Analogie, KU* §59; *Prol.* §56 and 57); the original synthetic unity of apperception, which is nothing but self-consciousness, hence thought altogether devoid of intuition ("das erste reine Verstandserkenntnis," *KrV* B 137); the philosopher's transcendental knowledge as a priori synthesis (*KrV* A 783/B 811, A 719/B 747); wisdom as knowledge of ignorance (*KrV* A 758/B 786); philosophical knowledge, which is itself superior to the sciences of "artists of reason" (the logician, the mathematician, the natural scientist: *KrV* A 839/B 867); and the science of the principles of sensibility that is the "Aesthetic" (*KrV* A 21/B 36). Whether these are examples of loose, sloppy, or intentionally plurivocal linguistic use, none of them seem to bother Hegel or the majority of interpreters who hastily identify one mode of cognition with all possible knowledge. In particular, Hegel denies the very concept of transcendental cognition and the *Critique of Pure Reason* as reason's self-knowledge when he holds that for Kant one must examine the faculty of knowledge prior to knowing. In claiming that Kant ignores the fact that "examining them [the forms of thought] is already itself a process of knowing" (*ENZ* §41 Z I), Hegel ascribes to Kant a form of ignorance that I am afraid is only his own.

Here again one can rejoin that Hegel does not invent anything. It is Kant who privileges the epistemic model of experience by obscuring, and almost disavowing, any other view of knowledge. It is Kant who speaks of the supposed necessity of combining intuition and concept without which it is not possible to speak of knowledge. But it is also Kant who directs us elsewhere, toward concepts and ideas that are no less important than the results, so crucial for him, of the Transcendental Deduction.

(3) The third premise is the thesis of transcendental idealism understood as subjective idealism. I say "premise" and not "conclusion" for this simple reason. Kant's thesis is achieved starting from the ideality of space and time and the nature of appearances. It is therefore an

CHAPTER 5

answer to the question of the unity of reason transcending itself toward the world and its a priori synthesis. By contrast, this thesis is in Hegel a starting point and a position of thought regarding objectivity from which it would make no sense to wish to free ourselves. It is as if for Hegel all Kant, primarily motivated by a speculative shyness, wants is to preserve the thing in itself and empty actual knowledge, confining it to a shadow of true reality.[7] It is as if for Hegel the interest in affirming the limits of reason had convinced Kant of its intrinsic weakness. As often happens to shy people, they work against themselves, sabotaging their own work: it seems to me that this is the picture we should get from Hegel's claims. Based on them, it would never cross the reader's mind that Kant believed he had given a definitive solution to the problems of metaphysics through the simple instrument of pure reason.[8]

Obviously, one could rejoin once again that Hegel is right. It is Kant who collapses representation and appearance and repeatedly muddles the notion of the thing in itself, arguing now one thesis and now another depending on the need or context. Had Kant simply argued that we can know only appearances and yet the noumenon has indubitable practical reality, he would have frozen the situation in the same configuration as the third antinomy of the Transcendental Dialectic. At that point, the only problem would have concerned our own twofold nature as citizens of two worlds, and the only complication, certainly not irrelevant but circumscribed, would have consisted in applying the categories of reality and causality to the noumenon and to its effects in the world of appearances, in contrast to the exclusive employment of categories in relation to appearances prescribed by the Transcendental Analytic.

Unfortunately, however, Kant does not only admit problematically a thing in itself as unknowable and a limiting concept. He also introduces pure intelligible beings as the ground of appearances (*Prol., Ak* 4, 315). It seems obvious to him that, if things are appearances for us, in themselves they cannot be but positively conceived noumena. If there is any appearance, it will be the appearing of something, so that noumena are causes of appearances which alone, owing to our constitution, are accessible to our knowledge. Attributing to noumena a causal action in the affection of our sensibility is the beginning of the downfall. Jacobi famously writes that without things in themselves he cannot enter the Kantian system, but with things in themselves he cannot stay in the system for long. Less known is Eric Weil's remark, which no less rightly suggests that the things in themselves are neither things nor in themselves.[9] The problem, it seems to me, consists in Kant's oscillation between the noumenon as a problematic possibility and as an incontrovertible, albeit unknowable, reality. If the thing in itself is given as the limiting concept of our sensibility, then it is not real but only thinkable. If, instead, the noumenon is a thing in itself that is positively albeit noumenically real, we suddenly end up having two contradictory notions of existence as well as of causality.

The fact that *this* appearance is the appearance of *this* thing in itself and not of another at random is obviously necessary. Once we uncover this problem, we cannot content ourselves with saying that I can know the appearance but not the thing in itself of which the appearance is the appearance. For I have established a relation—a determinate, although not further determinable relation—between noumenon and appearance. But if so, there is no way out. For either I am instituting a relation between a thing I do not know but must be able to identify somehow (and therefore I must know to a certain degree), or I only know my representations, in which case Kant cannot avoid the problem of Berkeley's idealism against which his *Prolegomena* are directed.

It appears, then, that besides two senses of noumenon we have two senses of appearance: as representation and as object in the experience of nature. In the former case, the review of Garve-Feder, though generally revealing a gross misunderstanding, cannot be circumvented, and it is not clear why Kant should complain that he has been misunderstood. In the latter case, representations have objective validity by virtue of the argument of the Transcendental Deduction thanks to the power of judgment, whereby the copula is the unification (however nonconceptual and blind as Hegel would have it) sanctioned by the original synthetic unity of apperception. It is off-putting to realize how Kant defends a thesis or its opposite depending on the context or on his argumentative needs. And it is destructive for this second sense to read that appearances are "der blosse Spiel der Vorstellungen" ("the mere play of representations") in us.[10]

However it may be, Hegel simply cuts all these hesitations and ambiguities short: "Kant's appearance is a given content of perception" (*WL* II, 21, *SL* 343). By ascribing to Kant a conventional form of empiricism, Hegel does not realize that, for Kant, it is not possible to speak of appearances given independently of any synthesis and there are no objects prior to my activity. According to Kant, only my constitution makes them possible, whereas for Hegel constitution is treated by Kant as an empty form tailored to different types of matter on a case-by-case basis.

We may wonder whether something would have changed in his reading, had Hegel paid more attention to the different meanings of the terms he criticizes, as well as to the greater richness and complexity of Kant's concepts. I lean toward a negative answer. First of all, at the time that Hegel wrote *Faith and Knowledge*, with Kant still alive, nobody was

CHAPTER 5

a convinced Kantian or took seriously critical philosophy per se, which was widely considered to have been "overcome" by Reinhold, Fichte, Schelling, and Hölderlin, especially with regard to the thing in itself.[11] But this is a consideration that pertains to historical influence and does not alter the respect we owe to a book like the *Critique of Pure Reason*, which many consider the founding text of modern idealism. More generally, then, I can say that my pessimism depends on something else: the dismissive, almost disinterested and negligent way in which Hegel portrays Kant's philosophy after *Faith and Knowledge*. After 1802 the impression is that Hegel often returns reluctantly and perfunctorily to those contradictions he had already taken the trouble of denouncing once and for all in his youth.

In Hegel's view, it goes without saying that transcendental idealism is a form of subjectivism. However, the associations implied by such subjectivism are less obvious. In the Logic of Essence, transcendental idealism amounts to a private world, namely, a world that has been literally deprived of objectivity. Since one starts with the empty abstraction of the thing in itself, all determination falls in consciousness, in a reflection foreign to the thing in itself. This is a "standpoint" that "falls *in me*, in the subject, whether I see the leaves of a tree not as black but green, the sun as round and not square, whether I taste sugar as sweet and not bitter" (*WL* II, 136, *SL* 428). "This crude display of subjective idealism is directly contradicted by the consciousness of the freedom in accordance with which I know myself as rather the universal" (ibid.). This I should be the true thing in itself, whereas the only absolute that is presupposed is the finite I standing against an equally finite world. For Hegel, even my positing representations as successive, instead of illustrating the Kantian concept, in a nutshell very Hegelian, of self-affection—my determination of sensibility through the understanding *in the apprehension* of the appearance, namely the activity at work in passivity—relies on "empirical conditions" (*WL* II, 254, *SL* 515).

Understandably, what counts as subjective and objective in transcendental and objective idealism has different meanings. In Hegel's exposition of Kant, "*the stages of feeling and intuition*" (as if feeling and intuition were on a par for Kant, *WL* II, 256, *SL* 517) must precede the understanding. This premise allows Hegel to construe the relation between objectivity and subjectivity in this way: the objective is the concept, truth in and for itself, a posited being, whereas the subjective is the appearance, immediacy (including feeling). According to Hegel, critical philosophy, by placing thoughts as a medium between us and things, excludes us from things, which are actually *entia rationis* (beings of reason, *WL* I, 26, *SL* 16). In particular, reason, as the dialectical faculty that is the source of ideas, is removed from any possibility of grasping truth or representing anything objective (*WL* II, 261–62, *SL* 520–21). Far from concluding that for Kant as for him the concept of objectivity means on the one hand what is against us and on the other the true (*WL* II, 408, *SL* 629), Hegel concludes that the I of subjective idealism is no different than Hume's, that is, the simple subject of consciousness devoid of objective reality (*WL* II, 490, *SL* 691; compare *ENZ* §41 and Z).

And yet if, as I said, I believe that things could not have gone otherwise, how can we hope for a verdict that is, if not fair, at least not useless? My hope is that the reader may call into question some established assessments so as to listen to Kant's own voice in a freer way, and also separate certain Hegelian jokes or formulaic phrases from Hegel's deeper thought. Whether this deeper thought is Kantian or anti-Kantian, it is interesting to examine in light of Hegel's relation to Kant's themes. Sometimes Hegel himself minimizes this sense of foreignness to critical philosophy such as when, for instance, he helps us understand Kant's philosophy by highlighting its deep core precisely as he is appropriating it. In such cases, he seems to be guiding us to reduce the distance separating his criticisms of Kant from Kant's thought. But at other times Hegel appears to make unbelievable blunders that are not even noticed, it seems to me, by interpreters. One example which I would like to dwell on for a moment is that Hegel shows that he has no clue as to what pure intuition means in Kant.

> The widespread nonsense regarding intuition that has grown out of this Kantian distinction between it and the concept is well known, and, in an effort to spare oneself the labor of conceptual comprehension, the value and the sphere of intuition have been extended to all cognition. What is pertinent here is only this, that space, just like intuition itself, must also be *conceptualized* if one wants to *comprehend conceptually* at all (*WL* I, 223, *SL* 162).

As we can see, conceiving is necessary because intuiting cannot be conceived. Intuition is called into play in order to save the concept all trouble. To understand space means to grasp it in concepts. This peculiar reading is on a par with that of the *Lectures on the History of Philosophy*, where we read that "space and time are pure, i.e., abstract intuitions" (*VGPh* 3, 340). Space and time are contrasted to perception, which always faces particularity, because they are rather "always one, and therefore a priori. But there is also and equally *one* blue" (*VGPh* 3, 342).

Facetious criticisms are allowed in philosophical prose, and we should not fret or get indignant about them. Hegel, who is well known for his

CHAPTER 5

gift of caustic and cutting polemics, often appeals to readers precisely for his sarcasm. After all, the Scholastic philosopher who cannot jump into the water without having first learned to swim is a good example, almost a topos, of a biting joke that is as recognizable as—some would think—it is gratuitous. By contrast, the fact that intuiting should serve the purpose of saving us the trouble of comprehending is no joke. This reading of the Kantian notion of sensibility is rather an example of what I called earlier a dismissive and superficial interpretation. Hegel does not see that the problem of space and time is not what we can learn about them once we have translated them into concepts, but the type of existence and the function they have. The uniqueness of space and time has nothing to do with the uniqueness of a concept of color. When Hegel translates it in these terms, he brings the problem back to his own ground, that is, the dialectic between universal and particular. The relation between color and blue, and moreover the relation between blue and singular instances of blue things, does not have anything in common with the relation between space and objects in space or portions of space. Hegel ignores—he refuses to understand—that, unlike a discursive concept, space exists as an undivided whole. A discursive concept is a class with an extension achieved by a composition (*Zusammensetzung*) of conceptual notes (*Teivorstellungen, Merkmale*), and an object is an instance falling *under* a concept. Space instead is undivided, uncomposed, continuous, as an infinite given magnitude in relation to which all particular spaces are not instances falling under space, but are "only thought *in it*" (*KrV* A 25/B 39) as *limitations* (*Einschränkungen*) of a presupposed continuum.

This is another example of the fact that even in Kant the one can make itself many. Space pluralizes itself into spaces (after all, intuition is only as pluralized) in a way that differs radically from the concept of blue and its various examples and plural instances. We shall come back to this point at the end of this section. Generally, it is safe to say for now that sensibility is a problem for Hegel (namely, for the thesis according to which the true in and for itself is only the concept) because he does not grant it any cognitive independence. The fact that sensibility may have an a priori form and be the source of intuitive cognitions must have been for him an exegetic absurdity that it was not even worth conceiving (indeed, he neither conceives nor names anything of the sort). What must have been inconceivable for him is that sensibility could be the source of independent representations, or even that Kant could write with ill-concealed pride that before him "it did not occur to anyone that the senses might also intuit a priori" (*Prol., Ak* 4, 375n.).

For Hegel, intuition must be translated into the concept; there cannot be any pure intuition; each intuition is empirical, including the intuition of space and time of mathematical construction.[12] But if intuition is sensible, then "intuition without form is blind" (*GuW* 327, *FK* 70). As we can see, for Hegel, form is provided only by the understanding!

The egregious Hegelian reduction of the faculties of pure reason to two, understanding and reason proper, goes incredibly unnoticed (at least I have not found any mention, let alone discussion of this, in the rich bibliography on Hegel's critique of Kant). Since sensibility is our way of accessing appearances, so goes Hegel's reasoning, it is not a faculty but only the vehicle of the presentation of things to thought. Differently stated, for Hegel, sensibility is indistinguishable from appearances: it is at one with the empirical (*GuW* 327, *FK* 69).

On the one hand, we cannot help but be surprised, given what Hegel teaches us about the reasons that permeate sensibility. What escapes him is not the activity in receptivity that is typical of sensibility in general, but pure intuition's independence, its irreducibility to the concept and ways of working. There is, on the other hand, a different viewpoint, the moral perspective, whereby Hegel's reduction of reason to two faculties is more correct (although he cares far less about it in that for him, as for Kant, what truly defines a philosophical position is its "principle," namely, its conceptual "logical-metaphysical" weft). In this case, his reading is not so outlandish. In the second *Critique*, Kant discusses the determination of the maxim in morality as belonging only to reason and the understanding. Here the inner division of faculties is different. Sensibility does not have an a priori principle. Although reason must have a motive or incentive, it cannot find it in sensibility, not even in the only autonomous feeling we can have, namely respect (reason finds such a motive in the rational form of universality, which is a much more revolutionary and fundamental novelty). Here sensibility in the form of inclinations and passions is a threat to the integrity of reason's self-determination. Hence, the presence of sensibility, and with it reason's inner division, is the very cause of the necessity of morality which first raises the demand of autonomous deliberation. Unlike the first *Critique*, reason's inner articulation is a division, a split. Sensibility is not regarded as an ally that can join forces in a common endeavor, but as the element from which to keep motivation free and the maxim separate.

However, Hegel recasts this internal difference as a contradiction. In his view, Kant considers reason as "a pure identity without intuition and in itself empty" (*GuW* 336, *FK* 81). As such, reason is nothing beyond its contrast to its opposite, while at the same time it is established as spontaneity and autonomy. This is contradictory, Hegel writes, because freedom is only through its opposite. "This contradiction, which remains insuperable in the system and destroys it, becomes a real inconsistency when this absolute emptiness is supposed to give itself content as practical reason and to expand itself in the form of duties" (ibid.).

Hegel's scheme of interpretation is reiterated: reason is the I, and the I is an empty identity as opposed to the empirical I (and to intuition). How this I can go out of itself is bound to remain unintelligible. Given Kant's affinity with empiricism, we might as well let Kant drown in the same whirlpool of incoherence until external determination ends up dismissing the I altogether, as in Hume. Hegel resists this, though, for there is something speculative worth rescuing in Kant, that is to say, the fact that reason wants to make itself world. I am referring to practical reason, naturally, for theoretical reason cannot cultivate such an ambition for Hegel.

As I mentioned earlier, Hegel is unable to see that the one can become the many in Kant, too. For Hegel, the Kantian I *originally* faces the many, a plurality that is presupposed and stands opposed to the I. Hegel laments the scarceness of movement in this juxtaposition. Reason is always already pluralized in various I's; the understanding is always already operative by means of categories it has not produced but found, and even lemmatically. And yet, quite often a production of this kind can be found in Kant, and it is highly important. More than this: Hegel, it must be acknowledged, does everything he can to obscure it. Space pluralizes itself in spaces, as we have seen. Above all, the subject is not an empty self-identity because in self-affection it determines itself in particular forms, and the pure concepts of the understanding make sensibility take up different forms. Schematism adapts pure concepts to pure intuitions and provides them with concrete meaning, while at the same time restricting the use of concepts and applying them to intuitions. This blindness is indeed remarkable for an early enthusiast of schematism such as Hegel.

We will come back to this disparity between theoretical and practical reason. For now, I would like to stress that generally in his version of Kantian philosophy Hegel contrasts the concept, which, as idealism teaches, should be the soul of the content, to its sensible existence. This is why Hegel does not appreciate the deep difference between transcendental and general logic that he nonetheless admits, as we have seen. In other words, he confuses content with matter, contrasting both of them to the understanding in the same way in which the empirical is contrasted to form.

Kant writes the Analytics of Principles to show how reason determines itself in *contents* that together give rise to the concept of object. These contents are schematized categories guided by ideas, which in turn guide the formation of empirical concepts, that is, concepts that refer to intuitively given objects. At the same time, however, these contents are nothing more than a form, foreign to the material existence in which each object will present itself to us in experience. All of this does not have any relevance for Hegel, for what exclusively matters to him is that concepts are opposed to appearances. What matters to him is that Kant claims he seeks the touchstone of the truth of our statements in appearances. As a result, he employs a representational, not a speculative concept of truth.

In other words, Hegel always separates and dissociates in isolated entities what Kant presents as distinct moments which he brings back to their original unity anyway. Here the separation has the following shape: on the one hand, contents are reduced to the intuitive and this to the empirical, whereas on the other hand, logical concepts are for Hegel empty, that is, they are considered in abstraction from reference. The realization that for Kant this is a deliberate abstraction should lead us to not lose sight of the relation between logical and transcendental concepts. However, Hegel does not only ignore this distinction. He also ignores that for Kant logic, far from being a form opposed to matter in all respects, is the understanding's self-knowledge (Ak 9, 14), in which reason has to do only with itself (KrV B ix).

In this regard, we could consider the affinity between Kant's general logic and Hegel's logic, which for Hegel is formal though not opposed to being (only to concrete disciplines and finite knowledge). Although the discussion of such affinities would be fruitful, their differences seem to me more important. For example, a passage from Hegel's introduction to the Logic of the Concept reminds us that logic does not investigate concepts as if they were the thoughts of an I. Insofar as concepts "belong to the *self-conscious spirit* [they do] not fall within the scope of logical science" (*WL* II, 257, *SL* 517).

Above all, it seems to me quite important to raise the question concerning what remains alien to reason in Hegel's philosophy. We have seen that Hegel opposes the forms of the Kantian understanding (subjective, empty, hence vacuous) to the reality of appearances or, alternatively, of things in themselves. Hegel wavers with respect to this (*WL* II, 259–60, *SL* 519–20), as well as to the Kantian thesis on truth. In the Subjective Logic he writes: "*truth is inaccessible to rational cognition*" (*WL* II, 264, *SL* 521). Yet, after one and a half pages he writes, quite inconsistently, that Kant asserts "as truth what it declared to be finite cognition" (*WL* II, 264, *SL* 522). After all—not that Hegel needs to be defended, certainly not by me—we have seen that incoherence already mars the concepts of reality and affection in Kant.

Hegel has a rare gift for images and a talent for penetrating other minds' prejudices like, in Proust's words from *Time Regained*, a radiographer.

CHAPTER 5

When Hegel criticizes Schulze's modern skepticism in the "Relation of Skepticism to Philosophy" (dated 1802, the same year as *Faith and Knowledge*), he writes that Schulze figures the Kantian thing in itself as a rock under the snow (*W* 2, 220). When it comes to the relation between the concept and the sensible content, it is as if we moved within this image: we look for a rock under an appearance that is doomed to melt like snow in the spring; then reality will become visible to us without veils or masks in its nakedness and hardness. It is a punitive concept of reality, if you will: when we stumble upon a rock under the snow we hurt our foot, and indeed Samuel Johnson objected to Berkeley's notion of *esse est percipi* that the pain in the foot kicking the stone shows the incontrovertible existence of things outside us. Still, it is the concept of reality that from Hobbes up to Dilthey and Heidegger reminds us of being's resistance to our temptations to assimilate it.

In this image, it is noteworthy that snow *hides* the rock. In fact, without snow, we would hardly stumble upon the rock and hurt ourselves. We may think—Hegel himself suggests this with insistence—that while for subjective idealism forms belong to a finite subject opposed to an equally finite world in relation to which all contents, in their diversity and infinite contingency, remain irremediably alien, in his idealism instead the actual is the rational and everything is saved in its concept. But such a contrast does not work that simply. Even though in Kant snow hides the rock, it is not as if we find in Hegel absolute transparency or being's nakedness either. Rocks keep hiding, that is to say, appearances as much reveal as conceal reality. And the Logic of Essence, dealing with the multiplicity of relations between essence and appearance over and above simple manifestation, is very clear in this respect.[13]

Now, I am convinced that Hegel is right when he complains about the unfortunate fate of his saying "the rational is actual," and we must defend him from those who understand that expression on the basis of the ordinary notions of actuality and reality.[14] When Hegel writes in the *Encyclopaedia* that existence is partly actuality (*Wirklichkeit*) and partly appearance, and that we must keep actuality distinct from chance, determinate being, and existence, he adds that "in ordinary life, we may accidentally call every idea, *error, evil, and the like, actual,* as well as every concrete existence, crippled and transitory though it may be" (*ENZ* §6 A). Nonetheless, a dilemma comes up, a virtually inevitable choice between a certain terminological confusion and a subtler, if haunting danger: that of a complete tautology.

If the actual is what Hegel's logic lexically defines as actual, it should not be confused with the contingent because it is the determination of an ideality that can work (*wirken*, "have effects") and rest on its feet. It is the logical *result* of the categories of essence and not *lazy* existence (*die faule Existenz*). But is the actual so defined because it is already thought as rational from the outset? If for Hegel the truth of things consists in their thought, can truth tolerate to leave outside itself all that does not belong to the actuality of the idea? If, as Hegel has been teaching us since the preface to the *Phenomenology*, the truth is the whole, how can it leave aside "error, evil, and the like"? In this way Hegel risks siding with a gnostic position, but more fundamentally he risks forgetting that for him evil is necessary, hence in some sense good. So is contingency. And if truth is *index sui et falsi,* error and falsity are integral to it. And how can we distinguish the motley peel of being from its core if not *post festum,* that is, on the basis of how *successful* something is at making itself actual? And how to distinguish between abstract possibility and the real potentiality that permeates the Hegelian concept of actuality? And why is it necessary that something *struggle* to be in order to be considered actual? Why should something find reasons to be—why is no gratuitous being admitted? Is it not circular to rule out from actuality *die faule Existenz,* i.e., that which we consider nonrational, precisely because it is not?[15]

Having clarified the *semantic-lexical* question and dispelled gross equivocations concerning the meaning of actuality, we can legitimately wonder about the distinction between transcendental and absolute idealism. What remains external to Kantian reason? I would answer on the basis of the Analytic of Principles (to which I shall return shortly): matter (contingency in its infinite variety and givenness), but not content.[16] And what is external to Hegelian reason? After all, does not lazy existence come down to the same as Kant's matter? Perhaps. Certainly, what cannot be the same is *the being of the finite*: givenness and transcendence for Kant's reason, and ideality (nullity in itself, inner dialectic, nonbeing, vanishing) for Hegel.

It seems to me that what separates Kant from Hegel is, more than reason, reason's other. Kant takes his bearings from the empirical and the alienness of the world that reason seeks to penetrate. Hegel ascribes to such a position a subordinate place as reflection (positing, external, and determining reflection in the "Logic of Essence"; see *WL* II, 25–32, *SL* 346–53) and has the more radical ambition of abolishing all transcendence. For Hegel, there is nothing *relevant* other than reason. For him Kant, who turns what is found into a product, should have followed through on this point and overcome givenness once and for all. Since reason is defined by its relation to its correlate, it is clear that in Hegel's absolute idealism reason is precisely by virtue of this relation which is far more ambitious than in Kant's transcendental idealism.

CHAPTER 5

A Priori Synthesis and Reason's
Self-Determination

I would like to stress that the truly philosophical question does not concern Hegel's occasional errors, but his fundamental judgment about a philosophy in which he overlooks something essential. He overlooks the concept of a priori synthesis, namely, nothing less than the Kantian concept of pure reason in its unity across the three *Critiques*. We can say that Hegel inaugurates a way of reading Kant that is still our own. Yet we must have the honesty of adding that this reading is successful because it was basically suggested by Kant himself.

Among the best-known outcomes of this reading I will call "standard" that Hegel contributes to shaping is the division of critical philosophy, and of pure reason in particular, into an epistemological part, a part devoted to morality, and finally a third part that pops up only after the first two *Critiques* have been completed. The suggestion is that Kant realizes that something had been left unthought in the division of theory and practice, nature and freedom: contingency, purposiveness, that which, while existing as an appearance in nature, cannot be brought back to the mechanism we call *natura formaliter spectata* (the universal thoroughgoing unity holding together all appearances) and is accessible to reflection. With regard to the first *Critique* on which I have mostly focused so far, I would say that the standard reading is a foundationalist one. According to this view, Kant reacts to skepticism, which in fact arises from Cartesian mentalism but has a disruptive effect on Kant thanks to Hume, and he seeks a foundation, usually isolated as the I, on which the objective knowledge of nature can rely. Hegel expresses this position by claiming that we first have: "(a) *The theoretical faculty*, knowledge as such. This philosophy identifies the *original identity of the I* in thinking as the specific *ground* of the concepts of the understanding" (*ENZ* §42).

The standard reading rests on an impressive number of undemonstrated identifications and presuppositions. This is not the place to discuss them.[17] Here I would like to dwell on some passages that offer a different portrayal of Kant's reason so as to make it interact with Hegel's reason. As a result, the comprehensive reading of critical philosophy that I end up voicing is to some extent incompatible with the presuppositions of the standard reading. If faced with the choice between primary texts and the almost unanimous approach on the part of scholars, I believe it is necessary to forsake the most widespread and authoritative consensus in favor of Kant's own writings.

The influence of the standard reading is such that one may be surprised to find certain themes in Kant before Hegel. I begin by briefly illustrating a presupposition of the standard reading: the way of proceeding by division. On the one hand, the three *Critiques* tend to be read as three works concerning different topics rather than three different discussions of one and the same underlying theme: reason in its unity. On the other hand, the *Critique of Pure Reason* in particular is divided into isolated parts. The division in two worlds we find in the 1770 *Dissertation* is transferred straight out to the 1781 dichotomy between the Aesthetic and the Analytic. Reason proper remains somewhat foreign to this opposition between sensibility and understanding. It is neglected more than in Hegel, but for the same reasons: reason is the seat of error and does not know anything objective.

This picture of the first *Critique* is not devoid of ground. It is only that it is the *solution* of an ambivalence, the result of a choice between elements that were originally fused together and are now divided so that some can be privileged at the expense of others. Indeed, it is Kant and not some tendentious and incompetent interpreter, not a Feder as it were, who at some point after 1781 lets this picture of the first *Critique* pass insensibly, among countless hesitations and second thoughts, in continually different contexts, for various reasons and sometimes without even fully realizing what he is doing. We are not called, let me repeat, to choose the picture we like better, but we must acknowledge both of them, for Kant's ambivalence is, over and above other choices and successive restrictions of thematic field, the important factor that is most obscured by the standard reading (and by Kant and Hegel themselves).

If the standard reading reduces the *Critique of Pure Reason* to epistemology, it comes as no surprise that some of the most fundamental themes of the 1781 edition are more and more confined to separate discussions and their relevance is downplayed, when they are not abandoned altogether. This applies to many key topics of the Doctrine of Method, and particularly of the Architectonic. Take the following. The critique is a propaedeutic to metaphysics. Reason is an organism that grows internally and not by addition, so that reason has a force and a life of its own, as well as a development in which each of its members exists and functions for the sake of the whole and of an idea. Reason is autarchic, self-contained, and interested only in itself, and it is a system and not an aggregate. The *Critique of Pure Reason* is a treatise on method, and hence an organization of contents and cognitions, one section of which is paradoxically devoted to method and contains fundamental indications regarding the unity, the functioning, and above all the ends of reason. Reason is the source of ideas which, though not having a corresponding object, are the guide for every use of reason. Reason has its own *life* and is driven by interests and ends that prescribe the form of its activities.

Reason is legislation and the a priori production of contents and cognitions that must be ordered architectonically. The philosopher, who in comparison with the mathematician is limited as to the extension of cognitions, is superior in vision to artists of reason (the mathematician, the logician, and the natural scientist, who represent the model to which according to many interpreters Kant has always already subordinated, when not reduced, the use of reason), because the philosopher's cognitions are oriented to the idea of the world and not to narrow fields of nature. Finally, Kant speaks of synthetic transcendental knowledge which, like many other types of cognition acknowledged and spelled out by him, is not reducible to the model of empirical knowledge (the model stretching, according to Hegel, as we have seen, between the poles of blind intuition and empty concept). All of this is so foreign to the standard reading that it is unintelligible to it. And yet, in this paragraph, I have done nothing but quote almost literally passages taken from the Doctrine of Method (and the preface to the second edition of the *Critique of Pure Reason*).

I have mentioned the distance of this account from the supposed epistemology to which the first *Critique* is reduced. It follows that the distance from the ideal of *mathesis universalis* held by modern philosophy is no less wide. In fact, it seems to me that Kant brings the modern idea of reason to a crisis. To put the point simply, in modernity reason becomes a logical and calculating tool whose goal is to make possible a scientific and definitive *mathesis universalis* of nature. It is the neutral, internally consistent, and indifferent seat of abstract forms—be they acquired or found in us—that stands opposed to its contents as well as to external drives and forces. Modern reason is a nature opposed to external nature and likewise inert, powerless, and unable to decide and motivate. It is a sort of mechanism which we must let run its course without encumbering it with metaphysical and teleological concerns, and make rigorous by adopting the scientific method that has fueled all our hopes of limitless progress since the scientific revolution.

To this picture of a heteronomous and instrumental reason, the slave of passions in practice and at the service of natural sciences in theory, Kant opposes a reason oriented to essential ends, an organism wherein each function is subordinated to the whole, an organized system of laws and principles. Thus, reason is as much an architect of its own use planning its inner articulation as an organism that develops by taking care only of itself, without receiving any structural modification from without. Both in metaphysics and in morality reason promotes itself, because its most proper activity is the institution of an order and rules. Indeed, to be self-governing, reason must be conceived as autonomous in each of its domains, not only in the practical one. There are no judges or authorities that are superior to reason in its tribunal.

Nonetheless, reason discovers that it is internally divided. It lives in two alternative worlds and is therefore unable to comprehend them in a unitary logos. These two worlds refer to each other; but they are its worlds, instituted by none other than reason itself according to an idea, a principle.

In all this, the difference between concepts of understanding and ideas of reason is essential. As we have seen, Hegel notices Kant's important novelty in this respect, but I am not sure he appreciates it enough. If concepts are rules we avail ourselves of in order to judge, ideas are models (*Urbilder*) and ends. The function of concepts is that of identifying and determining objects according to rules, whereas the function of ideas is to project a maximum, a totality or perfection to which we hold fast as to a standard.

To use an example from the *Metaphysik L1* (*Ak* 28, 240), in the statement "Cicero is learned" I use the predicate to judge Cicero's deeds. Therefore it is a rule for my judgment, and the understanding is at once the faculty of rules, of concepts, of judgments. By contrast, in "Cicero is just" the idea of justice is not related directly to experience, let alone derived from it. Ideas transcend all experience. In and through them we complete concepts, that is, we "think their objects completely with regard to their species," "without concerning ourselves with whether such a thing is actual or even merely possible" (*Refl.* 6206, *Ak* 18, 489–90). What matters is that nothing should be missing from the idea. Concepts aim at capturing the being of objects; ideas are at once a being (subjective, for reason) and an ought (for the objects it judges: *Sein-Sollen*). Concepts look to objects; ideas look past given objects—or, better, they look to objects in view of their normative standards, which, even though they point to something that does not exist, eventually turn out to be helpful for a better cognition of objects themselves. Ideas seek an encompassing view, a stereoscopic vision that keeps together near and far, presence and its horizon. And, sure enough, the fools who steadily direct their gaze toward *remote ends* and keep their head raised above the ground *looking for something that does not exist* are those at whom the Thracian maid pokes her fun: philosophers. "Philosophy is the true motherland of ideas," says Kant (*Refl.* 943, *Ak* 15.1, 419).

Ideas are plans to be realized; they are ends and at once principles of the organization of parts. We do not find this sense of project and realization in a concept. And yet, if ideas transcend experience and are not in relation to things, ideas are in relation to concepts. In fact, ideas are in themselves concepts of reason. They are results, obtained logically by extension and totalization of those concepts that we use in experience. The tendency to transcend the series of the conditioned in order to grasp it unitarily, starting with a principle that is external to the series, is logical in nature.

Take the idea of world: it is paradigmatic, and often, especially in Kant's *Opus Postumum,* it functions as the mirror image of the idea of God as the totality of all being. The world as such an all-encompassing totality does not exist, for it is our a priori thought. Nothing in reality corresponds to our idea, and we arrive at it not despite but precisely because we know it cannot denote any object. We know we cannot apply an idea for technical or even conceptual ends. The idea of world shows that our gaze is directed toward the whole, to the farthest and most comprehensive horizon. Such an idea can never become the means to something else. Instead, it affirms itself as an ideal that we may well never attain. In one sense, from the point of view of the concerns of experience, ideas appear as useless. In another sense, if our perspective is wider than this form of instrumentality, ideas are the most necessary guide, even for the application of our understanding to experience and the sciences (*KrV* A 645/B 673, A 651–54/B 679–82).

Ideas are therefore called regulative, whereas concepts are constitutive. But ideas are both regulative of the constitutive use of understanding and necessary even for empirical truth, so that it does not suffice to characterize them simply as "regulative." One may object that it is simply a matter of understanding correctly the sense of this term. But even understanding the term "regulative" correctly cannot be enough. We confront a problem: the Kantian ambivalence regarding ideas comes up and we cannot ignore it. As Hegel claims, Kant's solutions are often more disappointing than the pathways they open up (with stupefying intelligence, as I, but not Hegel, would add). There is nothing on which Hegel is more right than ideas. If ideas are necessary to concepts, their tension with concepts and intuitions is a vital relation, and not a dead end we must prudently avoid. More often than not, instead, Kant stresses the vanity of ideas in their attempt to grasp objects rather than their necessity.

Likewise, with the first *Critique* Kant does not intend to give us a censorship of reason's tendency to venture beyond the limits of experience. To be sure, we have that, but only because before it we have a comprehensive and global examination of reason's extent—its ambition and powers—as it strives to know itself. Reason knows itself as internally articulated. If we are in touch with things through sensibility, then concepts are not in touch with things but with intuitions. In turn, ideas of reason are the unitary use of the understanding's concepts. In other words, concepts represent the material basis for ideas, and the understanding as a whole is subordinated to reason as an executor of reason's plan. Thus, even knowledge is subjected to reason's project, but this should not be misunderstood (at least in the *Critique of Pure Reason*) as a leap to the primacy of practical reason. For, in truth, this dependency refers to the essential end of reason, which is the free and responsible use of itself as it is outlined in the Architectonic.

In this sense, the activity of reason is like the complete activity in Aristotle. The difference lies in the fact that it is a production, although of a particular type. It is not an Aristotelian *poiêsis*, but an a priori production of forms that are endowed with objective reality (even here, as in the Hegelian *Wirklichkeit*, "objective reality" means something different from sensible existence, that is, the possibility of experience). In turn this activity, this essential end, is oriented toward a final end (the highest good) which does not depend on reason but on freedom, the immortality of the soul, and a providential God.

"A priori synthesis" is the Kantian expression used to describe the power of reason to exercise its own causality in the world: in the form of a system of cognitions and principles, and of a moral order of motivations and actions. Let us consider the following two examples. If general logic deals only with conceptual relations and the coherent use of the understanding, *transcendental logic generates contents*. The logical concept of the self-identical subject can be employed indifferently for any object: a heptagon, a chimera, a table, a novel, justice. It denotes no more than a formal requisite, empty of content and reference. When I transform this concept into that of substance, I get a quite different result. The logical concept becomes a pure principle organizing my experience of objects. It is now a principle that allows me, rather than to sort out abstractly subject and predicate, to distinguish between change and permanence in experience. I have a rule (a rule excluding chimeras and justice from possible objects of consideration) under which I can subsume the particulars I experience and to which I can bring back all perception of alteration and becoming. I cannot anticipate anything of what I will each time experience, except that it will have to conform to this rule in order to be objective. In fact, all experience will have the form of an object in general that only my pure concepts and intuitions jointly have constituted. What allows me to turn subject into substance and, more broadly with other categories and pure intuitions, to generate rules for experience out of pure concepts is the addition of a supplementary condition to the logical concept: the schema of time—in this case as permanence.

This is an *a priori synthesis*, a production issuing from reason. The pure concept of substance has objective reality (i.e., the possibility of being applied to experience as a rule that makes it amenable to universal and necessary knowledge) and the possibility of reference (to whatever appearance I will each time experience). Last but not least, it also gives rise to a universal law in the general science of nature whose principles precede and make possible physics: substance remains and persists (*Prol.* §15).

Another example is this. When I promise my son to play with him, I have instituted something that previously did not exist. What interests Kant is not that the performative utterance makes an intention real, as in John Austin, but that once I make a promise I am bound by it. My reason has freely issued an imperative that I can break or make good on, but which determines my conduct. My afternoon changes accordingly, and, by extension, so do my time, my world, my history: who I am. The conduct to which I am bound once I have made a promise and thereby instituted something real is the product of my autonomous choice. Here, too, we have an a priori synthesis.

Through these syntheses I produce new objects. And this is the central question of critical philosophy as a whole, not only of pure reason: the evaluation and limits of the power that reason has to extend itself in the world. As we can see, unlike Hegel, I think that the cases of theoretical and practical production can be treated in an analogous way.[18] There are obvious differences: the theoretical production has in view the legislation of nature, while the practical has in view the realization of the law. Yet there is no disparity, for in both cases I produce a priori contents that remain simply forms (not objects as in a *poiêsis* or a *creatio ex nihilo*).

In transcendental logic the understanding synthesizes pure concepts by giving them an intuitive content (a pure, not empirical intuition), thereby bringing "a transcendental content into its representations" (*KrV* B 105). Transcendental logic is a logic of truth: a logic of the relation between concepts and their objects. As such, it is the source of all truth (*KrV* A 63/B 87, A 57/B 81, B IX). The power of reason consists in prescribing an order a priori. Its speculative a priori synthesis overturns three dogmas of empiricism. It claims: (1) experience is actually made possible by reason's constitutive activity; (2) the individual is made possible by the universal, the empirical by the a priori; and (3) the indefiniteness of experience is in principle intelligible, lawlike, and *familiar*. For I can experience particulars in a meaningful way because every particular is part of a universal and necessary connection that is the condition of all apprehension. Thus, what preexists from the point of view of experience is not a material particular, but a formal theory of the object of experience. Objectivity is the universal and necessary anticipation that we project onto things.

Likewise for practical production. It is not just a matter of saying that reason produces visible effects in the world. Even here, the important thing is that reason should act upon itself—that it be self-affection. The empirical effects of practical reason matter only because reason produces them to the extent that it *wills itself,* that is, the purity of a rational law it forms independently of inclinations. In this self-affection, reason determines itself to action.

The procedure is the inverse of that in the first *Critique.* We start from principles, pass to concepts (good and bad), and reach sensibility (the only pure feeling, respect). Furthermore, principles produce their own reality, unlike those of pure reason that have objective reality only once we show their reference to intuition. Finally, the human world is not an immutable order like nature; in fact, it becomes what we make of it. Still, here as well, reason is not confined to mere thought. Reason does not *think* a free will: it *determines* it by means of a law. In this way reason is causality through freedom: the force, motivation, and incentive to realize itself.

Thus, if I form the maxim of giving back a deposit, I institute a content of the categorical imperative by means of a resolution whose form is a certain relation to myself (variably definable as loyalty, integrity, truthfulness to oneself, a pledge or commitment over time). Content and form are two aspects of the same thing. They are not absolutely opposed in the way that universality and determinateness are. In the practical a priori synthesis, the content is the form's own product, not the surreptitiously assumed and empirically found content standing opposed to an empty rational form.

Unfortunately, it is precisely in these terms that Hegel interprets it.[19] He writes that the categorical imperative to return deposits presupposes a given matter (private property and the laws governing its existence) which it winds up sanctioning rationally, lending it a dignity and a necessity it does not have. For Hegel, since maxims are empty forms, the universalization of the maxim is a trivial test that all maxims can pass. For him, the form is external to the content; from the outset the form contradicts the content. As a result, the Kantian moral agent, by endorsing and legitimizing external, empirically found contents, lives in a necessary contradiction with the moral autonomy that it aspires to safeguard and implement.

Hegel thinks that Kant has not asked the critical question of what would happen if there were no deposits. He wonders why Kant is preoccupied with construing as a contradiction the absence of deposits from the world. What Hegel does not see, however, is that this is not the contradiction that Kant argues comes up if the maxim of returning the deposit is violated. Instead, it is the self-contradictory *world* in which deposits would disappear because reciprocal trust would vanish. How could deposits exist in such a world?

What Hegel does not realize is that the form—the will's agreement with itself—does not find or presuppose the content, but generates it because reason has the power of transcending itself and producing a world through its own legislation. If the content is not found empirically but produced by the form, then the formality of the imperative is not an "analytic unity and a tautology," as Hegel writes in "The Scientific Ways of Treating Natural Law" (*W* 2, 463), but an a priori synthesis. Hegel misses the identity of form and content; he also misidentifies "the empirical." What remains external and indifferent to the form-content that alone counts is the matter, not the content. It is indifferent whether the deposit is a book, money, or whatever else I promised to return.

The Kantian problem of how morality can become concrete and realize itself in specific and particular duties is not even acknowledged by Hegel. In the *Phenomenology*, Hegel criticizes the unconditioned character of duty. If the command is formal universality and lack of contradiction, all we have is an empty form that must be necessarily a "universality that lacks content" (*W* 3, 315, *PhS* 256). Laws are thought of from the start as ineffective. Similarly, in the *Lectures on the History of Philosophy*, Hegel says that with such a formal morality Kant cannot claim "*what* is moral, since he does not think of a system wherein spirit realizes itself" (*VGPh* 3, 369). One wonders whether Hegel has ever taken seriously *The Metaphysics of Morals*, on which he comments in relation to the discussion of abstract right in the *Outlines of the Philosophy of Right*. It is true, even obvious, that for Hegel, spirit's self-realization, and with it its satisfaction and happiness (as distinct from individual happiness), has an ethical content, so that for him morality is but a moment of spirit's self-realization. But it is false that Kant's moral philosophy is opposed to the content.

And the problem is ever the same. Recalling another memorable image used by Hegel, if skeptics inoculate the scab of the finite into the rational so they can scratch it (*W* 2, 247), we could say that Hegel empties Kantian reason in order to denounce its vacuity and impossibility of transcending itself. In *Faith and Knowledge* we read: "Kant's pure reason is this same empty thought, and reality is similarly opposed to that empty identity, and it is precisely the lack of concordance between them that makes faith in the beyond necessary" (*GuW* 395, *FK* 164). The problem, going back to the identification of Kant's starting point, is that Kant's reason is Hume's mind. Now, as in Hume, reason in Kant is admittedly absorbed only with itself, but, in contrast to Hume, it is focused on itself as it transcends itself toward the world, not because it is solipsistic. To put it differently, for Hegel Kantian reason is the child of the chain linking the Cartesian cogito and the mind in Berkeley and Hume. It necessarily follows that transcendental idealism is a private point of view.

All that we have seen in this section on Kant's reason is, in turn, only part of the story. For it is Kant who speaks emphatically of the dogmatic slumber from which Hume has awakened him. For various reasons which I cannot dwell on here, in the 1780s Kant progressively undermines the firm tenets we have examined in this section until he changes the whole architectonic structure of his system and the inner articulation of reason, including, in the retrospective consideration of the *Critique of Pure Reason*, the picture of reason he thinks he had given in 1781.[20] He progressively pushes out of the first *Critique* the noumenon to make it an exclusively moral problem of freedom. He also jumbles up the whole structure of the first *Critique* by calling reason the faculty of desire (in the second and third *Critiques*: *KpV*, *Ak* 5, 90, Eng. trans. 212; *KU*, *Ak* 5, 167, Eng. trans. 55). He expunges ideas, which migrate partly to the moral domain (the causality of freedom) and partly to the aesthetic domain (as aesthetic ideas, but especially in the notion of purposiveness and the representation of nature by reflection *as if* nature had been ordered systematically and providentially by a mind, so that the regulative function of ideas becomes the new principle of reflective judgment).

Reason, which was the only authority in its own tribunal, abdicates more and more clearly in favor of a newly appointed prosecutor, the understanding, which was one of its subordinate functions. Reason now becomes exclusively transcendent. At the same time, ideas are evaluated on the basis of a criterion that was elaborated for the understanding, that is, objective reality and the application of concepts to experience, and are judged on that basis. In turn, the understanding becomes synonymous with determining judgment and the quasi-mechanical execution—as the *Critique of the Power of Judgment* portrays it (*Ak* 5, 195, Eng. trans. 80–81)— of an intention that is now clearly identified as exclusively epistemological. The understanding has meanwhile removed from itself everything that cannot be reduced to the mechanism of nature; for example, the ideas of homogeneity, affinity, and specification, which in the Appendix to the 1781 Dialectic were nothing less than the criterion of empirical truth, disappear from the concepts of the empirical sciences.

The picture of Kantian reason described in this section may very well be only part of the story, but we cannot pretend it does not exist. Buying wholesale Kant's 1790 verdict on the 1781 Kant means to disrespect the latter. We can, and indeed, we must try to understand why Kant wants to downplay these results. But they cannot be erased or minimized only because Kant, and after him Hegel and a great many Kant scholars, have later made different choices. In particular, one cannot with Hegel ignore Kant's *ambivalence* in order to denounce his *one-sidedness* and the reduction of reason to the understanding. If anything, Kant strikes us by his continuous wavering and incredibly misleading and simplistic retrospective judgments, not for the supposed stubbornness in conceiving from the outset reason as consciousness and the I as an empty identity that is opposed to the finite.

The Logic of Being reads: "Kant's concept of *synthetic a priori judgments*—the concept of terms that are *distinct* and yet equally *inseparable*; of an *identity* which is within it an *inseparable difference*—belongs to what is great and imperishable in his philosophy" (*WL* I, 240, *SL* 174–75). This passage exemplifies what I meant earlier about what Hegel can teach us about Kant. It is too bad that he himself does not seriously believe what he claims. In the Logic of the Concept he writes: "In the a priori synthesis of the concept, Kant did have a higher principle in which it was possible to recognize a duality and therefore what is required for truth; but the material of the senses, the manifoldness of intuition, was too strong for him to be able to wrest himself away from it and turn to a consideration of the concept and the categories *in and for themselves,* and to a speculative form of philosophizing" (*WL* II, 267, *SL* 524). Hegel does not take seriously what he says in the former passage because he takes seriously Kant's depreciation of ideas. These, however, in Hegel have never been blessed with a favorable fate. As we read in *Faith and Knowledge* (*GuW* 336; *FK* 82), reason "cannot even get to the point of being able to produce an Idea" (as if the Transcendental Dialectic did not give us a metaphysical deduction of ideas!). This evaluation appears again in the chapter on the idea in the *Science of Logic,*[21] in the *Encyclopaedia,*[22] as well as in the *Lectures.* Here (*VGPh* 3, 351–52), Hegel says that "reason is thought that makes the unconditioned and infinite its object. Its product is the idea . . . but in Kant the idea is only the abstract universal, the indeterminate." But ideas are not just abstract and indeterminate; they are for Hegel nothing more than an empty *Sollen.* In ideas Kant has "stopped short at the negative and what merely *ought to be*" (*ENZ* §45 Z).

Nothing summarizes this point more poignantly than the seventh thesis of Hegel's 1801 *Habilitation*: "Philosophia critica caret ideis [*sic*] et imperfecta est Scepticismi forma" ("Critical philosophy lacks ideas, and is an imperfect form of skepticism," *W* 2, 533). Clearly, the portrayal of Kant as an epigone of Hume is established in Hegel very early on alongside the depreciation of Kant's ideas.

As we have seen, for Hegel the Kantian understanding is constitutive of the finite whereas it should be dialectical, realizing that the finite is an immanent "self-sublation" (*ENZ* §81 A). In turn, Kantian reason is conceived by Hegel only as the destruction of the finite (and not also as constitutive of a world, as we have seen in this section). Now, reason is indeed the destruction of the finite, but it is also conceived as understanding because it remains an abstract identity and the simple "systematizing [of] the material conveyed by perception . . . through the application of the categories" (*ENZ* §52 Z). In this way, reason must renounce its unconditionality.

Another way to put this can be inferred from the introduction to the *Science of Logic*. If the understanding separates and divides, then reflection must overcome the division and bring isolated determinations into relation. "This reflective activity of connection belongs in itself to reason, and to rise above the determinations and attain insight into their discord is the great negative step on the way to the true concept of reason. But, when not carried through, this insight runs into the misconception that reason is the one that contradicts itself" (*WL* I, 39, *SL* 26). We misunderstand reason if we hold contradiction to be its exclusive lot so as to protect things from it, out of soft-heartedness toward them. It is the finite that contradicts itself, not our reason when it is dialectical, as Kant argues.

This judgment returns in the Logic of the Concept. One would expect finitude to lose its grip in reason, says Hegel, but this expectation is disappointed. "For Kant defines the relation of reason to the categories as merely *dialectical.* Indeed, he even takes the result of this dialectic to be simply and solely an *infinite nothingness,* the result being that the synthesis is again lost, lost also to the infinite unity of reason, and lost with it is whatever beginning there was of a speculative, truly infinite, concept; reason becomes the well-known, totally formal, merely *regulative unity of the systematic employment of the understanding*" (*WL* II, 261–62, *SL* 520).[23]

The Hegelian critique can then be rephrased in these words: the understanding is conceived as static rather than vanishing; and reason is considered as the sheer overcoming of the understanding rather than as the actuality of the idea.

Hegel's Reason in Its Novelty Compared to Kant's

At this stage, it is worth examining the relation between Hegel's and Kant's reason as it results from the above section rather than in Hegel's critical

CHAPTER 5

evaluation. Here, too, no matter how many affinities we can establish, eventually we will see that some differences remain far more important.

Reason, too, can be said in many ways for Hegel. In the Philosophy of Subjective Spirit, reason appears at the end of the Phenomenology, where it is "the simple *identity* of the *subjectivity* of the concept with its *objectivity* and universality" (*ENZ* §438). This constitutes the premise for the Psychology, in which reason is the truth of the opposition that is internal to spirit (§467 A). In the logic, as we read in §214 of the *Encyclopaedia*, reason is properly speaking *idea*, namely, the unity of finite and infinite, concept and reality, ideal and real, soul and body, subject-object. In the words of the *Science of Logic*, reason is "the self-unveiled truth" (*WL* II, 271, *SL* 527). In general, reason is the identity of opposites.

If reason is the identity of opposites, it is not so originally, from the beginning: the identity must become. As we have seen, it is thinking (*das Logische*) that has different ways of existing, ranging from the concrete self-external manifestations of the idea in nature and unconscious thought up to understanding and reason. If thinking makes itself concrete, then it must be examined in light of its moments: the understanding, the negatively rational, and the speculative (*ENZ* §79). Reason "leads it [the understanding] back to unity" (*ENZ* §214 A). But which understanding is so led back? We know that the understanding separates and abstracts, and stops at isolated determinations. The understanding "works up the recollected representations into genera, species, laws, forces, etc., in general into categories" (*ENZ* §467). Notice the absence of that form of operation that in Kant defines the understanding: concepts. For Hegel, the concept is one activity, conceiving (*Begreifen*); forces, laws, and species are intellectual—abstract, separate, isolated, self-identical, and hence other-excluding—forms of the concept. The understanding explains the individual starting with its universal properties. It abstracts the essential from the contingent and holds it fast against itself. The content, which first appears as given, must be understood as the field of interaction of the universal and the particular.

This is not the only striking point. A sharp difference from Kant emerges already with the definition of reason as the unity of opposites: in Hegel, reason is not a faculty in any sense of the word. Even when it could appear as a faculty—for instance, as observing reason or as examining laws in the *Phenomenology*—reason is consciousness's certainty to be actual, and is therefore thinking's instinct (*Trieb*) to look for itself in the world. Reason is described as an instinct because it must produce itself in the world. It wants to find and possess itself; it wants to rule the world, be at home in it (*Beisichselbstsein*), and when it is not, it is the drive to become so. This is the most basic trait of Hegel's reason.

We have seen that reason is properly speaking idea, and the idea is the unity of concept and reality. When reason appears in the form of consciousness (a finite I standing against the world), an opposition takes place between consciousness, understood as the seat of the concept, and the real, understood as the given. Here reason appears as a degree (*ENZ* §467 A), one activity of consciousness among others. The content here remains indifferent to its form.

In turn, once reason realizes that it is not a finite consciousness opposed to a no less finite world but is spirit, *Geist*, the formative principle of the world in which it is beginning to feel at home (once, that is, the opposition is sublated), reason is "the truth of the opposition" (ibid.). "Truth" means that we finally get the authentic relation: no longer the external one between a given content and a form imposed on it from without, but the universal that particularizes itself and produces its own content. This is why actuality appears to reason as its own, as posited, as something that reason has freely produced.

We have seen that, in Hegel's view, Kant opposes the sheer form of thinking to matter, and thereby to truth. Thinking receives the material and limits itself to shaping it, and thus cannot "transcend itself" (*WL* I, 37, *SL* 25). What Hegel does not realize is that appearances and nature in general are already translated into their laws by pure reason. Form is not opposed to content. In fact, transcendental logic is but their identity, in the concept of an object in general. An appearance is nothing other than the relations that unite it, says Kant in the Amphiboly. His principle *forma dat esse rei* (form gives being to the thing) can be hardly reduced to an empty form, an inert vessel to be filled by the given sensible content. Differently stated, Kant does not think of the objective content as preexisting, given before and independently of the conceptual form.

In Hegel, the law as "a *constant* image of fleeting appearance," "its calm copy" (*W* 3, 120, *PhS* 90–91; *WL* II, 153–54, *SL* 440–41), and "the inversion of the world of appearance" (*WL* II, 161, *SL* 446), is the law that reflection *discovers* in nature. He believes that this holds for all modern philosophies of reflection, including Kant, who might want to retort that law is actually the product of a law-giving reason which *generates* contents by operating on its own forms. This is what it means for it to posit laws of nature, which are not the inverted world, but its inner form.

To put it differently, the relation between appearance and law in Kant is not that distant from what we read in Hegel's Logic of Essence. With the ambiguities and hesitations we have seen, for Kant, too, the appearance is a posited being. For him as for Hegel, it is "the concrete existent mediated through its negation" (*WL* II, 150, *SL* 438). If the ground of appearances is the law, then law and appearance have one and the same content and "law is the reflection of appearance into self-identity" (*WL* II, 153, *SL* 441). "The law, therefore, is not beyond appearance but is immediately present in it" (*WL* II, 156, *SL* 441). As a result, "the concrete existing world tranquilly raises itself to a kingdom of laws" (*WL* II, 156, *SL* 443). "Thus appearance reflected-into-itself is now *a world that discloses itself above the world of appearance as one which is in and for itself*" (*WL* II, 158, *SL* 444).

As we can see, Hegel distances himself from Kant even when he seems to share his theses. Yet Hegel is impervious to this realization because he has reduced Kantian philosophy to a residual version of Hume's. Thus, when Hegel writes that his logic is the "system of pure reason" (*WL* I, 44, *SL* 29) and writes that the form, as the law of appearances, is the content (*ENZ* §133), it comes as no surprise that he believes he is criticizing Kant instead of making claims analogous to his.[24]

We have also seen that at other times Hegel expresses himself differently. Before we cherish this, we had better consider what this means for the coherence of his critique of Kant. For instance, in the General Division of the Logic, he writes that transcendental logic "does not abstract from all the content of objective cognition . . . , contains the rules of the pure thinking of an intended object; and it thereby goes to the source of our cognition" (*WL* I, 59, *SL* 40). Hegel refers to Kant as to the initiator of the view of metaphysics as logic. And he is right: transcendental logic is contrasted by Kant to general logic, and it is no longer the vestibule, propaedeutic, or organ of sciences, external to them. As an analytic of the understanding, transcendental logic actually replaces ontology, as Kant writes in a famous passage that Hegel shows he has in mind when he describes objective logic (*WL* I, 45, *SL* 30). This is the logic of the concept as object, which has to be followed by the logic of the concept as subject, as comprehension of reason.

At other times, with regard to themes brought back to life by Kant against modern philosophies of reflection, Hegel manifests an unexpected attitude. He undermines these themes by taking them as expressed in defective and merely reflective ways. Hegel uses them as motives to return to their genuinely speculative formulation which he finds in Aristotle. Consider the instance of finality.[25] For Hegel, Kant overcomes the antinomy of necessity and external teleology, but does not arrive at the Aristotelian conception of an immanent finality in nature. Having myself written a book showing the importance of Aristotle for Hegel, I can hardly criticize him for this critique, and yet I would like to point out that Kant has not discussed purposiveness only in the "timid" *Critique of the Power of Judgment*. In fact, in the Architectonic it is Kant who speaks of reason as an organism. It is Kant who, speaking of the concept of a teleology of reason, *teleologia humanae rationis,* describes its system as an edifice to build and at once as a living being that develops out of itself. Regardless, when in the preface to the *Phenomenology of Spirit* Hegel writes that reason is "das zweckmässige Tun" (*W* 3, 26: "purposive activity" at *PhS* 12), he does so in order to praise Aristotle against Kant and the moderns with whom for him Kant is in line. In Aristotle we find a subject as pure negativity, "the unmoved that is itself mover" (ibid.).[26]

Similarly, Hegel contrasts the system of sciences with their aggregate—a distinction that comes from these very pages of the Architectonic—and goes to the point of calling philosophy a "science of freedom" (*EA* §5 A) which, like reason in the Architectonic, cannot feed on anything external but grows *per intus susceptionem* (internally), not depending on any given contents but organizing them and endowing the exposition with a necessary shape (*ENZ* §12 A). When Hegel expresses himself thus, Kant seems a conspicuous specter in his absence.

If the criterion of the scientificity of reason in its self-examination is the comprehensive systematic totality of all rational cognitions, for both Kant and Hegel properly speaking, only philosophy can be science. And for both of them reason is in its innermost essence restlessness, need and search for logos. And yet, for Kant, restlessness is the symptom of reason's need for order; reason's interest can be either practical or speculative; and its hope is the highest good that is not of this world but presupposes faith in ideas—or postulates for practical reason—that cannot be brought back to any form of knowledge. By contrast, for Hegel, the need is philosophy's need, and this is the production of a unification, a *re-conciliation*, and thereby a return to itself from a division. Such interest is both practical and speculative, or, better said, it is the unification of theory and practice. Lastly, beyond this world there is none other, so that the concept of hope has a completely different weight and role to play than in Kant.

For Kant, if reason's need is that of finding itself in its laws, its final motivation is quite clearly in the Doctrine of Method the desire for wisdom, so that the basic inspiration of the *Critique of Pure Reason* is the Socratic self-knowledge of reason as knowledge of its limits: knowledge of non-knowledge as a science.[27] For Hegel, instead, every activity of reason is but its own manifestation in the world, and as a result it is to Aristotle (*his* Aristotle, of course) rather than to Socrates that he feels close: philosophy has left behind the name of desire for knowledge to become accomplished knowledge.

The destiny of Kant's reason is to explore new ways and venture across a vast ocean, leaving behind what is familiar.[28] In Hegel, reason discovers that it is, or must become, at home everywhere; it need only

CHAPTER 5

realize this by transforming what is familiar into what is known. Hegel's reason therefore has a latitude and depth that Kant's reason neither can nor aspires to have. To begin with, for Hegel, reason is the tendential unity of theory and practice, and thereby of ideas and the passions that tend to realize it, whereas in Kant the gap between reason and passions is as unbridgeable as that between reason and history. Hegel's reason does not rule the world because it gives it a lawlike structure, but because it promotes and objectifies itself in the world: it makes the world its home. Its end is that of producing freedom in objective spirit, and with that historical progress.

Reason's relation to faith changes accordingly. Faith and reason are no longer alternative at all. In German the term *Glaube*, as we know since Jacobi's reading of Hume on belief, encloses in itself both senses of "faith," faith in transcendence and subjective faith or trust. In Hegel, faith begins to take on the unitary sense of subjective certainty; and this is first of all the certainty that modern individual freedom is the founding principle of institutions and the mores of a people, including their religious community (*Gemeinde*). Therefore, legislation is no longer the activity of a reason that is embodied but trans-individual; it is rather the result of the work of each and every one. On the one hand, this gives the individual's political responsibility a much greater weight; on the other hand, it is as objective, actual, shared, and even reified that reason can be what Kant in the Architectonic called the form and end of the whole. As a consequence, the relation between the individual and objectivity is no longer framed in Enlightenment republican terms as in Kant (to get out of the state of minority, we must adopt the maxim of *Selbstdenken*), but in the form of something substantial that must recognize itself as a subject. Hegelian individuals, that is, are pervaded by norms and reasons belonging to an objective tradition they have not created but in which they were born and which they must validate by participating in the activities of their community and State. Individuals become the co-creators of objective norms insofar as they use them; and they must make fluid and appropriate that which tradition has handed down to them as a reified whole.

For Hegel, self-conscious reason realizes itself in the life of a people (*W* 3, 264 ff., *PhS* 211 ff.). In fact, reason is called the resolution to finitude (*GPR* §13, *W* 7, 64), its self-realization in concrete forms. This does not mean that Hegel's reason realizes itself thoroughly in history, for it is only in absolute spirit, that is, in an ahistorical dimension, that it considers itself retrospectively and knows itself as realized. But it does mean that its relation to history, including the relation between philosophy and its history, changes dramatically. Indeed, Kant offers a sketch of a

History of Pure Reason at the end of the Doctrine of Method, but it is the ideal transition of three philosophical positions (dogmatism, skepticism, critique) that has nothing historical. One could say it is as little historical as the three positions of thought concerning objectivity in the Preliminary Concept of the *Encyclopaedia* Logic. There, much as Kant has done, Hegel has empiricism, with its skeptical results and up to Kant himself, supersede the dogmatism of the understanding's metaphysics (Hegel then adds the further and final stage of immediate knowledge). In his concept of the history of philosophy, Hegel uses several Kantian notions (from the concept of systematic and organic development guided by an idea, to reason as autonomous self-determination and an internal end which does not depend on sciences but gives them their form and end). But it is not surprising, given his very different relation between truth and history, that Hegel both stresses Kant's ignorance of the history of philosophy (*GuW* 338, *FK* 84)—evident if compared to Hegel's knowledge of Greek philosophy in particular, I would add—and founds an altogether new discipline, the history of philosophy, of which not even the Kant of *What Real Progress* . . . with its concept of an a priori history of reason had any inkling.

More fundamentally, several key concepts change. The concepts of reality and actuality, which for Kant are different categories of quality (*Realität*) and modality (*Wirklichkeit*) but in general denote givenness, become for Hegel reason's self-realization. In Kant, the problem of the objective reality of our concepts is discussed in the Transcendental Deduction and in the Analytic of Principles through the difference between the logical and real use of reason. Pure concepts obtain meaning and reference, and thus objective reality, through exhibition (*Darstellung*). This is the translation of a logical concept into a schematized concept, that is, a concept that finds its reality and reference to possible experience in an intuition. In general, this is the way in which Kant gives an account of the mediation between abstract and intuitive planes, between rules and their application (to experience as well as to action).[29] In Hegel, the problem becomes that of the reality of the concept; it is the concept *in the singular* which realizes itself in different particular modes (*WL* II, 505, *SL* 702). The *Darstellung des Begriffs* (exhibition of the concept), which in Kant is typical of the construction of mathematical concepts as well as of schematism, in Hegel means the self-objectivation of the concept which acquires a spatiotemporal reality. Curiously, Hegel takes up—unwittingly, as I suggest—certain themes from Kant's philosophy of mathematics. The *Selbstthätigkeit*, which in Kant designated the spontaneous activity of mathematical concepts as exhibition in intuition, in Hegel becomes the fundamental and immanent trait of organisms, their very manner of being:

CHAPTER 5

here internal finality, which is instinctual, takes the place of constructive and deliberate activity.[30] The genetic definition in Kant concerned mathematical concepts alone in their difference from pure and empirical concepts, because only mathematics gives rise to real objects that it sees arise through its construction. For Hegel instead, the genetic definition is the standard definition of each concept, because every determination is a determinate negation, that is, the nothingness of that from which it results, and must be expounded in its genesis.

Everything changes, naturally. The subject of the process of the concept's self-realization is no longer reason as I-think, a self-affection that makes pure concepts sensible and concrete. It is rather thought—as objective thought, *das Logische*, the unconscious and natural thought deposited in tradition, language, history, and objective spirit—that must be brought to self-consciousness. If a historical moment is a rational concretion, in reason we do not have a form and a concept as opposed to matter, but forces and movements animated by a logic we must understand. The relation between essence and manifestation changes: whereas for Hegel essence is taken as active and is its appearing, without which it is neither actual nor knowable, for Kant their difference can never be canceled, and the relation concerns the facticity of our subjective faculties.

The Kantian problem of schematism is taken up at different levels by Hegel. For Hegel, reason's need is to alternate and integrate concept and representation, the familiar and the known (*bekannt—erkannt*). Purifying familiar concepts from representation is philosophy's specific work; but giving a sensible content to concepts—in Kant's words, exhibiting them *in concreto*—is no less important, for the true must be expressed sensibly in order to be able to speak to everyone. This is why God has made Himself flesh, and the speculative has given itself a sensible shape. A movement shuttles back and forth between two sides of meaning: philosophical, essential meaning, as opposed to the concrete exemplification and fulfillment of empty intentions with concrete associations. And this movement helps both.

And yet, as we have seen in chapter 4, the movement is neither complementary nor symmetrical. Philosophy's work is an effort at purification, while the desire to clothe bare concepts is a concession to the subjective need to come down from the conceptual to the representational level of examples and illustration of concepts. If the movement were symmetrical, Hegel would not call representations the "metaphors of thoughts and concepts" (*ENZ* §3 A), whereby "metaphor" is not Ricoeur's living metaphor but signals a defective implication: the crystallization of thought into images and sensible figures from which we philosophers must divest it in order to grasp it purely.

This two-way movement, as we have seen in chapter 4, involves several cultural and symbolic aspects in a broad sense, and it is in the *Lectures on Philosophy of Religion* (besides the introduction to the Berlin *Encyclopaedia* and scattered writings from the Berlin years) that Hegel talks about this translation from one medium to another. This movement can be illustrated by the relation between absolute spirit and world; this relation is philosophically analyzed in the system, but it can also be translated for the sake of representation in the popular theme of the creation of the world, and the descent to earth of the divine. In all this, what Kant treated under the rubric of the symbol (the intuitive exhibition of the supersensible) and of analogy in the *Prolegomena* and the third *Critique* (*KU* §59) becomes in Hegel the problem of the different modes of embodiment of the divine.

A further dimension involved in Hegel's retrieval of the schematism is the progression internal to the concept of representation (and more specifically of *Erinnerung* and imagination) in the Philosophy of Subjective Spirit in the *Encyclopaedia*. And another dimension concerns the absolute idea's self-release in nature, where it assumes a spatiotemporal, external, and natural being (notoriously one of the most controversial and misunderstood theses in Hegel's philosophy).

Finally, in Kant, the problem of exhibition is used in the *Critique of the Power of Judgment* to introduce the concept of a technique of nature. Nature is seen as if it had been made by an intelligent creator in view of ends, that is, as if in its harmonious forms it had to exhibit a rational design. In this way the relation of concepts, intuitions, time, and imagination which structured the first *Critique* is now recast in the context of reflecting judgment as the cluster of problems including a bridge between particular and universal, the symbol, aesthetic ideas, and purposiveness. Hegel takes up this concept of exhibition in his reading of the intuitive understanding and in the extension of the concept of reason to include imagination, genius, and aesthetic ideas (e.g., *GuW* 322, *FK* 86).

When in a construction you alter even only a small detail or element, says Kant, the whole acquires a totally different configuration. So, as the global frame of concepts defining reason changes between Kant and Hegel, so do some fundamental concepts. Let me briefly turn now in the conclusion of this section to the concepts of method, dialectic, limit, and ideas of reason.

1. *Method*. For Kant as for Hegel, method is not a structure or procedure that is ready-made and imported into philosophy from without, as, for example, it is in mathematics in modern physics or in the very proof-structure of philosophies such as Spinoza's or Wolff's. For both Hegel and Kant, method is the arrangement and form that reason gives its contents

CHAPTER 5

and cognitions; for both, that is, method and object do not fall asunder, unlike in all disciplines other than philosophy.

For Kant method is the design and plan of the whole, the scientific form that guides the organization of cognitions (*KrV* A 707/B 736, "V-Lo/Dohna," *Ak* 24, 780). This naturally means that you cannot treat determinate contents apart from their organization. Incidentally, this implies that Kant's critics from Schopenhauer to Adickes to Kemp Smith and Lehmann, who wish to liberate the living core of Kant's philosophy from the external and baroque fetters of the system, show a remarkably poor understanding of Kant's key novelty in comparison to the modern tradition. Likewise, Hegel writes that the method is the consciousness of the form of its inner movement (*WL* I, 49, *SL* 33; *W* 3, 47, *PhS* 28). Possibly appealing to the etymology of method, Hegel writes in the *Science of Logic* that the method is "the way" for the construction of concepts (*WL* I, 49, *SL* 33).

But even here, unfortunately, Hegel never considers Kant as an example or a precursor or a positive role model. He writes in the *Logic*: "Hitherto, philosophy had yet to find its method" (*WL* I, 48, *SL* 32). He thinks that we must adopt a new concept of scientific treatment in which science does not borrow any direction from without, but lets the content move and progress without imposing upon it any external reflection (*WL* I, 16, *SL* 9). About this first point, I think we must conclude that the difference between Kant and Hegel is that for the former the method is architectonic, while for the latter it is the immanent objective development animated by determinate negation.[31]

2. *Dialectic.* The transformation of the meaning of method grounds the shift in the meaning of dialectic. In Hegel we no longer have, as in Kant, a "dialectic," let alone a transcendental one. Hegel introduces the substantivization of an adjective and speaks of "das wahrhaft Dialektische" (*WL* I, 51, *SL* 34–35) as one element or moment of every concept. In other words, the Dialectic is no longer one section opposed to the Analytic as the logic of illusion is opposed to the logic of truth. The dialectic is no longer simply the seat of antinomies and paralogisms and ideal, that is, the inability on the part of reason proper to know its objects. For Hegel, it constitutes the second moment of development that is internal to each concept: the negative side of determinacy. Hegel writes in the *Science of Logic*: "It is in this dialectic as understood here, and hence in grasping opposites in their unity, or the positive in the negative, that the *speculative* consists" (*WL* I, 52, *SL* 35). As we have seen, the consequence is that it is not only transcendental ideas that are dialectical, or reason insofar as it does not pay attention to the limits of its use: every concept has a negative-dialectical and determinate moment (*WL* I, 217–18, *SL* 158–59). The dialectical moment is the soul of scientific progress (*ENZ* §81). A

necessary mutual relation links method and dialectic, while nothing of the sort holds for Kant.

3. *Limit.* This transformation is tied in turn to that of limit. Both Kant and Hegel follow Aristotle's notion of *peras.*[32] A limit is the principle of determinateness of every thing, and at the same time it is that in which each thing knows its end and is no longer what it is—in Hegel because it has its immanent moment in its other and in negation (the limit is determinate being posited together with its negation, *ENZ* §92 and *WL* I, 137–38, *SL* 99–100), in Kant because it sends us beyond itself. Thus, for both of them, the limit is the negation of the thing. But for Hegel *Grenze* and *Schranke* are equivalent,[33] while Kant separates them neatly: the limit (*Grenze, terminus*) is formal and constitutive, while the boundary (*Schranke, limes*) refers to an indeterminate magnitude that can change size over time. Unlike a boundary, which can be seen, as in scientific progress, as something that scientific research works to push back progressively so as to increase our cognitions, the limit does not change over time and is understood as essential to distinguish parts and whole. It is of decisive importance for the philosopher who must gain consciousness of reason in its internal division and articulation.

In the *Prolegomena*, the limit has a symbolic meaning in an etymological sense. In Greek, *sumbolon* was the half of a severed whole which, if made to match its other half, allowed for the reconstitution of the whole. For this reason, it helped recognize in the broken half its necessary complement (significantly, it is the word used by Aristophanes in the *Symposium* to talk about the circular beings that Zeus cut into halves). Put differently, for Kant, the limit is constitutive of the two heterogeneous realms (the sensible and the supersensible) that are internal to reason, which is assumed as their unity (*Prol.* §57). The question of the limit is crucial to understand reason in its internal division and is fundamental for reason's self-knowledge, because only by focusing on the limit can reason know why it cannot know.

In Hegel, on the contrary, the limit is no longer the essence of reason in its inner division. It is rather the essence of all determinacy and of the finite in general. This is why he says that everything is contradictory, not only some ideas of reason as it is caught in its illegitimate and transcendent use.

4. *Ideas.* Ideas, in turn, have no being in Kant. They are concepts of reason, which depend on its use and their referent.[34] The idea of God can be used in an empty and illusory rational theology, or in an ethicotheology that is quite necessary to reason. And the idea of world is different from the idea of an ideal State, and this latter from the idea of God. In Hegel, instead, the idea is not something other than reason, nor

is it the idea of something. In fact, it is the several ideas that are the determination of the one idea; and the idea is the substance and subject—the process—of its own realization. In Hegel's view of the idea, the problem is not the ambivalence between a legitimate regulative use as opposed to its lack of reality, as in Kant. The problem, if anything, is the necessity for the idea to objectify itself in the soul and body of the finite and be appropriated by subjective spirit in its concrete life until it comes to know itself in us.

The Becoming of Reason

From a Hegelian point of view, all that we have seen so far risks remaining abstract unless it is, as any concept has to be for Hegel, fluidified and seen at work in the multiplicity of its forms—especially in its genesis. In the case at hand, *the becoming of reason* is the issue with which we have not yet dealt. Hegel can proceed by successive identifications, as he does in section 214 of the *Encyclopaedia*,[35] but he can do so because these identifications have been shown in their genesis elsewhere. Reason, that is, the identity of subject and object, constitutes the premise of the logic, but it has been earned painstakingly through a journey that opens up the logic and yet remains external to it, like a vestibule to a systematic building. I am referring to the *Phenomenology of Spirit*, but not only to it. For, as the idea makes itself objective in different concretions, so does reason *become* in different contexts.

Investigating reason, which is the result of a process of mediation, in its becoming means that we must examine how it becomes aware of itself. This implies that it is necessary to respect the essential differences proper to the several contexts in which reason is at stake. In the logic of which it is the premise, reason is idea, the congruence between concept and reality, the original identity of subject and object. But an identity that does not produce itself and is not the process of its own becoming cannot be or know itself as such. And since reason means the overcoming of division, we must consider each time what the division at stake is and how we can make sense of it.

It is noteworthy that in the *Phenomenology of Spirit* reason appears as the result of self-consciousness. Differently stated, the world that consciousness had up to that point of the phenomenological development desired and elaborated is now for reason its own world (*W*3, 178–79, *PhS* 527–28). It has lost its alienness not by virtue of a particular *theoretical* position, but because through desire and work—the shaping of the will—

self-consciousness has progressively transformed and vanquished it. The world has been conquered by reason through desire and work, through the struggle and recognition between self-consciousnesses, as we have seen in chapter 1. As the result of self-consciousness, reason must then be understood as consciousness's certainty of being every reality insofar as it has been penetrated and appropriated by the I, earned with the sweat of one's brow and at the risk of one's own life.

Yet, in the *Phenomenology* reason, despite its self-certainty, is only in search of itself in the world. Reason here still belongs to an individual consciousness that must yet come to terms with the opposition to the object. Reason must first observe nature as a domain of universality, driven by its instinct to design experiments and find laws (*W* 3, 194, *PhS* 152). Here, as later in the chapters entitled Law of the Heart and the Spiritual Animal Kingdom, it is still the individual that realizes the universal. To put it differently, in the *Phenomenology* this reason is not yet knowledge of the truth. It is only as spirit that reason becomes effectively aware of the world as of itself (*W* 3, 324, *PhS* 263). It is only as spirit that reason understands it is the universal realizing itself in actuality through the individual. It is only as spirit that reason knows itself as absolute being and as the only substantial subject. Reason knows itself then as the concept that has the form of the self, the identity of subject and object, as we read in the Absolute Knowledge chapter that preludes to speculative logic.[36]

After the *Phenomenology*, in the courses held at the Nuremberg gymnasium and then in Heidelberg and Berlin, "reason" takes on a wider and more self-sufficient meaning. It is no longer simply the rational knowledge of nature. Since self-consciousness and reason have removed the alienness of the object, reason now represents that position of thought with respect to objectivity that can be characterized as true idealism. It becomes the overcoming of all dualism and subjectivism. It thereby also becomes the overcoming of the difference between certainty and truth, as well as the difference between subject and object which still marked phenomenological reason. Both differences turn out thus to be derivative concepts.[37]

In Hegel's mature system, then, reason is not only the premise to the logic, but also to the Psychology and the free will of the *Encyclopaedia*. For here reason presents itself as the self-conscious rationality of intelligence and will that has overcome the opposition between the concept and reality, between consciousness and object. Hegel also calls it "I," self-knowing truth (§§437–39), "knowledge of the substantial totality that is neither subjective nor objective" (*ENZ* §440). As it has become out of Anthropology and Phenomenology, reason is the premise to spirit as knowledge of the modes of its activity.

In sum, all different senses of reason are tied and connected, and it can be shown how each of them derives from, or generates, or is anyway linked with, the others.

An interconnection of this kind cannot be found in Kant. This is not to say that Kant gives us an abstract or ahistorical view of reason, as if it were a metaphysical hypostasis. For Kant, human reason is always embodied in an I; it is that which is in but cannot be reduced to experience, that which is in but cannot be reduced to body and nature. It is that which is active in our finite existence but cannot be reduced to finitude.

In the brilliant essay "Conjectural Beginning of Human History," Kant shows how reason awakens as it establishes connections and comparisons until it comes to rise above nature, discovering that it is independent and free from it. The subject of the process is not an abstract I or reason as we know it, but human *needs*. Humans realize at some point that they can be at variance with natural impulses and can even invent unnatural desires thanks to their imagination. The first stage of the elevation of humans above nature is refusal (*Weigerung*, "MAM," *Ak* 8, 113), the suspension of natural impulses. In this way, we suspend the voice of nature while still remaining in it. At this level, "reason" is nothing more than the inhibition of desire that discloses our freedom from it. Through successive steps, we get to civilization as well as to practices and customs dictated by reason.

Kant too, then, has a conjecture about the genesis of reason, albeit a "naturalistic" and not a dialectical one. However, in this framework the most important question, from my point of view as well as from Hegel's, is the transition from pre-historical reason to history, from natural reason developing from—though exceeding—desires, needs, and imagination to pure reason asserting itself positively as free and unconditioned, as the source of knowledge and rational actions illustrated by the three *Critiques*. Regarding this transition, it would be generous to say that Kant is reticent. His silence is deafening and reminds us of the analogous silence on the problematic unity of the different senses of freedom in Rousseau, who inspires these pages.

About the inner articulation of reason we cannot have any doubts. For Kant, the relation between faculties is architectonic: the relation is immanence and reciprocal reference, inner distinction within a unity, in a well-defined hierarchy in which distinct functions can be activated and have effects only through collaboration and reciprocal mediation. Hegel is simply wrong when he holds that in Kant faculties are amassed side by side at random and superficially, like a pile without any order or criterion (*ENZ* §182 Z) in which in "the sack of the soul" (*im Seelensack*) we eventually *also* come across reason proper (*VGPh* 3, 351). At its best, architectonically ordered, Kantian reason is legislation and a principle of order in different fields with clear ends. The exercise of its activity and the affirmation of its own freedom are necessary to answer the three questions of the Canon of the *Critique of Pure Reason* (What can I know? What should I do? What may I hope?). As the three questions can be summarized, says Kant, in the further question "What is man?" likewise, I believe, the first two questions find their ultimate goal in the third one, with its reference to the highest good. Reason is therefore the power of generating a priori a legislation of cognitions and actions, but aiming to an end that transcends it. Its finitude is not the historicist or hermeneutic finitude, but the realization that its autarchy, its self-enclosed completeness and autonomy, are insufficient to satisfy its deepest aspiration. In other words, reason is a cause, but among all its possible effects the most desired one, the highest good, is not in its power and essentially escapes it.

Reason as legislation is the cause of a world, whether this is nature as a system of laws or the world of moral action in which reason is causality through freedom. Even inside itself, in the relation between faculties, reason acts through causality. For instance, in self-affection it is clear that there is no *poiêsis* (the production of a real and self-subsistent object), and yet the understanding acts and has effects (*wirkt*) upon imagination and sensibility, and time is schematized according to the causal action of pure concepts on pure intuition. Generally speaking, an active side acts upon a passive side. Kant's pure reason is cause in a twofold sense: efficient—a legislation claiming to be binding for objects outside us—and immanent, that is, it is an activity which unlike the poietic model is immanent in its effects and knows itself in them. In Kant, reason is productive in this sense. In sum, even when Kant does not privilege the procedure and the results of the Transcendental Deduction, the model of his determination is a causal one.

Hegelian reason is not causal in the sense of efficient causality, and at the same time it is *causa sui*, substance that becomes subject.[38] The model for reason cannot be that of a causal action on to a passive side. The model is rather the constitution of a unified and substantial totality that is permeated by reciprocal relations and interaction. From a Hegelian point of view, the problem of Kantian reason is that self-determination remains the non-unified sum of relations falling asunder. Thus, Kant deprives of authority that same reason which he claims to defend (*ENZ* §60). However, the problem—and I believe we must interpret Hegel by going beyond what he writes—is not that the I remains external to its determinations or, as Hegel writes, that "the *how* and *in what respect* of this self-determination of thinking has not yet been demonstrated by Kant" (§60 Z). The problem is that such self-determination has no thickness or substantiality.

CHAPTER 5

Therefore, the criticism that Kant does not deduce the forms of thinking touches upon the epiphenomenon of a more fundamental point. For Hegel, thought is not the production of ever new syntheses, but rather movement and an ongoing power of formation that is intrinsically dialectical, unstable, active. "Das Wirkende" (that which has effects) is not reason, but the concept as such (*ENZ* §163). The difference is relevant, because the action of the concept does not produce effects "as the *cause* with the semblance of producing another, but as what produces its very self" (§163 A).

We need to see in some texts how this happens for Hegel. With regard to Fichte, Hegel writes in the *Difference between Fichte's and Schelling's System of Philosophy* that the identity I = I of transcendental idealism lacks substantiality insofar as "one element is dominant, the other is dominated, the subjective is not identical to the objective, but they stand in a mutual relation of causality" (*Diff.* 50). What matters to philosophy is that every movement forward is a return back to the ground and that the origin is immanent in the conclusions, as we have seen (*WL* I, 70, *SL* 49).

I am not interested in going back to the topic of circularity, which is admittedly a good symptom of what I mean. I would rather like to seal this conclusion in a sort of gnomic way. From a Hegelian point of view, it is the model of the Aristotelian *hexis* as formed power, as the becoming of itself through its own action, that cannot be found in Kant. To put this in a more direct and recognizable though different form, transcendental idealism lacks Spinozan substantiality (against Kant Hegel sometimes uses Spinoza, and sometimes Aristotle). In Kant reason does not have any being, however autarchic and self-determining it is. To be sure, Spinoza argues in an intellectualistic way and his substance misses subjectivity, personality, and the becoming of identity (*WL* I, 291, *WL* II, 195 and 198; *SL* 212, 472, and 474–75; this does not apply to the Aristotelian *hexis*). However, in order to begin to philosophize we must find ourselves on the ground of Spinozism (*VGPh* 3, 165). And this point was already present in Hegel since the Jena writings (the eighth thesis of the 1801 *Habilitation, W* 2, 533). Hegel writes in the "Relation of Skepticism to Philosophy" that by establishing the concept of God as the immanent cause of the world Spinoza has practically *negated the concept of cause and effect* (*W* 2, 229–30).

The Logic of Essence reads: "The passive substance is *preserved* or *posited* by the active . . . ; but, on the other hand, it is the *act of the passive substance* itself to rejoin itself and thus to make itself into what is originary and a *cause.* The *being posited* by another and its own *becoming* are one and the same" (*WL* II, 236, *SL* 502). This is what Kant's reason, with all its autonomy, can never be: the becoming itself of passive substance.

Conclusions

A human being *is* what he *does* and the mendacious vanity
that comforts itself with the consciousness of an inner splen-
didness must be countered with the words of the Gospel: "By
their fruits, you shall know them". . . . Conversely, it is then also
frequently the case that, in judging others who have brought
about something right and respectable, people avail themselves
of the false distinction of inner and outer in order to claim
that what those others have brought about was merely external,
while internally it is about something quite different for them,
such as the satisfaction of their vanity or some other reprehen-
sible passions. This is the sentiment of envy that, itself incapable
of achieving greatness, strives to put down and belittle what is
great. We should remember, by contrast, Goethe's beautiful saying that, in the face of the great superiorities of others, the only
means of saving ourselves is love.
—*ENZ* §140 Z

It is striking that Kant and Hegel, driven by the same goal of understanding reason, employ certain verbs (*vernünfteln* in Kant, *räsonieren* in Hegel)
in order to denounce some of its distorted, defective, when not caricatu-
ral senses. "Reasoning" so understood is not an excess of reason—as if
the spirit of the Enlightenment belatedly found that it had something to
regret—but rather a use of it that is futile or misunderstood as merely
formal or technical. There is also an inner necessity for this sense, which
is what Hobbes already stressed when he said that *ratio* is, starting from
its etymology, calculation. In this way, however, reason is reduced to one
of its functions. Reasoning hovers over the thing but remains external to
it, since it is more engrossed in itself and its own distinctions than in the
thing at stake.

CONCLUSIONS

Kant highlights the fundamental difference between understanding and reason proper as well as between their respective correlates, that is, concepts and ideas. For both Kant and Hegel, understanding and reason are two inseparable functions that stand in a vital mutual relation, to the point that there cannot be any understanding without reason and vice versa. There cannot be any whole without particularity; conversely, without the idea of the absolute, there cannot be any determinate truth. While for both of them the understanding is the rectilinear logic of the finite and reason is the logic of the unconditioned, unlike Kant, Hegel recognizes in the logic of the understanding that dialectic which for Kant is instead typical only of reason in its effort to go beyond experience. Kant, who admittedly made the dialectic a necessary work of reason, separates the logic of truth, the Analytic, from the logic of illusion, the Dialectic. Hegel shows that no determination can claim validity in the fixity it pretends to have. True and false are not opposed to each other, nor are identity and negation.

Kant's system of reason, though far more complex than Hegel concedes, remains nonetheless opposed to the empirical, whereas for Hegel it is the empirical realm philosophically understood that counts as speculative truth. The system must count as the universal that has made itself concrete in the world. Reason cannot be dissociated from what has been classically understood as objective rationality. In Hegel's view understanding and reason are not distinct faculties, but different forms with which thought operates. And thought equally needs affirmative determination and skeptical negation, which sanctions the finitude of all determinacy. What for a subjective understanding is the need to fluidify all fixed determination is from the point of view of the concept what I called the movement of spontaneity and reification.

Reason is not without its relation to actuality; conversely, actuality has different ways to support itself and is thus rational in different ways. It is the truth of actuality that is called into question; conversely, truth has the urge to become actual or it is not truth for Hegel. The logic is not separate from being or nature: properly speaking, it is the logic of actuality. The opposition in the *Lectures on the History of Philosophy* between Platonic ideas, taken as separate and static idealities, and the Aristotelian *energeia*, which is the movement of the concept that becomes real and is therefore called subjectivity (*VGPh* 2, 154), is among the most amazing and eloquent illustrations of this view. The nexus between logic and subjectivity moves to center stage starting with the concept of actuality and Hegel's interpretation of the Greeks.

Categories weave together all forms of thinking and acting; they are thought that is sedimented in nature, tradition, language, and history. However, they are at work implicitly and unconsciously, and the task of

CONCLUSIONS

philosophy consists in making them an object of consideration for themselves. Philosophy and speculative logic understand what is spontaneously at work in the world as well as in us. For this reason, the pervasive tendency on the part of philosophy (from logic to analytic philosophy and neo-pragmatism)—as well as of some interpretations of Hegel's philosophy—in the last decades, namely the reduction of reason to discursive knowledge, is incompatible with Hegel. The reduction of reason to reason-giving practices of justification and inference in which rationality only comes down to the normative level of rules and concepts leaves aside all that for Hegel must actually be understood in its logical web: the sensible, the unconscious, the body, nature. If norms, besides being valid *of* something, must count *for* someone who appropriates them discerningly, this reduction is a presupposition that makes the intimate link between discursivity and first-person perspective, between knowledge and self-consciousness, an opaque core that is neither investigated nor understood.

The dissociation of rationality from objective logos is the core of every assimilation of Hegel's philosophy to anthropology and human history, which not by chance, ever since Kojève, concentrates on the *Phenomenology of Spirit* at the expense of the *Science of Logic* and the *Encyclopaedia*. But this formalism is a dead end. The search for a post-metaphysical Hegel leads at best to what the second syllogism at the end of the *Encyclopaedia* describes thus: "Science appears as a subjective *cognition*, whose aim is freedom and which is itself the way to produce its freedom" (*ENZ* §576).

The semantic reconceptualization of our language, the plurivocity of the names of all fundamental philosophical concepts, is essential to understand its dialectic. Meanings shift, not because we intend them differently in turn in our reflection, but because each identity is in itself dialectical, and every determinacy must be understood as one of the ways in which reason makes itself world. Thus we come back to the substance that is equally subject, insofar as it is self-development.

As we have seen, we need to invert our discourse and say that each determinate concept is the self-determination of thought. I would like to conclude by going back to this point. Saying, for instance, that "truth becomes objective in Democritus or Bacon," or that "the concept gives itself a determinate form in the laws of thermodynamics" sounds estranging because it leads us to assume some truth, concept, or idea, like some mysterious absolute entities that, at some point and without any understanding of how and why, take on a finite shape. This is, as we have seen, the position I have dubbed realist. However, it seems to me that there would be hardly any objections if one said that beauty is expressed differently in Monteverdi or Debussy. The beautiful is not an archetype separate from the world, and it can only exist in its diverse manifestations,

CONCLUSIONS

whether it is taken as natural beauty or as the beauty of Praxiteles's and Donatello's sculptures. Thus, aesthetics wonders about the beautiful—in itself, not in Praxiteles or Donatello—without anyone batting an eye over the ghost of dogmatic metaphysics or onto-theology. Like beauty, truth exists in its particular forms alone, and if we seek to understand it, we must take it as a movement of development. This is why Hegel speaks of truth as the subject that makes itself finite in determinate forms, and of truth as the universal that abides in the particulars that are its way of realizing itself. Universality would be empty without particulars. At the same time, putting the universal and the particulars on the same level would be as if "someone were to ask for fruit and then rejected cherries, pears, and grapes simply because they are cherries, pears, and grapes, but *not* fruit" (*ENZ* §13 A).

There cannot be any view of the whole other than as an immanent movement. Even the most infamous examples of a dialectic of this type, such as the development bud-flower-fruit in the preface to the *Phenomenology* (I remind the reader that this is an analogy which, like others in Hegel, is introduced by the expression "one might say": *W* 3, 12, *PhS* 2), show something decisive. If I want to talk about the pear tree, I mean the whole, but the whole can be indicated only through the form of one of its moments. When I let one moment count, I am aware that it applies at the expense of others; when I describe a finite moment, I contradict other ways of describing the pear tree (it is potentially contained in a tiny bud, and is deployed in wide foliage and thriving blossoms; it is bare, and in bloom, etc.). Every moment rules out other possibilities and can exist as successive in time with respect to another only because the other moment existed as its condition. The condition now removed is not thereby a nothing but is the negation of one state; and every state is the present of a past that survives in it; the fruit is the posthumous life of the flower. The development is the process of becoming something other than itself, wherein each moment is equally necessary and functional to the organic unity. The present must be understood in its thickness as the co-presence of negated possibilities, and as the sign of all moments of the whole.

If each of the forms we consider is the negation of an antecedent moment, then, conversely, in each positive form we can find the vanished moment that has become internal to that form. What has been sublated survives unnoticed and yet is active in what is. It is up to us to consider the pear tree here and now as a contradiction with respect to another description or as the development of what it is, as Hegel says (*W* 3, 12, *PhS* 2). Yet, if we have to see something as a negation, then every falsity (the assertion of the moment that is no longer there which makes us say: "the pear tree is not the bud") is a mode of the true. Negation implies that

CONCLUSIONS

the sublated moment is lowered to virtuality, and at the same time raised to a necessary moment of the whole. This entails the *recognition* of the negative in the identical. Negativity abides as a virtuality that does not immediately appear in the present, but must be affirmed in the understanding of the whole. Negativity is the vanished moment which no longer appears. The whole cannot do without the moment that does not appear—the negated, the unconscious—and yet is internal to it. As is clear, the identification of rationality with consciousness is for Hegel the most pernicious form of one-sidedness. This virtual and inner permanence—this immanence—of the negated moment in being is the dialectic.

In my opinion, Hegel's view of action is another excellent illustration of this relation between actuality and possibility, of this virtuality without which actuality is flattened to a positive given, at which we are often content to halt. Hegel says that action is the resolution to finitude (*GPhR* §13 A). Before I act, an open series of possibilities is available to me. Acting means choosing, and choosing amounts to favoring one possibility, which ends up eliminating all the others. Being able to do so is a sign of strength of character (and one of the most common neuroses is the inability to decide, when one anticipates the annihilation of possibilities and fearfully steers clear of the destruction that choice implies). Acting means denying possibilities, and the beautiful soul is repelled by this violent act. What applied to the pear tree applies to action, too: it is an actualization that, to be fully understood, must lead back to its excluded possibilities.

When Hegel praises the strength of the understanding which as the force of the negative holds "fast to what is dead" (*W* 3, 36, *PhS* 19), he does not have in mind an event like natural death. The negative is an independent part and not the member of an organic unity because it has been isolated from the whole—it has been killed—by the understanding. Hegel means that it takes great resoluteness to separate and hold fast to the negative. It requires a break. But only such a power holding fast to the separate can then comprehend what vanishes, thereby "converting [the negative] into being" (*W* 3, 36, *PhS* 19). Only in this way does thought remain faithful to itself (*ENZ* §11).

As we can see, Hegel's provocation that the "blossom refutes the bud" can be ridiculed only by those who have already decided that negation is a syntactical and linguistic function external to things—only by those who maintain that dialectic is a discourse and not an objective force. Rationality is in the world, not in our sciences alone.

Notes

Introduction

1. T. W. Adorno, *Negative Dialectics*, trans. E. B. Ashton (London, 2004), 233. Should we decide to take seriously Adorno's remark and read the lied, the paradoxical character of Adorno's misinterpretation would stand out. It is not conceivable that the musicologist Adorno could ignore the lied's sarcastic element and its close. It is the prisoner in a tower who rejoices that his thoughts sweep away bars and walls ("Denn meine Gedanken zerreissen die Schranken / und Mauern entzwei, die Gedanken sind frei"). The new Epictetus in chains who laughs and sings the freedom of his thoughts is the loser who is bitterly aware of the renunciation caused by his captivity, not the confident representative of the modern bourgeois Enlightenment self-consciousness.

2. Again regarding the line "No person can know them" (*kein Mensch kann sie wissen*), Adorno, who wrote in *Minima Moralia* that "true thoughts are those alone which do not understand themselves" ("Wahr sind nur die Gedanken, die sich selber nicht verstehen," aphorism 122, trans. E. F. N. Jephcott [London, 2005], 192, recalled in *Negative Dialectics*, 48), could have shown more sensitivity.

3. As we will see in the following, it is not in itself but when it is "turned against reason" that "this understanding behaves in the manner of *ordinary common sense*, giving credence to the latter's view that truth rests on sensuous reality, that thoughts are *only* thoughts" (*WL* I, 38, *SL* 25).

4. *WL* I, 45, *SL* 30. In Hegel's history of philosophy, this principle mirrors the belief that it is possible to reduce every determinate philosophy to a unitary guiding principle which Hegel calls "the truth" of that particular philosophy, that is, its logical-metaphysical polar star. In my view, besides sacrificing plurality to unity and making irreducible and often recalcitrant elements homogeneous, this line of thought creates serious problems for Hegel when it comes to the political or moral philosophy of past thinkers. For example, if each philosophy is reducible to one logical principle, then Rousseau's thought, which more problematically than others can be condensed into a unitary logic, becomes immediately a compressed mention in Hegel's discussion and is for all practical purposes irrelevant for his picture of the philosophy of the second half of the eighteenth century. Other examples are the following: for Hegel as for Kant, Hume is the author of the manifesto of modern epistemological skepticism, the *Treatise of Human Nature*, not the naturalist of history and human nature that he aspired to be in his various works. For Hegel, Plato's main principle is the destruction of the particular,

NOTES TO PAGES 13–15

both in his dialectic and his political philosophy. Hobbes's fundamental idea is atomism. In all this it is difficult to see how, and even whether, a logical principle can rule or animate a political philosophy and generate further connections and fruitful arguments. On this problem, let me refer to my works *Hegel and Aristotle* (Cambridge, 2001), 34–37; and "Hegels Idee einer Geschichte der Philosophie und Aristoteles," in *Die modernen Väter der Antike*, ed. A. M. Baertschi and C. G. King (Berlin, 2009), 276–302, esp. 291–92.

5. "Similarly, the concept is also not to be considered here as the act of the self-conscious understanding, not as *subjective understanding*, but as the concept in and for itself which constitutes a *stage* of *nature* as well as of *spirit*. Life, or organic nature, is the stage of nature where the concept comes on the scene, but as a *blind concept that does not comprehend itself, that is, is not thought* [my emphasis]; only as self-aware and as thought does it belong to spirit. Its logical form, however, is independent of such shapes, whether unspiritual or spiritual" (*WL* II, 257, *SL* 517).

6. If metaphysics refers to a foundationalist attitude wherein the principle is other than what is founded, then Hegel is obviously not a metaphysician. Otherwise, I would like to recall what for Hegel goes without saying. "Logic thus coincides with *metaphysics*, i.e., the science of *things* captured in *thoughts* that have counted as expressing *the essentialities of things*" (*ENZ* §24). The older metaphysics "had in this respect a higher concept of thinking than now passes as the accepted opinion. For it presupposed as its principle that only what is known of things and in things by thought is really true in them. . . . This metaphysics thus held that thinking and the determination of thinking are not something alien to the subject matters, but are rather their essence" (*WL* I, 38, *SL* 25). The Enlightenment which no longer finds vital the interest in metaphysics displays "the singular spectacle of a cultivated people without metaphysics—like a temple richly ornamented in other respects but without a holy of holies" (*WL* I, 14, *SL* 8). The reason is plain: metaphysics is the diamond net of concepts that weave together everything we do, such that "every cultured consciousness has its metaphysics, its instinctive way of thinking. This is the absolute power within us, and we shall only master it if we make it the object of our knowledge" (*ENZ* §246 Z). If so, then metaphysics is inescapably present in us and we can either comprehend it (thereby mastering it, as in this quote), or undergo it without knowing it. This is precisely what happens to empiricism, which uses logical and metaphysical categories (matter, force, one, universal, infinite, etc.) but fails to notice that "in so doing it itself contains and pursues metaphysics and . . . uses those categories and their relationships in a completely uncritical and unconscious fashion" (*ENZ* 38 A). The idea that you can presume to steer clear of metaphysics is a delusion: "Indeed only the animals are pure, unadulterated physicists, since they do not think, whereas a human being as a thinking being is a born metaphysician. The only thing that matters, therefore, is whether the metaphysics one applies is of the right kind" (*ENZ* §98 Z 1).

7. What I said with regard to Hegel as a philosopher is well expressed from the reader's point of view in Adorno's description: "No one can read any more out of Hegel than he puts in. The process of understanding is a progressive self-correcting of such projections through comparison with the text. The content itself contains, as a law of its form, the expectation of productive imagination on

NOTES TO PAGES 15-22

the part of the one reading" (T. W. Adorno, *Drei Studien zu Hegel* [Frankfurt am Main, 1963]; translated into English by S. Weber Nicholsen as *Hegel: Three Studies* [Cambridge, Mass., 1993], 139).

8. See K. Rosenkranz, *Hegels Leben* (Berlin, 1844; Darmstadt, 1977), 398: "Hegel is certainly a rare and profound mind, but I cannot understand how such a philosophy can have deep roots. . . . It is as if the language and the author were not interpenetrated. This might be owing to a great lack in imagination."

9. *ENZ* §396 Z; *W* 10, 80. In this regard, the main difference between the moderns and Hegel lies in the different concept of "bringing back to origin." For the former, genesis is fundamentally material, whereas for Hegel it is the genesis in the concept. "The procedure involved in the formation and preliminaries of a science is not the same as the science itself, however, for in this latter case it is no longer experience, but rather the necessity of the Notion, which must emerge as the foundation" (*ENZ* §246 A). In the *Elements of the Philosophy of Right,* Hegel criticizes the explanation of laws which draws exclusive attention to historical genesis and to the justification of material circumstances without taking into account the essential, the concept of the thing: "the external appearance is put in place of the thing [*Sache*] itself" (*GPR* §3 A).

10. Ferrarin, *Hegel and Aristotle.*

11. Let us not underestimate the importance of analogies, as if they were inadequate expedients compared to the direct characterization of the thing itself. An analogy (as Kant writes in the *Critique of Judgment* §59) is not something vague and inaccurate, but rather a formal equivalence between relations made up by two pairs of terms. In the analogies he uses to talk about reason, Kant aims to introduce the subject matter starting from what is most familiar, so that after the affinities the differences stand out by contrast. This enables him to better define the status and function of reason. Many of the greatest philosophers in our tradition have approached the object of their investigations by proposing analogies in a similar fashion. Aristotle introduces the intellect in *De Anima* III 4 by analogy with perception, and the active intellect in III 5 by analogy with nature.

12. A. Ferrarin, *The Powers of Pure Reason: Kant and the Idea of Cosmic Philosophy* (Chicago, 2015).

13. We may think that this tension is the child of the modern concept of reason since Descartes. In the *Regulae ad directionem ingenii,* Descartes seems to anticipate Kant when he writes that the mind needs discipline and has to be ruled methodically. And yet "the human mind possesses something, I know not what, of the divine, in which the first seeds of useful thoughts have been sown in such a way that, however neglected and stifled by interfering studies, they often yield spontaneous fruits" (Regula IV, AT 10, 87). Actually, the differences between Descartes on the one hand and Kant and Hegel on the other are fundamental, especially with regard to the notion of reason. Descartes aims to eliminate every opinion and to discriminate between truth and error (whereby verisimilitude is equated to falsehood). For Descartes, only the rectilinear movement of a thought built on firm foundations is true (the second maxim in the third part of the *Discourse on Method* insists on firmness and resoluteness, such that—when lost in a forest—the only way not to wander vainly in a circle is to choose to march straight on until we get to any destination whatever). In Kantian and Hegelian terms, this

NOTES TO PAGES 26–27

resoluteness to hold fast to determinacy is the understanding's way. By contrast, Kant and Hegel define the understanding by reference to and difference from reason: neither can subsist without the other. Between straightness and circularity there is no strict opposition. Falsehood is not the subjective error that one can correct once and for all with discipline and vigilant conduct, for it is unavoidable and necessary. This applies strongly to Hegel, for whom falsehood cannot be opposed to truth like oil to water, but rather the false represents the one-sidedness of the true. It also applies partly to Kant, for whom illusion is necessary to the thought of the unconditioned, except that Kant considers his critical philosophy to be the remedy for reason's errors.

Chapter 1

1. We could conjecture that Freud and Husserl meet on the ground prepared by their common teacher Brentano. After all, they attended his lectures precisely in those years in which Brentano adopted the Aristotelian thesis according to which self-consciousness is not original, but rather concomitant (*en parergôi*, as Aristotle writes in *Metaphysics*, Lambda 9, 1074b 35) with the intentional consciousness of its object. However, the theory of inner consciousness as well as of the unity of the acts of presentation developed in the *Psychology from an Empirical Point of View* seems to me hardly compatible with the unconscious in Freud and Husserl. On the relationship between Brentano and Freud, I share Jones's skepticism (E. Jones, *Life and Work of Sigmund Freud*, vol. 1 [New York, 1953], 55–56).

2. When Freud writes that "the ego comes up against limits to its power in its own house, the mind," he imagines that psychoanalysis "can speak thus to the ego: "You feel sure that you are informed of all that goes on in your mind if it is of any importance at all. . . . Indeed, you go so far as to regard what is *mental* as identical with what is *conscious*—that is, with what is known to you in spite of the most obvious evidence that a great deal more must constantly be going on in your mind than can be known to your consciousness. . . . You behave like an absolute ruler who is content with the information supplied him by his highest officials and never goes among the people to hear their voice." See Freud, "A Difficulty in the Path of Psycho-Analysis" (1917), in *Gesammelte Werke*, vol. 12 (London, 1940–52), 3–12; translated by J. Strachey in *The Complete Psychological Works of Sigmund Freud, Volume 17 (1917–1919): An Infantile Neurosis and Other Works*, edited by Strachey in collaboration with A. Freud (London, 1999), 137–44.

3. For a development of this thesis, see my "Hegel and Husserl on the Emergence of the I Out of Subjectivity," *Hegel Bulletin* 75 (2017): 7–23.

4. §387 Z; *W* 10, 41. I quote a bit more extensively the English translation (27): "Out of this immediate oneness with its naturalness, soul enters into opposition and conflict with it (the states of derangement and somnambulism belong here). The outcome of this conflict [*Diesem Kampfe*] is the triumph of the soul over its bodiliness, the process of reducing, and the accomplished reduction, of this bodiliness to a sign, to the portrayal of the soul."

NOTES TO PAGES 30–33

5. *ENZ* §415 A (trans. corrected). It has not always been so in Hegel. If this book were not a theoretical analysis that focuses on the conceptual positions of the mature Hegel but a historical reconstruction aspiring to completeness, then it should start with the Kantian I, and soon move to Fichte's transformations of the I-think and to the post-Kantian debate on thinking and the I. Here such debate is inevitably bound to remain in the background. From the point of view of the relationship between the I and Spinozism, an analysis of the reactions to Fichte and to Schelling's *Vom Ich* (1795) would be particularly important. There is nothing more instructive than reading the correspondences of the year 1795 between those involved in such a debate. Hölderlin, who attended Fichte's lectures in Jena, writes to Hegel on January 26, 1795 (Hoff I, 19–20) that the absolute Fichtean I is like Spinoza's substance, since it contains every reality. In his letter to Hegel of February 4, 1795 (Hoff I, 22), Schelling contrasts the dogmatism that begins with the non-I or absolute object and leads to Spinoza's system with the critical philosophy that starts from the absolute I in its purity and freedom and leads to the Kantian system. The same positions are voiced in Schelling's printed work (*Vom Ich als Prinzip der Philosophie*, in *Sämmtliche Werke*, vol. 1 [Stuttgart and Augsburg, 1856–61, rpt. Darmstadt, 1967], 149–244, §4, §10, §12n). In his letter to Reinhold of July 2, 1795, Fichte claims that he is more than happy with that reading ("Above all, I like his way of looking at Spinoza: from his system mine can be explained in the best way"; *Gesamtsausgabe der Bayerischen Akademie der Wissenschaften*, ed. R. Lauth and H. Jacob, vol. 3, no. 2 [Stuttgart, 1962], 347–48). In his letter of August 30, 1795, Hegel, having expressed his gratitude and friendship to Schelling who had sent him his writings, raises very quickly a substantial criticism. Bestowing on the ego the attribute of the one substance conflates the absolute and the empirical I. The concept of substance, being correlative to that of accident, does not apply to the absolute I but only to the empirical I (Hoff I, 29–33). All these elements, which are indispensable to track the post-Kantian genesis of Idealism during a crucial phase of its evolution, reflect genuine concerns which, however, were successively overcome and are absent in the mature positions of both Hegel and Schelling. For this reason, besides the fact that Hegel's position in such a debate is not explicitly expressed and can only be gleaned from heterogeneous references, the value of these considerations is historical but not systematic, and I do not avail myself of them for this book.

6. Karl Marx, *Grundrisse der Kritik der politischen Ökonomie* (Berlin, 1953), translated into English by M. Nicolaus as *Grundrisse: Foundations of the Critique of Political Economy (Rough Draft)* (London, 1973), 83 (Marx quotes the *zôon politikon* on page 84).

7. With the words of the *Phenomenology of Spirit*, "we already have before us the notion of *spirit*. What still lies ahead for consciousness is the experience of what spirit is—this absolute substance which is the unity of the different independent self-consciousnesses which, in their opposition, enjoy perfect freedom and independence: 'I' that is 'We' and 'We' that is 'I'" (*W* 3, 145, *PhS* 110–77).

8. L. Siep, *Anerkennung als Prinzip der praktischen Philosophie* (Munich, 1979); I. Testa, *La natura del riconoscimento: Riconoscimento naturale e ontologia sociale in Hegel (1801–1806)* (Milan, 2010).

NOTES TO PAGES 33-39

9. Siep, *Anerkennung*, 121–31.

10. I have discussed this and other differences between Hegel's various Phenomenologies in my commentary on the Philosophy of Subjective Spirit in *Hegel and Aristotle*, 284 ff.

11. Among others, Sartre ascribes—mistakenly, in my view—this position to Hegel (*L'Être et le néant: Essai d'ontologie phénoménologique* [Paris, 1943]; translated into English by H. E. Barnes as *Being and Nothingness* [New York, 1966], 290–92).

12. Adrian Peperzak writes: "The concrete identity of the I with itself is the ground (or essence or truth) of the mutual recognition that is the appearance of that ground" (*Modern Freedom* [Dordrecht, 2001], 156).

13. At the end of the 1970s, Ernst Tugendhat criticized Dieter Henrich's theory of self-consciousness for being modeled upon the subject-object relation. As an alternative, Tugendhat proposed a theory based on the Wittgensteinian use of the pronoun I (*Selbsbewusstein und Selbstbestimmung: Sprachanalytische Interpretationen* [Frankfurt am Main, 1979]). Henrich replied that the semantic explanation of the I is circular, because the I cannot say "I" unless it assumes an elementary form of self-knowledge or self-acquaintance (*Vertrautheit mit sich*). We do not achieve either self-consciousness or the I as a subject from the reflexive use of the personal pronoun. Self-consciousness cannot be derived or objectively demonstrated (see "Noch einmail in Zirkeln: Eine Kritik von Ernst Tugendhats Erklärung von Selbstbewusstein," in *Mensch und Moderne*, ed. C. Bellut and V. Müller-Scholl [Würzburg, 1989], 93–132). Henrich did not have Hegel in mind when he replied to Tugendhat, who in turn provocatively entitled the last part of his book "Clean Sweep of Hegel!" ("Kehraus mit Hegel!"). See also my discussion in "Autocoscienza, riferimento dell'io e conoscenza di sé," *Teoria* 12 (1992): 111–52.

14. R. Brandom, "The Structure of Desire and Recognition: Self-Consciousness and Self-Constitution," in *Von der Logik zur Sprache*, ed. R. Bubner and G. Hindrichs, Stuttgart Hegel-Kongress 2005 (Stuttgart, 2007), 426–49 (quote at 435). I have discussed Brandom's arguments in my essay "What Must We Recognize? Brandom's Kant and Hegel," *Verifiche* 41, nos. 1–3 (2012): 203–19.

15. Brandom, "The Structure of Desire," 447.

16. Ibid., 435.

17. See Robert Pippin, *Hegel's Practical Philosophy* (Cambridge, 2008), 221: "A social status exists by being taken to exist by members of some community. A priest, a knight, a statesman, a citizen, are not, that is, natural kinds. One exists as such a kind by being treated as one, according to the rules of the community, reciprocally available to all, . . . being an individual already presupposes a complex recognitional status." I agree with what McDowell writes: the status of a rational agent can be conferred, but it does not depend on its being conferred (*Having the World in View: Essays on Kant, Hegel, and Sellars* [Cambridge, Mass., 2009], 171).

18. Robert Pippin, *Hegel on Self-Consciousness* (Princeton, 2011), vii.

19. "Hegel's presentation is motivated by the internal inadequacies of the Kantian notion of apperception *in general*" (Pippin, *Hegel on Self-Consciousness*, 16n.). Testa comes to an analogous conclusion, too. See *La natura del riconoscimento*, 38, 65.

NOTES TO PAGES 40–45

20. "The whole expanse of the sensuous world is preserved for it" (*W* 3, 138, *PhS* 105). The singularity of opinion, the universality of perception, and the inner truth of the understanding (the first three chapters of the section "Consciousness") are no longer freestanding essences, but rather moments of self-consciousness.

21. "This unity must become essential to self-consciousness; i.e., self-consciousness is *desire [Begierde]* in general" (*W* 3, 138, *PhS* 105).

22. H.-G. Gadamer, *Hegels Dialektik* (Tübingen, 1971), translated into English by P. C. Smith as *Hegel's Dialectic* (New Haven, Conn., 1976), 62 ff.

23. Personally, however, I believe it would be even more interesting to imagine alternative accounts, and a good example of this is, in my opinion, the tradition to which Pascal refers when he takes *amour-propre* as a result. According to Pascal, self-love is the result of the split of an original innocence, as well as the choice to silence the love for God so as to isolate and contrast it to self-love which, precisely by virtue of this choice, is not original and natural as in Spinoza and Hobbes. For Pascal, who adopts the neologism "amour propre" coined by La Rochefoucauld, desire is certainly marked by lack, but this is due to the mutilation of the original undivided unity that enabled Adam before the fall to love himself without sin. After the fall, self-love loses its innocence and becomes immoderate and arrogant in that it competes with the love for God. This is the reason why Pascal hates the I ("le moi est haïssable"). Pascal admits his debt to the tradition initiated by Saint Paul and Augustine (*Oeuvres complètes*, vol. 2 [Paris, 1998], 20; see I. Gaspari, "Étude des passions et conscience de soi chez Spinoza et Pascal," Ph.D. diss., Pisa-Paris, 2015).

24. See S. H. Rosen, *G. W. F. Hegel: An Introduction to the Science of Wisdom* (New Haven, Conn., 1974), 30.

25. For Lacan, desire makes self-consciousness opaque to itself, whereas self-consciousness would like to transform desire into logos and self-transparent reflexivity. For this as well as for the French readings of recognition and the struggle of self-consciousnesses inspired by Kojève, see J. Butler, *Subjects of Desire* (New York, 1999), 175–238.

26. For the history of this relationship between desire and reason, as well as for the role of reason in Kant, which is not driven by passions but finds in its own universal form the motivation to actualize itself in the world, see my *The Powers of Pure Reason*, 128 ff.

27. He "posits himself as a negative in the permanent order of things, and thereby becomes *for himself*, someone existing on his own account" (*W* 3, 154, *PhS* 118).

28. *W* 3, 153–54, *PhS* 117–18, 195. See Peperzak, *Modern Freedom*, 155.

29. Rosen, *Hegel*, 163, italics mine.

30. "From this equality of ability ariseth equality of hope in the attaining of our ends. And therefore, if any two men desire the same thing, which nevertheless they cannot both enjoy, they become enemies; and in the way to their end, which is principally their own conservation, and sometimes their delectation only, endeavour to destroy or subdue one another" (Thomas Hobbes, *Leviathan*, ed. E. Curley [Indianapolis, Ind., 1994], bk. 1, chap. 13, 75).

NOTES TO PAGES 45–50

31. Hobbes, *Leviathan*, bk. 1, chap. 6, 32.

32. See J. Taminiaux, *Dialectic and Difference* (Atlantic Highlands, N.J., 1985), 24.

33. For Hobbes, human beings obey *laws of nature*. Thus they are not *without a nature proper* as in the humanistic tradition from Pico's *Orazione* and Bacon's Prometheus, according to which they can become whatever they make of themselves. For these themes in Hobbes, see my book *Artificio, desiderio, considerazione di sé: Hobbes e i fondamenti antropologici della politica*, 2nd ed. (Pisa, [2001], 2015).

34. This is true of the 1807 self-consciousness, but less so of the *Encyclopaedia* recognitive self-consciousness. There Hegel does mention a concern for the future ("The form of universality thus arising in satisfying the want creates a *permanent* means and a provision which takes care for and secures the future," §434), but the whole context of the deduction of self-consciousness changes. (I wish to thank Heikki Ikäheimo for reminding me of the §434 passage.) The differences between the 1807 *Phenomenology* and the parallel treatment of this theme in the *Encyclopaedia* are fairly obvious. Here (§433) the relation is unequal in that by preferring life the bondsman "gives up his claim to recognition." By working for the lord, which means by silencing his natural being, he forms his individual will. Here the beginning of wisdom is still the fear of the lord (whose will instead remains immediate and is reflected back to him in his own image of the slave), but at the same time it means more clearly the transformation of the bondsman's appetites. This self-externalization, the bondsman's great conquest, is the freedom from his natural being through which his self-consciousness becomes (§§435–36) without further ado universal self-consciousness. In both versions, through the pages on the struggle for recognition we have certainly attained to freedom (which explains why Hegel leaves the struggle in its main gist roughly unaltered from 1807 to 1827, whether it leads to stoicism or to universal self-consciousness as the premise for spirit), but in the new form that inequality has taken, that is, the conquest made possible by the bondsman's work. In §433 Hegel goes to the point of mentioning the "external or phenomenal commencement of states" through force which had no role to play in the 1807 *Phenomenology* (or in his argument in §433 or beyond, anyway).

35. The title of §430 in the Philosophy of Subjective Spirit, "Das anerkennende Selbstbewusstsein," is therefore proleptic for the aims of Hegel's deduction there.

36. "But for recognition proper the moment is lacking that what the lord does to the other he also does to himself, and what the bondsman does to himself he should also do to the other. The outcome is a recognition that is one-sided and unequal" (*W* 3, 152, *PhS* 116).

37. For a discussion, see Butler, *Subjects of Desire*, 81 ff.

38. A brilliant and concise exposition of the *Phenomenology* is S. Houlgate's *Hegel's "Phenomenology of Spirit"* (London, 2013).

39. It is noteworthy that reason in the *Phenomenology* designates a stage that is inferior to spirit and which therefore has a narrower meaning compared to the later works, in which reason is synonymous with idea. See chapter 5 in this volume.

Chapter 2

1. Among the most recent contributions after W. Jaeschke, "Objektives Denken: Philosophiehistorische Erwägungen zur Konzeption und zur Aktualität der spekulativen Logik," *Independent Journal of Philosophy* 3 (1979): 23–37, and C. Halbig, *Objektives Denken: Erkenntnistheorie und Philosophy of Mind in Hegels System* (Stuttgart, 2002), are F. Cirulli's and S. Houlgate's essays in *La realtà del pensiero,* ed. A. Ferrarin (Pisa, 2007); and the articles by L. Illetterati, C. Halbig, P. Cesaroni, D. De Pretto, S. Furlani, P. Livieri, G. Mendola, F. Perelda, B. Santini, and S. Soresi in L. Illetterati, ed., *L'oggettività del pensiero: La filosofia di Hegel fra idealismo, anti-idealismo e realismo, Verifiche* 36, nos. 1–4 (2007). I also recommend two excellent texts: S. Soresi, *Il soggetto del pensiero: Modi e articolazioni della nozione di pensiero in Hegel* (Trent, 2012); and F. Orsini's brilliant "Il problema dell'ontologia nella Scienza della logica di Hegel," Ph.D diss., Padua, 2014.

2. Ernst Bloch expresses well this aspect when he writes that "here [in the logic], thinking wants to be all that is worthy of being" (*Subjekt-Objekt: Erläuterungen zu Hegel* [Berlin, 1949; Frankfurt am Main, 1962], 155).

3. *WL* I, 29, *SL* 19; *ENZ* §21, §24. *Die Sache selbst* is usually translated as "the thing itself."

4. The vocabulary of reality and actuality is plurivocal because this concept has "different, even opposite determinations" (*WL* I, 119–21, *SL* 85–88). Existence (*Existenz,* translated as "concrete existence" by De Giovanni, as "existence" by Miller) is a category that follows being and determinate being and is the achieved satisfaction of all conditions (at that point, the thing "comes forth into existence," *WL* II, 122, *SL* 417). Actuality proper (*Wirklichkeit*) is the "unity of essence and concrete existence" (*WL* II, 186, *SL* 465). And the actual is not still and fixed, as something sensible and externally given, but rather coincides with what can have effects (*wirken*), such that the definition of actuality is self-movement, the production of effects in a relation to itself (*WL* II, p, 208, *SL* 482). Thus, actuality must be understood as the substance that is cause (*WL* II, 223, *SL* 493). If so, it is irrelevant and accidental that in nature there are 137 species of veronica and 67 species of parrots (*WL* II, 375, *SL* 605); strictly speaking, this is *unreal.* Indeed, in the fuller sense, what counts as real is such only "to the extent that it has the idea in it and expresses it" (*WL* II, 464, *SL* 671; reality and actuality are here as often elsewhere interchangeable). It follows that in Hegel's vocabulary "reality" is equivalent, if anything, to truth (*WL* II, 465, *SL* 672). Hegel's analysis becomes interesting precisely at this point, that is, in regard to his theory—itself counterintuitive and anti-subjectivist—of truth as adequation between the concept and its actualization (*WL* II, 571–78, *SL* 712–13).

5. *WL* I, 44, *SL* 29. Perhaps Hegel's students showed some resistance to this conception of objective thought. Perhaps this difference between thinking and consciousness was obscure to them, and they may have pressed Hegel to shed more light on it. The fact is that some of the most insightful and interesting remarks among the oral additions to the Berlin lectures concern this point. In his comment on §24, Hegel says: "When it is said that thought as objective thought constitutes the core of the world, it may seem as if, by this, consciousness is sup-

NOTES TO PAGES 57-61

posed to be attributed to natural things. We feel a certain resistance to construing the inner activity of things as thinking. We would therefore have to speak of nature as the system of unconscious thoughts, a 'petrified intelligence,' as Schelling puts it. Instead of using the expression *thoughts*, it would thus be better to speak of *thought-determinations*."

6. The same applies to the 1831 lecture notes on logic (see *Logik 1831*, 5–8, 18–20; *LL* 3–5, 15–16).

7. *W* 12, 23 ff. The French Revolution makes Anaxagoras's *nous* come true because "only then man comes to know that thought must rule spiritual reality" (*W* 12, 529).

8. Hegel states this explicitly in *ENZ* §24 Z I, as well as in his 1831 lectures when he comments on Anaxagoras: "If one says 'God by His wisdom rules the world,' God is thereby in the world, not outside it" (*Logik 1831*, 20, *LL* 16).

9. "There cannot be two reasons and two spirits, a divine and a human reason that would be absolutely different from one another in their core and in the modes of its activity" (*VPhR* 43).

10. In the Hegelian example, the sun is determined by its concept, yet its concept is not for the sun, but only for us who think of it (*WL* II, 555, *SL* 740). In other similar passages, the sun and the animal *are* their concept, but they do not *have* it (*VPhR* 220; *ENZ* §24 Z 1). In other words, their concept is their truth and substance, except that they do not know it as a concept. The concept does not acquire a subsistent and known reality: it only lives as the soul of the thing. Paradoxically, in this example the soul and the animal are their concept subjectively but not objectively, whereas from another point of view it would have been more reasonable to consider them as examples of objective and subjective logic respectively.

11. In subjective thinking, which Hegel also calls the formal concept, we have an externality that "is manifested in the fixed being of its determinations that makes them come up each by itself, isolated and qualitative, and each only externally referred to the other. But the identity of the concept . . . sets them in dialectical movement, and through this movement their singleness is sublated and with it also the separation of the concept from the subject matter, and what emerges as their truth is the totality which is the objective concept" (*WL* II, 271, *SL* 527).

12. "What are also called concepts and, to be sure, determinate concepts, e.g., human being, house, animal, and so forth, are simple determinations and abstract representations, abstractions that, taking only the factor of universality from the concept while omitting the particularity and individuality, are thus not developed in themselves and accordingly abstract precisely from the concept" (*ENZ* §164).

13. Consider Reflexion 945 in *Ak* 15/I, 419. The idea is "Ganz im Gantzen und Ganz in iedem Theil." For a commentary, see Ferrarin, *The Powers of Pure Reason*, 43 ff.

14. "In the case of a judgment one usually thinks first of the *self-sufficiency* of the extremes, subject and predicate, such that the subject is a thing or a determination for itself and the predicate, too, is a universal determination outside

NOTES TO PAGES 61–66

that subject, in my head somehow. I then bring the predicate together with the subject and, by this means, I judge. However, since the copula asserts the predicate of the subject, that external, subjective *subsuming* is sublated in turn and the judgment is taken as a determination of the *object* itself. The etymological meaning of judgment [*Urteil*] in our language is profounder and expresses the unity of the concept as what comes first [*das Erste*] and its differentiation as the *original* division [*Teilung*] that the judgment truly is" (*ENZ* §166 A).

15. In the words of the 1831 logic lectures: "The subject is something universal and at once determinate. These are the simple moments of the self-concept. The horse is first an animal, and that is its universality. It then has its determinacy, which is particularity—the species horse. But third it is *this* horse, the singular subject . . . Its subjectivity emerges as a quite trivial determination within the definition of the thing" (*Logik 1831*, 180, *LL* 180).

16. See *ENZ* §19 A: "The logical dimension constitutes the absolute form of the truth and . . . it is something completely different from anything merely *useful*."

17. "The *concept* of the thing, *the universal which is present in it*. . . . The profounder foundation is the soul standing on its own, the pure concept which is the innermost moment of the objects, their simple life pulse, just as it is of the subjective thinking of them. To bring to consciousness this *logical* nature that animates the spirit, that moves and works within it, this is the task" (*WL* I, 27, *SL* 16–17).

18. It is Bloch who speaks of Hades in this regard, even though as we shall see, this has in my view a meaning antithetical to his (see n. 35 in this chapter).

19. "O mother, my urgent need has been to go down to the house of Hades to seek an oracle from the breath-soul of Theban Tiresias," says Odysseus (Homer, *The Odyssey*, trans. B. B. Powell [Oxford, 2014], XI.156–57).

20. Analogous to Plato's "the good," the substantivized adjective *das Logische* finds parallel uses in Hegel in expressions such as "das Wahre" (the true), "das Erste" (the first), "das Absolute" (the absolute), "das Bekannte" (the familiar), and so on. I will occasionally use "the logical" in my text.

21. Hegel refers explicitly to such duplicity from the very beginning of the first preface to the *Science of Logic*: "There is a period in the formation of an epoch in which, just as in the formation of the individual, the foremost concern is the acquisition and reinforcement of the principle in its undeveloped intensity. But the higher demand is that such a principle should be made into science" (*WL* I, 15–16, *SL* 9).

22. See G. Frilli, "Sapere speculativo e teleologia della ragione," *Il cannocchiale* 38, no. 3 (2013): 139–61.

23. While the analogy of soul or nature can coexist with that of the shadows, this passage from Hegel is less problematic because of the changed meaning of "nature": "If we however contrast nature as such, as the realm of the physical, with the realm of the spiritual, then we must say that logic is the *supernatural* element that permeates all his natural behavior, his ways of sensing, intuiting, desiring, his needs and impulses" (*WL* I, 20, *SL* 12, italics mine).

24. "*The absolute idea* . . . is *the pure form* of the concept. . . . It is *content* for itself. . . . This content is the system of *the logical*. Nothing remains here of the idea, as *form*, but the *method* of this content—the determinate knowledge of the

NOTES TO PAGES 67–68

validity of its moments" (*ENZ* §237). In this way, philosophy bestows "upon this content [the logical element] the value of a universal" (*WL* I, 55–56, *SL* 38).

25. My translation. I think that here Brinkmann's and Dahlstrom's translation ("moments of every proper logical content") is mistaken. Hegel is speaking of *das Logische* in its objective form. Equally debatable is the translation of *das Logische* in the same section as "the logical domain."

26. Recall my note 13 in the introduction regarding Descartes's *Regulae.*

27. For one of the many praises of the understanding, see *WL* II, 285–88, *SL* 538–40. At the end of this passage, Hegel writes about the understanding's concepts: "The determinate and abstract concept is the *condition,* or rather an *essential moment, of reason*; it is form quickened by spirit in which the finite, through the universality in which it refers to itself, is internally kindled, is posited as dialectical and thereby is the *beginning* of the appearance of reason" (*WL* II, 288, *SL* 540).

28. Joyce's *Finnegans Wake,* like Queneau, Guimaraes Rosa, and Gadda in their experimental works and in those by other twentieth-century masters of literary invention, uses the fluidity of language on a phonetic and semantic, not a grammatical, level. It is certainly possible to subvert an order from the inside, that is, one can create a new order with its dancing stars out of an original chaos. But it is not possible to assume an original chaos in order to create a different chaos. Determinacy is necessary even when we want to go beyond it.

29. In my view, David Lachterman's objections to the attempts at formalizing dialectic and turning it into a method are unsurpassed. See "Hegel and the Formalization of the Logic," *Graduate Faculty Philosophy Journal* 12, nos. 1–2 (1987): 153–235. F. Berto's *Che cos'è la dialettica hegeliana?* (Padua, 2005) and D. Marconi's earlier "Contradiction and the Language of Hegel's Dialectic" (Ph.D. diss., University of Pittsburgh, 1981) are two of the most interesting and intelligent attempts at interpreting Hegel's dialectic as an analytic method. Berto offers a reconstruction that can be understood as a semantics of the determinacy of meanings rather than as a theory of objective thought (210 ff.). For Berto, negation is propositional in nature, and contradiction is the semantic isolation of nonidentical concepts (379 ff.). For an equally complex discussion of the dialectic in its relation to contemporary philosophy, which, however, restores the ancient spirit of the dialectic, see P. Masciarelli's *Un'apologia della dialettica* (Bologna, 2014).

30. "It can only be the *nature of the content* which is responsible for *movement* in scientific knowledge, for it is the content's *own reflection* that first posits and *generates what that content is*" (*WL* I, 16, *SL* 9–10). "For it is the content in itself, the dialectic which it possesses within itself, which moves the subject matter forward" (*WL* I, 50, *SL* 33). "The dialectic is far more the proper, true nature of the determinations of the understanding, of things, and of the finite in general. . . . The dialectic is, by contrast, this *immanent* process of going beyond [such determinacy] wherein the one-sided and limited character of the determinations of the understanding presents itself as what it is, namely as their negation. Everything finite is this, the sublating of itself. Thus, the dialectical moment constitutes the moving soul of the scientific progression and is the principle through which alone

an immanent connection and necessity enters into the content of science" (*ENZ* §81).
"The dialectic makes up the very nature of thinking" (*ENZ* §11 A).

31. See *W* 3, 73, *PhS* 51; and *WL* I, 49, *SL* 32.

32. For this "inequality" regarding the motor of the dialectic, see *W* 3, 39, 59–60, 74; *PhS* 21–22, 38–39, 50–51. The passages on the dialectic and the negative in the preface to the *Phenomenology* are one of the clearest demonstrations of the fact, with which all students of Hegel are familiar, that the preface was indeed written to introduce the system as it was conceived in 1807, not to introduce the book known as the *Phenomenology of Spirit.*

33. On the three syllogisms, the most instructive essays are R. Bodei, *Sistema ed epoca in Hegel* (Bologna, 1976), 309 ff., now *La civetta e la talpa: Sistema ed epoca in Hegel* (Bologna, 2014), 335–62; and A. Peperzak, *Selbsterkenntnis des Absoluten* (Stuttgart, 1987), 125–65.

34. A similar consideration applies to the characterization of the absolute idea as "the original *word*" (*WL* II, 550, *SL* 736) or to the logic as "science only of the divine *concept*" (*WL* II, 572, *SL* 752).

35. One of the most influential examples of this aprioristic reading of the logic—to be identified as a Platonic one, although it is clearly indebted to Marx's 1844 *Manuscripts*—is Ernst Bloch, according to whom Hegel, "as an *a priori* thinker [*als Apriorist*], presents his categories as a logical *prius* with respect to the world, and thereby as *universalia ante rem*, as the *Hades of a beginning, not of an end*" (Bloch, *Subjekt-Objekt*, 160).

36. By a realist reading, I mean all those interpretations (mostly, though not always, aiming at discrediting Hegel's philosophy as an aprioristic or theologically inspired metaphysics) of the primacy of thought, which is understood as the cause of the world, irrespective of whether this reading is that of Marx, neo-Kantianism, phenomenology, hermeneutics, or Heidegger.

37. *VPhR* 51–52. See this passage from the beginning of the lectures edited by Lasson: "Our concern here is therefore not with God as such or as object, but with God as He is in His community. For as spirit He is not simply an abstract self-relating being, but He makes Himself into the counterpart of a knowing community . . . ; the knowledge of God as a self-knowing absolute divine spirit is to be grasped as the doctrine of religion" (*VPhR* 8).

38. I have dealt with this theme in *Hegel and Aristotle*, and with regard to practice in *Saggezza, immaginazione e giudizio pratico: Studio su Aristotle e Kant* (Pisa, 2004). For the concept of truth in Hegel, see *Hegel and Aristotle*, 373–93.

39. "It is wrong to assume, first that there are objects which form the content of our representations and then our subjective activity comes along behind them, forming the concepts of objects by means of the earlier mentioned operation of abstracting and gathering together what is common to the objects. On the contrary, the concept is what is truly first and the things are what they are, thanks to the activity of the concept dwelling in them and revealing itself in them" (*ENZ* §167 Z).

40. A way to illustrate such primacy is this. Typically, we say that we grasp a concept when we are able to isolate its fundamental core and derive further particular aspects from it, or at least understand such aspects in light of the concept. Similarly, we distinguish a good dictionary from a poor one because the

NOTES TO PAGES 77–79

latter enumerates a list of meanings for each word, whereas the former provides a fundamental root and shows how the different nuances or meanings the word acquires deviate from the original sense.

41. When Nietzsche writes that philosophers "take what comes at the end . . . , the 'highest ideas,' which means the emptiest, most universal ideas, the last wisps of smoke from the evaporating end of reality—and they put it at the beginning, *as* the beginning," saying that "none of these could have become, and so they must be *causa sui*" (*Twilight of the Idols*, in Nietzsche, *The Anti-Christ, Ecce Homo, Twilight of the Idols*, ed. A. Ridley and J. Norman [Cambridge, 2007], 168), he charges philosophers with "Egypticity" (167), that is, mummified concepts that decontextualize, kill, and stuff becoming. Nietzsche's denunciation attacks Platonism, the world behind the alleged world, but Hegel's notion of *causa sui* is not the mummified truth that lies *beyond* the sensible.

42. "Since it contains *all determinateness* within it, and its essence consists in returning through its self-determination and particularization back to itself, it has various shapes, and the business of philosophy is to recognize it in these. Nature and spirit are in general different modes of exhibiting its existence, art and religion its different modes of apprehending itself and giving itself appropriate existence" (*WL* II, 549–50, *SL* 735).

43. Angelica Nuzzo's works, with a methodological view of the absolute idea considered as *Erinnerung* at the end of the *Science of Logic*, are the most valuable among the essays I know about the Hegelian notion of absolute idea. See "The Idea of 'Method' in Hegel's Science of Logic—A Method for Finite Thinking and Absolute Reason," *Hegel Society of Great Britain* 39–40 (1999): 1–17; and "The End of Hegel's Logic: Absolute Idea as Absolute Method," *Cardozo Public Law, Policy and Ethics Journal* 3 (2004): 203–24. Before these, see Nuzzo's *Logica e sistema: Sull'idea hegeliana di filosofia* (Genoa, 1992); and her beautiful essay "'Idee' bei Kant und Hegel," in *Das Recht der Vernunft: Kant und Hegel über Denken, Erkennen und Handeln*, ed. V. C. Firke, P. König, and T. Petersen (Stuttgart, 1995), 81–120; and finally the notes on method as process without subject in "The Language of Hegel's Speculative Philosophy," in *Hegel and Language*, ed. J. P. Surber (Albany, N.Y., 2006), 75–94.

44. Peperzak, *Selbsterkenntnis des Absoluten*, 165.

45. The concept is "*foundation and truth*" of its becoming (of its previous moments, being and essence; *WL* II, 245, *SL* 508). Yet it "cannot be a first, an immediate. Essentially the absolute is rather *its result*" (*WL* II, 196, *SL* 473).

46. "The logical determinations in general can be regarded as the definitions of the absolute, as *metaphysical definitions of God*" (*ENZ* §85). The determinations of essence, Hegel writes in *ENZ* §115 A, are "predicates of a presupposed subject that is '*everything*.'" All partial determinations of the absolute are certainly its definitions, but they are finite. By contrast, "the definition of the absolute, that it is the idea, is itself absolute. All previous definitions go back to this one" (*ENZ* §213 A). Indeed, "the absolute idea alone is *being*, imperishable *life, self-knowing truth, and is all truth*" (*WL* II, 549, *SL* 735).

47. "One may well say, therefore, that every beginning must be made with the *absolute*, just as every advance is only the exposition of it, in so far as *implicit*

NOTES TO PAGES 81-87

in existence is the concept. But because the absolute exists at first only *implicitly, in itself*, it equally is not the absolute or the posited concept, and also not the idea" (*WL* II, 555, *SL* 740).

48. With regard to the logical absolutism that he identified with Husserl (this is not the place to argue whether rightly or wrongly), Adorno wrote: "They use their subjectivity to subtract the subject from truth, and such a residue is their idea of objectivity." See Adorno, *Zur Metakritik der Erkenntnistheorie* (Stuttgart, 1956), translated into English by W. Domingo as *Against Epistemology. A Meta-Critique* (Cambridge, 2013), 15 (trans. modified).

49. See D. Henrich, "Anfang und Methode der Logik," in *Hegel im Kontext* (Frankfurt am Main, 1971), 82 ff.

50. "The I, the I! The most lurid of all pronouns! . . . Pronouns! They are the lice of thought. When thought has lice, it scratches itself like those who have lice . . . and then in the nails . . . it finds there again pronouns: personal pronouns" (C. E. Gadda, *La cognizione del dolore*, ed. E. Manzotti [Turin, 1987], 176). If we compare this resentment to the epigraph from Nabokov ("the square root of I is I"), we can say that while Gonzalo in Gadda's novel would be an excellent commentary on the unavoidability of the indexical pronoun, Nabokov's Krug would give voice to the transcendence of the I in Sartre, as a spectator and a nucleus that is opaque to consciousness.

51. "This absolute universality which is just as immediately absolute *singularization* . . . constitutes the nature of the '*I*' and of the *concept*" (*WL* II, 254, *SL* 514–15). The concrete universal is "the unity of the singular content and of abstract universality, therefore it is something *concrete*, the opposite of what it is supposed to be. . . . Singularity is not, however, only the turning back of the concept into itself, but the immediate loss of it. Through singularity, where it is internal *to itself*, the concept becomes external to itself and steps into actuality" (*WL* II, 298–99, *SL* 547–48). Thus, singularity does not appear to be opposed to universality, for it is rather a moment. It is one way in which universality refers to itself (*WL* II, 300–301, *SL* 549–50).

52. "'*I*,' however, taken abstractly and as such, is the pure relationship to itself in which abstraction is made from representing, sensing, indeed from every state as from every particularity of nature, talent, experience, etc. I is in this respect the concrete existence of the entirely *abstract* universality, the abstractly *free*. This is why the I is *thinking* as a *subject*, and because I am at the same time present in all my sensations, representations, and states, etc., thought is present everywhere and permeates all these determinations as a category" (*ENZ* §20 A).

53. This true meaning of the universal, says Hegel in the Addition to section 163 of the *Encyclopaedia*, "cost millennia before entering into human consciousness." Not even the Greeks got it: for them, both the human being and God were particulars. It is only Christianity that discovered the infinite value of the human being and God. It is because the human being has value as infinite universality that for Hegel, Christianity is the religion of absolute freedom.

54. "Everywhere the abstract must constitute the starting point and the element in which and from which the particularities and rich shapes of the concrete spread out" (*WL* II, 522, *SL* 715). "Thus in *learning to read* for example, the

NOTES TO PAGES 89-91

more rational way to begin is also not with reading whole words or even syllables, but with the *elements* of words and syllables and with the signs of abstract sound inflections; in alphabetic script the analysis of concrete words into their abstract sound inflections and their signs is already accomplished" (*WL* II, 521, *SL* 714). We begin to learn when abstraction into simple elements has already taken place.

Chapter 3

1. "... dass sich die Intelligenz dadurch zu einem *Sächlichen* macht," *ENZ* §462 Z.

2. *W* 3, 36, *PhS* 18. See also *WL* II, 285, *SL* 538–39, on the "infinite force of the understanding in splitting the concrete into abstract determinacies and plumbing the depth of the difference." The way of being of the understanding consists in the form of analysis, and we must reiterate that the understanding is essential for knowledge, even when its limits are highlighted. For an eloquent exemplification thereof, recall this passage: "The sort of knowing that wants to take things as they are thereby falls into self-contradiction. Thus, for example, the chemist brings a piece of meat to his test-tube, breaks it down in a variety of ways, and then says that he has found that it consists of nitrogen, carbon, hydrogen, and so on. However, these abstract bits of material are then no longer meat. . . . The analytically treated object is regarded, as it were, as an onion from which one peels one skin after the other" (*ENZ* §227 Z).

3. In the Jewish and Islamic religions, God is "*only* as the Lord," an absolute force to be feared. This has the flaw that it does not give justice to the finite (*ENZ* §112 Z), for it prevents us from the true concept of God that reconciles with man in religious community. "Only God is; but God is only by virtue of His being mediated with Himself. God wills the finite, posits it as His other and so Himself becomes an other of Himself, a finite, for he is confronted by another. God is in Himself this movement, and only thus is He a living God" (*VPhR* 147). "The divine, in order to be spirit in this way, finitizes itself so as to become human, i.e., knowledge. . . . This is not on the other hand the affair of the single human being; rather, what is singular is precisely sublated thereby, and religion is the self-knowing of divine spirit through the mediation of finite spirit" (*VPhR* 151).

4. "The infinite is only as the transcending of the finite; it therefore contains its other essentially, and it is thus within it that it is the other of itself. The finite is not sublated by the infinite as by a power present outside it; its infinity consists rather in sublating itself" (*WL* I, 160, *SL* 116).

5. In light of what we have seen about the Hegelian critique of concepts as fixed and determinate products, it is idle to raise objections to the view of thought as movement. Another thing is to raise objections to the *arbitrariness* of the movement and its supposed tacit assumptions, as in Schelling's and Trendelenburg's critique. For a convincing Hegelian answer to this kind of objection, see A. White, *Absolute Knowledge: Hegel and the Problem of Metaphysics* (Athens, Ohio, 1983); K. Brinkmann, "Schellings Hegelkritik," in *Die ontologische Option*, ed. K. Hartmann (Berlin, 1976), 117–210; S. Houlgate, "Schelling's Critique of Hegel's *Science of Logic*," *The Review of Metaphysics* 53, no. 1 (1999): 99–128; and

NOTES TO PAGES 91–92

S. Houlgate, *The Opening of Hegel's Logic: From Being to Infinity* (West Lafayette, Ind., 2006), 294 ff.

6. S. Rosen, "Il pensare è spontaneo?" *Teoria* 12, no. 1 (1992): 31–58 (this essay appeared originally in Italian translation, but was later published in English with the title "Is Thinking Spontaneous?" in Rosen, *Essays in Philosophy: Modern*, ed. M. Black [South Bend, Ind., 2013], 129–52). Franco Chiereghin points me to a third use, attested by Cicero (*Verr.* II.1.111), which fits in very well with what I am going to show: *sponte* also means "unprecedented," "without prior examples," or "instituted for the first time." See Chiereghin, *Possibilità e limiti dell'agire umano* (Genoa, 1990).

7. "We are only to regard it as a gentle force which commonly prevails," in David Hume, *A Treatise of Human Nature*, ed. Selby Bigge, rev. P. H. Nidditch, (Oxford, 1978), part 1, §4, 10.

8. Reason is this force, not Hume's nature of which imagination is the spokesman: more precisely, subjective reason as force of the spontaneous connections between ideas. With regard to this gentle force, a reciprocal attractive force between images, Hegel writes in the Philosophy of Subjective Spirit without ever mentioning Hume: "If this *superimposing* is not to be entirely a matter of *chance*, with no trace of a concept, a *force of attraction* [*Attraktionskraft*] between similar images must be assumed, or something of the sort, which at the same time would be the negative power of rubbing off their remaining unlikeness against each other. This force is in fact intelligence itself" (*ENZ* §455 A).

9. See *WL* I, 20, *SL* 12; and *WL* I, 114, *SL* 82 on the speculative character of natural language and of the German language in particular, in which many words have opposite meanings.

10. No single term covers the whole spectrum of Hegel's usage of this key point without exceptions, not even *Entäusserung* or "objectification" (which is admittedly a good candidate). "Reification," in which, unlike the German *Verdinglichung*, the reference to "thing" (*res*) is weak, has the advantage of highlighting the (momentary) fixity that thought gives itself. If I had called this objectification "determinacy," I would have run the risk of sacrificing the universality of the notion which must be able to be applied to Hegel's thought in general, including its particular logical categories and its several embodiments (for example, in natural organizations or historical and ethical institutions). Since in the *Science of Logic* one category of Being is "determinacy," using this term for thought's objectification in general would have restricted the usage of the term and generated confusion in the reader. But then again, it is natural language we are speaking of, and with this come many compromises that are no less interesting than their solutions. For example, it is pertinent to remember that the word chosen by Hegel to refer to categories is *Denkbestimmung*, which is itself the fusion of one category (*Bestimmung*, the "vocation" of the Doctrine of Being, *WL* I, 131, *SL* 95) with the trans-categorial principle of thought. Regarding the concept of reification from Lukács until the most recent developments, see A. Honneth, *Verdinglichung: Eine anerkennungstheoretische Studie* (Frankfurt am Main, 2005, exp. ed. 2015); and the essays edited by A. Bellan in *Teorie della reificazione: Storia e attualità di un fenomeno sociale* (Milan, 2013).

NOTES TO PAGES 92-95

11. If thought is devoid of content, it can be regarded as nothingness that must become something. Bloch speaks beautifully of "a function of nothingness" which Hegel took over from Nicholas of Cusa (Bloch, *Subjekt-Objekt*. 152): "nothingness becomes an objective Mephistopheles, who stimulates and creates in the world" (153). But this is precisely an image, and Hegel would treat it in representational, not speculative terms. For example, the representation of the creation of order from chaos among the Greeks is a "mythical form" which presupposes a demiurge that shapes the world. Another representational image, "the intuition that God created the world out of nothing," is superior to it because it aims to express that "the form does not reach the matter from the outside" (*ENZ* §128 Z). R. D. Winfield (*From Concept to Objectivity. Thinking through Hegel's Subjective Logic* [Farnham, Eng., 2006], 51–65) speaks of a determinateness that constitutes itself out of indeterminacy. Given that K. Hartmann, who is not quoted by Winfield ("Hegel: A Non-Metaphysical View," in *Hegel: A Collection of Critical Essays*, ed. A. McIntyre [Notre Dame, Ind., 1972], 105), raises specious objections as to how indeterminacy can generate determinacy, Winfield's thesis sounds convincing, provided that "indeterminacy" is not hypostasized into an independent principle.

12. "Crystallization" is a term used by Stendhal in these very years (*De l'amour*, 1823) by analogy with the natural formation of salt crystals around a tiny dead tree bough. A lover, claims Stendhal, projects onto the beloved an image until eventually the act of this projection effaces itself and results in the shining crystals that a lover is so keen on admiring as if they were natural diamonds. "Leave a lover with his thoughts for twenty-four hours, and this is what will happen: At the salt mines of Salzburg, they throw a leafless wintry bough into one of the abandoned workings. Two or three months later they haul it out covered with a shining deposit of crystals. The smallest twig, no bigger than a tom-tit's claw, is studded with a galaxy of scintillating diamonds. The original branch is no longer recognizable. What I have called crystallization is a mental process which draws from everything that happens new proofs of the perfection of the loved one" (*Love*, trans. G. and S. Sale [London, 2004], 84). It is worth remembering that this is once again an analogy, and the affinities with Hegel must be stressed no less than the differences. In Hegel, crystallization is not the work of nature but of thought. There is no deception, illusion, or sublimation that must convince the lover of the value of the beloved independently of his or her intrinsic value. Still, as in Stendhal, the movement of crystallization is presupposed as having happened in the past, and it exercises its power over us precisely because we have forgotten about it: it is unknown or unconscious to us.

Curiously, Hegel also speaks of metaphysics as a "diamond net" of categories that are operative in everything we do or say (*ENZ* §246 Z, §98 Z 1; about the web of categories, without diamonds, see *WL* I, 27, *SL* 17).

13. "Bewusstein ist eine Einheit. Ein Akt ist nichts für sich, es ist Welle in Bewusstseinsstrom," Ms. L I, 15 2 b, quoted D. Zahavi, in *Self-Awareness and Alterity: A Phenomenological Investigation* (Evanston, Ill., 1999), 77.

14. On this last point, see the discussion between Becker and Wiehl (W. Becker, "Das Problem der Selbstanwendung im Kategorienverständnis der dialektischen Logik," and R. Wiehl, "Selbstbeziehung und Selbstanwendung

dialektischer Kategorien"), *Hegel-Studien Beiheft* 18 (1978): 75–82; 83–113, respectively. On recursivity, see F. Chiereghin, *Rileggere la "Scienza della logica" di Hegel: Ricorsività, retroazioni, ologrammi* (Rome, 2011).

15. See my *Hegel and Aristotle*, 308–25; and "Hegel's Intepretation of the Aristotelian NOUS," in *The Impact of Aristotelianism on Modern Philosophy*, ed. R. Pozzo (Washington, D.C., 2004), 193–209.

16. This is not the same as the *pathêtikos nous*, an expression which occurs in one passage of *De anima*, book III (5 430a24), in which it clearly refers to the corruptibility of our human intellectual life, that is, the individual intellect as a first potency or formed habituality.

17. Like Aristotle, Kant also understands thought as spontaneity without receptivity. Think, among other examples, of the maxim of *Selbstdenken*, or the concept of a history of reason that can be arrived at *ex principiis* (from principles). If all objectification of thought is a product that appears foreign to thinking and is not understood as thinking's self-production, then reason and history are bound to remain mutually alternative. History and the history of philosophy in our particular case can teach us something and even be constituted as disciplines only if we admit that we are shaped by them, that is, provided that receptivity is integral to spontaneity (see my *The Powers of Pure Reason*, 67–80).

18. For Hegel, Rousseau's merit, which consists in establishing the will as the principle of the State, is immediately undermined by the fact that Rousseau understood the will as individual, so that the universal will is nothing more than a "common" will, the product of different conscious wills, and each union becomes the outcome of a contract as an expression of a subjective consensus (*GPR* §29 A, §258 A).

19. Regarding this movement and the identification of freedom and concept, see A. Nuzzo, "La 'verità' del concetto di libertà secondo Hegel: *Dasein* e idea di libertà nell'eticità," in *La libertà nella filosofia classica tedesca*, ed. G. Duso and G. Rametta (Milan, 2000), 147–70; and also her earlier book *Rappresentazione e concetto nella "logica" della filosofia del diritto di Hegel* (Naples 1990).

20. I have discussed more extensively Brandom's and Heidegger's interpretations in my works, respectively: "What Must We Recognize? Brandom on Kant and Hegel," and *Hegel and Aristotle*, 229–33.

21. "On the other hand, it is just as important that philosophy come to understand that its content is none other than the basic content that has originally been produced and reproduces itself in the sphere of the living spirit, a content turned into a world, namely the outer and inner world of consciousness, or that its content is *actuality* [*die Wirklichkeit*]" (*ENZ* §6). As we have seen, reality and actuality have different gradations. It necessarily follows that even reification must assume different forms, depending on the rationality and permeability of the medium in which it takes place.

22. *ENZ* §12. The beginning of the philosophy of nature reads as follows: "It is not only that philosophy must accord with the experience nature gives rise to; in its *formation* and in its *development*, philosophic science presupposes and is conditioned by empirical physics. The procedure involved in the formation and preliminaries of a science is not the same as the science itself, however, for in

this latter case it is no longer experience, but rather the necessity of the Notion" (*ENZ* 246 A).

23. With regard to the problem of speculative memory in relation to the logic, see E. Magrì, *Hegel e la genesi del concetto: Autoriferimento, memoria, incarnazione* (Trent, 2017).

24. Already in Jena Hegel wrote: "The image is preserved in its treasure, in its night—it is unconscious, i.e., it is not displayed as an object for representation. The human being is this night, this empty nothing which contains everything in its simplicity" (*JSE* 3, 186–87).

25. See W. Kern, "Die Aristotelesdeutung Hegels," *Philosophisches Jahrbuch* 78 (1971): 252–54.

26. "The *conceptual comprehension* of a subject matter consists in nothing else than in the 'I' *making it its own*, in pervading it and bringing it into *its own form*, that is, into a *universality* which is immediately determinateness . . . In *thinking* it, the 'I' pervades it. . . . Thought sublates the *immediacy* with which it first comes before us and in this way transforms it into a *positedness*; but this, its positedness, is its *being-in-and-for-itself* or its *objectivity*. This is an objectivity which the subject matter consequently attains in the *concept*" (*WL* II, 255, *SL* 516).

27. In the Idea of Cognition of the *Science of Logic* we read this important passage: "It is just as one-sided to portray analysis as though there were nothing in the subject matter that is not *imported* into it, as it is to suppose that the resulting determinations are only *extracted* from it. The former way of stating the case corresponds, as is well known, to subjective idealism, which takes the activity of cognition in analysis to be only a one-sided positing, beyond which the thing-in-itself remains hidden. The other way belongs to the so-called realism, for which the subjective concept is an empty identity that *imports* the thought determinations *from outside*. Since analytical cognition, the transformation of the given material into logical determinations, has shown itself to be a positing that immediately determines itself to be equally a *presupposing*, to be both in one, the logical element can appear on account of this presupposing to be in the subject matter as something already *completed*, just as because of the positing it can appear as the *product* of a merely subjective activity. But the two moments are not to be separated. In the abstract form to which analysis raises it, the logical element is of course only to be found in cognition, just as conversely it is not only something *posited* but something that rather exists *in itself*" (*WL* II, 503, *SL* 701).

28. *Nachdenken* literally means "to think afterward" and is the proper philosophical reflection in the *Encyclopaedia*. As such, it should not be confused with the reflective understanding or the modern philosophy of reflection.

29. In his 1762 dissertation, Merian raises this criticism against Descartes. Rather than *cogito, ergo sum*, Descartes should have claimed "I *have thought*, therefore I am," because we cannot have as the object of our thought an object and our reflection on it at the same time. The simultaneity is excluded in self-thinking because as we focus on our thought it has evaporated, like the fleeting moment we pretend to grasp and arrest. We are always one step behind. Kant must have been aware of this point in Merian at least indirectly, because Tetens makes much of it in his discussion of representations of inner sense. See J. N. Tetens, *Philosophische*

Versuche uber die menschliche Natur und ihre Entwicklung (Leipzig, 1777; Hildesheim, 1979), vol. 1, 46 ff. After Jacobi's critique of the shortcomings of the understanding and finite knowledge and the necessity of intuition, this is then the key question of the notions of the Absolute and intellectual intuition in Fichte after his Jena years. The disparity between the act of positing and the vision of that act is inevitable: beginning and origin escape the I.

30. See, for instance, *WL* II, 253, *SL* 514: the free concept is "the 'I' or pure self-consciousness." The absolute idea is "self-knowing truth" (*WL* II, 549, *SL* 735).

31. See W. Carl, *The First-Person Point of View* (Berlin, 2014).

32. "When we wish to see an oak with its massive trunk and spreading branches and foliage, we are not content to be shown an acorn instead. So too, Science, the crown of a world of Spirit, is not complete in its beginnings" (*W* 3, 19, *PhS* 7). "When I say 'all animals,' this expression cannot pass for a zoology" (*W* 3, 24, *PhS* 11).

33. When Hegel writes that "the *absolute idea* . . . is the *pure form* of the concept that intuits its content *as itself*" (*ENZ* §237), the act of grasping the absolute idea he refers to cannot literally be an intuition, a concentration of the whole in a unity. Similarly, "the objective totality" that is the idea cannot literally be an "intellectual intuition," as Hegel nonetheless writes in *WL* II, 286, *SL* 539. Finally, when considering the different forms of exposition of the absolute in art and philosophy, Hegel cannot go down the path he nonetheless suggests in a handwritten note on §477 of the Heidelberg *Encyclopaedia* ("Totales Wissen, das nich subjektiv ist . . . so daß das Allgemeine in mir wirkt—Wie im Kunstwerk," in "Hegels Notizen zum absoluten Geist," ed. H. Schneider, *Hegel-Studien* 9 [1974]: 9–38).

34. For different senses of "knowledge" and "cognition," see the beautiful, albeit habitually neglected, pages in the *Lectures on the Philosophy of Religion* edited by Lasson (*VPhR* 86–92).

35. This is the *exaiphnês* in Plato's *Parmenides* (156d–e), which for Hegel is also the position of Descartes and Jacobi with regard to objectivity (*ENZ* §§64 ff.).

Chapter 4

1. The content "which is grounded in thought does not at first appear in the form of thought, but rather as feeling, intuition, representation" (*ENZ* §2).

2. Philosophy and religion "have the truth for their object, and more precisely the truth in the highest sense" (*ENZ* §1). "The way in which spirit becomes object for itself is representation" (*VPhR* 67). "Religion is for everybody. It is not philosophy, which is not for everybody" (*VPhR* 69).

3. The content of philosophy is "the basic content that has originally been produced and reproduces itself in the sphere of the living spirit, a content turned into a *world*, . . . *actuality*" (*ENZ* §6).

4. "When deprived of its manner of representing, consciousness feels as if it had lost the ground in which it is otherwise so firmly rooted and at home. When it finds itself transposed into the pure region of concepts, it no longer knows *where* in the world it is" (*ENZ* §3 A).

NOTES TO PAGES 114–117

5. For a commentary on the Philosophy of Subjective Spirit, see my *Hegel and Aristotle*, 234–347. For a commentary on the philosophy of practical and objective spirit, see Adriaan Peperzak, *Hegels praktische Philosophie* (Stuttgart, 1991) and his *Modern Freedom*. I will give further indications concerning particular aspects of spirit in the next notes.

6. This liberation does not necessarily lead us elsewhere, for example, to a sail to the *logoi* like Socrates in the *Phaedo*. I may want to occupy myself with the color red all my life long. Yet it is one thing to hope to come across new nuances of red, and it is quite another to devote myself to the study and the scientific experiments on the visible spectrum of colors—or investigate the use of red in the paintings of Tuscan Mannerism or Mark Rothko. The difference is the same as that between depending on the given and knowing it thoroughly, limiting the impact of chance as much as possible and reducing the sense of foreignness of the given.

7. Intelligence that knows, "theoretical spirit . . . has a world opposite itself, but it approaches the world with the faith that the world is rational" (*Erdmann* 200). "This singling out isolates the yellow, and constitutes it as self-relating (the yellow is only as yellow). The determination thus becomes universal, an abstract representation. The content is taken from the given, but the form is a process of analysis, the determination is isolated. . . . Representation is the general name for the fact that the object is mine, in my possession, and that I am the subject of the object" (Erdmann 221).

8. *ENZ* §457 A. Often, the second draft of the Jena lectures on the philosophy of spirit (1805–06) expresses as best as can be desired the points to which Hegel returns later on in the *Encyclopaedia*: "The I makes itself into a *thing*, in that it fixes the order of names within itself. It fixes them *within itself*, i.e., it makes itself into this unthinking order, which has the mere appearance of order" (*JSE* 3, 194).

9. I wrote on habit and second nature in Hegel and Aristotle in my *Hegel and Aristotle*, 278–83; besides the essays I referenced there, see V. Verra, "Storia e seconda natura in Hegel," in *Su Hegel*, ed. C. Cesa (Bologna, 2007), 65–82; I. Testa, "Seconda natura e riconoscimento: Hegel e la teoria dello spazio sociale," in *Lo spazio sociale della ragione: Da Hegel in avanti*, ed. L. Ruggiu and I. Testa (Milan, 2009), 315–42; D. Forman, "Second Nature and Spirit: Hegel on the Role of Habit in the Appearance of Perceptual Consciousness," *Southern Journal of Philosophy* 48, no. 4 (2010): 325–52; C. Cesa, "La 'seconda natura' fra Kant e Hegel," in *Verso l'eticità: Saggi di storia della filosofia*, ed. C. De Pascale, L. Fonnesu, and A. Savorelli (Pisa, 2013), 147–66; F. Ranchio, "Reificazione e seconda natura: Le origini hegeliane di un'idea," in *Teorie della reificazione: Storia e attualità di un fenomeno sociale*, ed. A. Bellan (Milan, 2013), 47–69; and E. Magrì, "The Place of Habit in Hegel's Psychology," in *Hegel's Philosophical Psychology*, ed. L. Ziglioli and S. Herrmann-Sinai (London, 2016), 74–90.

For the notion of *Erinnerung*, see the essays by V. Ricci, M. Bordignon, F. Sanguinetti, E. Magrì, F. Orsini, G. Cecchinato, S. Achella, and P. Ktenides in *Hegel on Recollection: Essays on the Concept of Erinnerung in Hegel's System*, ed. V. Ricci and F. Sanguinetti (Newcastle, Eng., 2013).

Regarding language, I published a bibliographical commentary, "Hegel e il linguaggio: Per una bibliografia sul tema," *Teoria* 7, no. 1 (1987): 139–59; and, above all, "Logic, Thinking, and Language," in *Von der Logik zur Sprache: Stuttgarter Hegelkongress 2005*, ed. R. Bubner and G. Hindrichs (Stuttgart, 2007), 135–58. Besides the secondary literature I discussed there, I would like to recommend the works by A. Nuzzo, "The Language of Hegel's Speculative Philosophy," in *Hegel and Language*, ed. J. P. Surber (Albany, N.Y., 2006), 75–94; G. Rametta, "La 'proposizione speculativa' nella Prefazione alla *Fenomenologia dello spirito* di Hegel," *Fenomenologia e società* 32, no. 2 (2009): 105–16; and L. Ziglioli, "Linguaggio e oggettività in Hegel," *Rivista di filosofia* 2 (2014): 223–46.

10. "The *disposition* of the individuals is *awareness* of the substance and of the identity of all their interests with the whole; and when the other individuals are actual and reciprocally aware of themselves only in this identity, this is *trust*, the genuine, ethical disposition" (*ENZ* §515).

11. For different critiques of reification, particularly in the Frankfurt school, see L. Cortella's essay in Bellan, ed., *Teorie della reificazione*, 17–43.

12. "But if it is simply *identical* with the actuality of individuals, the ethical, as their general mode of behavior, appears as *custom*; and the habit of the ethical appears as a *second nature* which takes the place of the original and purely natural will and is the all-pervading soul, significance, and actuality of individual existence. It is spirit living and present as a world, and only thus does the substance of *spirit* begin to exist as spirit" (*GPR* §151).

13. See the *Vorlesungen über die Philosophie der Geschichte* (*W* 12, 57): "Die Sittlichkeit aber ist die Pflicht, das substantielle Recht, die zweite Natur, wie man sie mit Recht genannt hat, denn die erste Natur des Menschen ist sein unmittelbares, tierisches Sein." See also the *Vorlesungen über die Philosophie der Religion* II on ethical life as constitutive of the second nature of the individual as a result and work of education and culture ("Werk der Erziehung und Bildung," *W* 17, 146).

14. Habit is an ability acquired through the repeated exercise of one's own power (*Ak* 7, 147; Eng. trans. 259), and for this reason it does not have anything to do with virtue. In fact, in the preface, Kant explains that "habits which, as we say, are second nature, make it hard for us to decide what view to take of ourselves" (*Ak* 7, 121; Eng. trans. 233). In the *Lectures on Pedagogy* (*Ak* 9, 463), we read that the more habits we have, the less free we are.

15. *ENZ* §20 A. In the *Lectures on the Philosophy of Religion*, we read that representation is still immersed in the sensible. It "needs the sensible and this conflict against it to be itself. The sensible therefore belongs to representation essentially, even though it never counts as independent. . . . Therefore representation is now in a constant restlessness between immediate and sensible intuition and proper thought" (*VPhR* 115–16).

16. It is possible to move back and forth between the two: "ein Herüber-und Hinübergehen" (*W* 11, 378). Hegel misquotes Homer, as Geraets, Suchting, and Harris (*ENZ*, 309, n. 9) document by referring to the *Iliad*'s book 1.401, 14.290, and 20.74. However, Hegel himself makes amends in 1830 by replacing "constellations" with "things."

17. This has been pointed out by Soresi, *Il soggetto del pensiero*, 45. I have in mind here the essential difference between metaphor and denomination highlighted by P. Ricoeur in *La métaphore vive* (Paris, 1975), translated into English by

R. Czerny as *The Rule of Metaphor* (Toronto, 1977). For the "gap" between meta-phorical and abstractive uses, see 106 ff.

18. In the Philosophy of Nature in the *Encyclopaedia*, shortly after the passage quoted above ("The procedure involved in the formation and preliminaries of a science is not the same as the science itself," *ENZ* §246 A), we read: "As it is our procedure to ask how the thought which has been established *as a necessity by means of the Notion looks in our sensuous intuition*, the further requirement is that *the intuition of space shall correspond to the thought of pure self-externality*" (§254 Z, italics mine). Kant, too, conceived of space as the form of the *Aussereinandersein*, but because he aimed to establish space as intuition; this was the problem he intended to solve. Hegel here is saying that the logical truth of exteriority has an intuitive equivalent in space. Space is the concept of exteriority become intuitable. The Philosophy of Nature proceeds to investigate this, whereas the necessity of speculative logic seeks only the purity and essentiality of the concept.

19. Preface to the second edition (1831) of the *Science of Logic*, *WL* I, 22, *SL* 13: "And what could be more familiar than just those determinations of thought which we employ everywhere, and are on our lips in every sentence that we utter?"

20. I am quoting from the famous essay by H.-G. Gadamer, "Die Idee der Hegelschen Logik," in *Hegels Dialektik: Fünf hermeneutische Studien* (Tübingen, 1971); translated into English by P. C. Smith as "The Idea of Hegel's Logic," in *Hegel's Dialectic: Five Hermeneutical Studies* (New Haven, Conn., 1976), 92.

21. Ibid., 99.

22. Bloch, *Subjekt-Objekt*, 19. In this regard, Bloch writes that "there are precious gems that are not transparent [*undurchsichtige Edelsteine*]," 20. Obviously the preface to the *Phenomenology* deserves from this point of view a special place. For a stylistic and literary analysis, see M. Züfle, *Die Prose der Welt* (Einsiedeln, 1968), 303–62. While this book may not be memorable, an interpretative essay that deserves to be taken again into consideration is "Skoteinos oder Wie zu lesen sei," the third essay in Adorno's *Drei Studien zu Hegel* (Frankfurt am Main, 1963), translated as "Skoteinos, or How to Read Hegel" by S. Weber Nicholsen in *Three Studies on Hegel* (Cambridge, 1993).

23. See Hotho's recollection in the introduction to Adorno, *Three Studies on Hegel.*

24. Rosenkranz, *Hegels Leben*, 361.

25. Referring to Ben Jonson, Stephen Daedalus says: "The language in which we are speaking is his before it is mine. . . . His language, so familiar and so foreign, will always be for me an acquired speech. I have not made or accepted his words. My voice holds them at bay. My soul frets in the shadow of his language" (J. Joyce, *A Portrait of the Artist as a Young Man* [Harmondsworth, Eng., 1960], 189). If a master of elegant prose like Stephen, to whom Hegel certainly cannot be compared, says so, he is to be trusted.

26. This is the core idea of F. Chiereghin's book *Dialettica dell'assoluto e ontologia della soggettività* (Trent, 1980).

27. "The exposition should preserve the dialectical form, and should admit nothing except in so far as it is comprehended [in terms of the Notion], and is the Notion," *W* 3, 62, *PhS* 41.

NOTES TO PAGES 128–138

28. "The form of the positive judgment is accepted as something perfectly correct in itself, and whether the judgment is true is made to depend solely on the content. No thought is given to investigating whether this form of judgment is a form of truth *in and for itself*; whether the proposition it enunciates, '*the individual is a universal*,' is not inherently dialectical" (*WL* 2, 268, *SL* 525).

29. "A proposition [*Satz*] can indeed have a subject and predicate in a grammatical sense without however being a judgment [*Urteil*] for that. The latter requires that the predicate behave with respect to the subject in a relation of conceptual determination, hence as a universal with respect to a particular or singular. And if what is said of a singular subject is itself only something singular . . . then this is a mere proposition, not a judgment" (*WL* II, 305, *SL* 553). This excludes from philosophical consideration a type of proposition that still holds its right to be for ordinary communication: "non-speculative thinking also has its valid rights which are disregarded in the speculative way of stating a proposition" (*W* 3, 6, *PhS* 39).

30. We owe Rametta and Yovel two exhaustive commentaries on the preface: G. Rametta, *Filosofia come "sistema della scienza": Introduzione alla lettura della Prefazione alla "Fenomenologia dello spirito" di Hegel* (Schio, 1992), and Hegel, *Hegel's Preface to the "Phenomenology of Spirit,"* trans. and commentary by Y. Yovel (Princeton, N.J., 2005).

31. This is why Russell's complaint about the Hegelian confusion between identity and the attribution of the copula is an equivocation. See Lachterman, "Hegel and the Formalization of Logic," 168.

32. In the *Lectures on the Philosophy of Religion* (*VPhR* 30–32), we read that asking for meaning can point in two opposite directions: I may have a name and want to know what to think of it (how to fill it by means of representations and examples), or else I may have a representation and ask for its conceptual meaning. In the latter case, "the opposite need pushes us *to give externality to thinking*"; that is, we ask for an example of the given content in pure thought; but "already in the word 'example' it can be recognized that the role of externality is merely transitional, for the substantial element is pure thought" (*VPhR* 31, italics mine). As we have seen, there is an asymmetry here: representation and concept are alternative, and it is only for the latter that "each true progression returns to itself" (*VPhR* 64). Once again, thought gives itself an externality in representations and examples, and the concept consists in returning to itself from them.

33. See Rametta, "La proposizione speculativa," 110.

Chapter 5

1. Occasional references to my recent book on Kant (*The Powers of Pure Reason*), driven by the desire to understand Kant's philosophy beyond certain interpretative readings such as Hegel's, are intended to direct interested readers to further analyses that I cannot spell out here.

2. "In this work I make frequent references to the Kantian philosophy because . . . it constitutes the foundation and the starting point of the new German

NOTES TO PAGES 145–163

philosophy, and this is a merit of which it can boast undiminished by whatever fault may be found in it" (*WL* I, 59n., *SL* 40n.). See *EA* §12; *ENZ* §20.

3. This is evident from the 1817 review of Jacobi's works (*W* 4, 440). But see also *WL* II, 539, *SL* 727; and *ENZ* §50 A.

4. See, for instance, besides the famous discussion of antinomies, Kant's view of matter in *WL* I, 200–208, *SL* 145–51.

5. Letter dated July 3, 1792, in *Ak* 11, 346–48.

6. For a thematic discussion of this non-identity, see *The Powers of Pure Reason*, 254–59.

7. L. Lugarini underlines this point clearly: see "La confutazione hegeliana della filosofia critica," in *Hegel interprete di Kant*, ed. V. Verra (Naples, 1981), 13–66, esp. 37.

8. Or that he could write: "Thus we cannot evade the obligation of giving at least a critical resolution of the questions of reason before us by lamenting the narrow limits of our reason and confessing, with the appearance of a modest self-knowledge, that it lies beyond our reason to settle whether the world has existed from eternity or has a beginning, . . . whether there is a generating and producing through freedom or everything depends on the causal chain of the natural order. . . . For each of these questions concerns an object that can be given nowhere but in our thoughts, namely the absolutely unconditioned totality of the synthesis of appearances" (*KrV* A 481/B 509).

9. E. Weil, *Problèmes kantiens* (Paris, 1963), 41.

10. The problem that either we have a play of representations or we refer representations to rules is well known. Among other interpreters, I recommend Adickes, Prauss, and Allison for a further discussion of this issue. I limit myself to naming a few examples of these oscillations: the appearance as "the undetermined object of an empirical intuition" (*KrV* A 20/B 34) is equivalent to an empirical not yet conceptualized intuition (e.g., A 198/B 243). As the A Deduction claims, "if it is combined with consciousness, [it] is called perception" (A 120). Kant often writes that the objects we experience are nothing but representations (A 494/B 522), *blosse Vorstellungen* (A 563/B 591, A 491/B 519, A 369). The great ambivalence that follows is equally known: "appearance" is, on the one hand, what is spatiotemporally given, and, on the other, what is constituted by our a priori forms. In turn, "object" can be the appearance understood as a material object, or its objective concept ("that in the concept of which the manifold of a given intuition is united," B 137).

11. In respect to this, all handbooks and textbooks on the history of German idealism express themselves in the same terms as Hegel, to whom they can be brought back: "In its more consistent form [Hegel is referring to Fichte], transcendental idealism did recognize the nothingness of the spectral thing-in-itself, this abstract shadow divorced from all content left over by critical philosophy, and its goal was to destroy it completely" (*WL* I, 41; *SL* 27). In the Addition to §41 of the *Encyclopaedia*, Hegel says: "Nowadays, the Kantian philosophy has been left behind, and everybody wants to be at a point further on."

12. It is because Hegel does not understand the concept of pure intuition that he misunderstands the concept of mathematical construction in Kant (which

NOTES TO PAGES 166-179

for him is "the process of giving an account of *sensory* determinations taken up from *perception* [sic]," *ENZ* §231 A). It does not fare any better for the concept of a priori synthesis in mathematics (which he treats as a completely analytic synthesis, *WL* I, 238, *SL* 173; *ENZ* §256 A). After all, Hegel jumbles intuition as an object with intuition as a way of knowing when he denounces the superficiality of modern geometry, which holds that its demonstrations rely on intuition when in fact "no science can be brought about by intuition, but only by thought" (*WL* II, 535, *SL* 724).

13. See F. Cirulli, *Hegel's Critique of Essence: A Reading of the "Wesenslogik"* (New York, 2006).

14. We saw at the beginning of chapter 2 some differences between the concept of *Wirklichkeit* and that of *Realität* (besides the notions of *Dasein* and *Existenz*). I myself have illustrated the concept of reality and actuality in Hegel in comparison with the Aristotelian notion of *energeia* to stress their distance from the ordinary concept (*Hegel and Aristotle*, 138–40).

15. "A reality that does not correspond to the concept is mere appearance, something subjective, accidental, arbitrary, something which is not the truth" (*WL* II, 464, *SL* 671).

16. For a detailed discussion of form, content, and matter, see chapter 2 of *The Powers of Pure Reason*. For the sake of brevity, I am leaving aside here the further problem that in the *Metaphysische Anfangsgründe der Naturwissenschaft*, matter is a concept as well as the balance resulting from the opposite forces of attraction and repulsion. Similarly, I cannot discuss here the problem, no less important, of the modal status of contingency and the difference between the contingent and the accidental.

17. My book *The Powers of Pure Reason* is devoted to the critique of these theses. In this section I summarize some of its results.

18. For Hegel, "what Kant had denied to theoretical reason, namely free self-determination, he explicitly vindicated for practical reason." Theoretical reason is "only the negative faculty of the infinite" (*ENZ* §54 Z).

19. See *Über die wissenschaftlichen Behandlungsarten des Naturrechts* (1803), in *W* 2, 453 ff., later summarized in the *Phenomenology* (*W* 3, 322–23, *PhS* 261–62).

20. For the circumstances and motivations behind these radical transformations, see the third chapter of *The Powers of Pure Reason*.

21. *WL* II, 462–64, *SL* 670–72.

22. "Thinking determines itself out of itself . . . , whereas *the how and in what respect* of this self-determination of thinking has not yet been demonstrated by Kant," *ENZ* §60 Z.

23. "In accordance with this, there is also a tendency to distinguish mere concepts of the understanding and concepts of reason, which is nevertheless not to be understood as though there *were* two distinct species of concepts but instead much more so that it is *our* doing either to stand pat merely with the negative and abstract form of the concept or to construe it, in keeping with its true nature, as at the same time positive and concrete. Thus, for example, the concept of freedom, insofar as it is a mere concept of the understanding, is freedom considered as the abstract opposite of necessity, while the true and rational concept of free-

dom contains in itself necessity as sublated. Similarly, the definition of God put forward by so-called deism, is the concept of God insofar as it is a mere concept of the understanding, while by contrast the Christian religion, knowing God as the triune God, contains the rational concept of God" (*ENZ* §182 Z). See also the *Zusatz* to §467 of the *Encyclopaedia.*

24. Recall that the *Critique of Pure Reason* gives us a "complete system of pure reason" (*KrV* A 708/B 736; A 832/B 860).

25. Further instances include the idea of activity (*Tun* and *Handeln*); time in the philosophy of nature; ethics as politics, happiness, and the unity of character, which in Kant instead is divided and opposed to all natural aspect; and much more. I, soul, and spirit but above all thought are speculative concepts in Aristotle and empty representations in Kant (*WL* II, 489–92, *SL* 690–91; *ENZ* §378; *EA* §321 A, §368 A, §370 A). In the idea of cognition, the immanent passage from sensation to intellect in Aristotle is superior to the relation between intuition and concept in Kant. Regarding the Eleatic antinomies, the Aristotelian solution is superior to the Kantian one. For all these issues, see my *Hegel and Aristotle.*

26. Hegel is driven by the enthusiasm for his recent discovery of Aristotle and the link between *Metaphysics* Lambda 7–9 and *De Anima* III 4–5, which was unforeseen until then and is read in a Neoplatonic light as a theory of divine life as thought thinking itself, a theory that will represent the core of Hegel's view of the Absolute from them on. I have discussed this point in *Hegel and Aristotle,* 409–11, and in "Hegel on Aristotle's *Energeia,*" *Bulletin of the Hegel Society of Great Britain* 53 (2006): 69–80.

27. "The former cognition of ignorance, which is possible only by means of the critique of reason itself, is thus *science,*" Kant writes in the conclusion of the *Critique of Pure Reason* (A 758/B 786).

28. There is a fine Reflexion (5073, *Ak* 18, 79–80) where Kant says that the critique of pure reason is "the prophylaxis against a malady of reason," its nostalgia or homesickness, a desire to lose itself and cover other worlds ("Die Critik der reinen Vernunft ist ein Präservativ vor eine Krankheit der Vernunft, welche ihren Keim in unserer Natur hat. Sie ist das Gegenteil von der Neigung, die uns an unser Vaterland fesselt [heimweh]. Eine Sehnsucht, uns ausser unserm Kreise zu verlieren und Andre Welten zu beziehen").

29. For the role of imagination in Kant, see my "Kant and Imagination," *Fenomenologia e società* 32 (2009): 7–19. For the problem of schematism in Kant's practical philosophy and the interconnection of imagination, rules, and power of judgment in action, see my *Saggezza, immaginazione e Giudizio pratico: Studio su Aristotle e Kant* (Pisa, 2004).

30. Hegel also speaks of *Selbstthätigkeit* negatively with regard to the emptying of Kant's freedom, conceived as merely formal, on the part of Fries (*GPR* §15).

31. For further discussion, see my "Method in Kant and Hegel," *British Journal of the History of Philosophy* 27 (2019).

32. But only Hegel does this with full and conscious appreciation. Kant, uninterested in knowing Aristotle in depth, never read Aristotle seriously and in the original text. On the concept of limit, he has with Aristotle a spontaneous thematic affinity.

33. This is so in the *Encyclopaedia* Logic (*ENZ* §92), but not in the *Science of Logic*. Regarding this difference, and generally on the notion of limit, see L. Illetterati, *Figure del limite* (Trent, 1996).

34. See A. Nuzzo, "'Idee' bei Kant und Hegel," 81–120.

35. "The idea can be grasped as *reason* (this is the genuine philosophical meaning of *reason*), further as *subject–object*, as the *unity of the ideal and the real of the finite and the infinite, of the soul and the body, as the possibility that has its actuality in itself*."

36. "In dieser selbstischen *Form*, worin das Dasein unmittelbar Gedanke ist, ist der Inhalt *Begriff*" (*W* 3, 589, *PhS* 491).

37. See P. Giuspoli, *Verso la scienza della logica* (Trent, 2000), 49–63.

38. See E. Magrì, *Hegel e la genesi del concetto: Autoriferimento, memoria, incarnazione* (Trent, 2017).

Index of Names

This index includes all names with the exception of Hegel, Kant, and editors and translators of works cited.

Achella, S., 222n9
Adam, 207n23
Adeimantus, 79
Adickes, E., 226n10
Adorno, T. W., 3, 16, 19, 25, 31, 62, 77, 92, 117, 201n1, 202n7, 203n7, 215n48, 224nn22–23
Augustine, 207n23
Allison, H., 226n10
Almaviva, Count of, 42
Anaxagoras, 57, 210n7, 210n8
Antigone, 49
Aristophanes, 35, 45, 189
Aristotle, 8, 17, 20, 33, 35, 36, 43, 56–57, 60, 66, 76, 95–96, 101, 103–5, 139, 173, 182–83, 189, 194, 202n4, 203n11, 204n1, 219n15, 219n17, 222n9, 228n25, 225n26, 228n32
Arnim, A. von, 13
Austin, J., 174

Bacon, F., 155, 197, 208n33
Becker, W., 218n14
Bellan, A., 217n10, 222n9
Benjamin, W., 64
Berkeley, G., 159, 166, 177
Berto, F., 212n29
Bloch, E., 209n2, 211n18, 213n35, 218n11, 224n22
Bodei, R., 213n33
Bordignon, M., 222n9
Bramhall, J., 91
Brandom, R., 37–39, 98, 206nn14–15, 219n20
Brentano, C., 3
Brentano, F., 204n1

Brinkmann, K., 212n25, 216n5
Butler, J., 207n25, 208n37

Carl, W., 221n31
Cecchinato, G., 222n9
Cesa, C., 222n9
Cesaroni, P., 209n1
Chiereghin, F., 217n6, 219n14, 224n26
Cicero, M. T., 217n6
Cirulli, F., 209n1, 227n13
Cortella, L., 223n11
Cusa, Nicholas of, 218n11

da Ponte, L., 23
Debussy, C., 197
Democritus, 197
De Pretto, D., 209n1
Descartes, R. (also: Cartesian), 5, 7, 104, 143, 144, 168, 177, 203n13, 203n26, 203n29, 221n35
Dilthey, W., 166
Diotima, 69
Donatello, 198

Epictetus, 201n1

Feder, J. G., 159, 169
Ferrarin, A., 202n5, 203n10, 203n12, 204n3, 206n10, 207n26, 210n13, 213n38, 219n15, 219n17, 219n20, 222n5, 222n9, 225n1, 226n6, 227n14, 227nn16–17, 227n20, 228n29, 228n31
Fichte, J. G., 29, 78, 153, 160, 194, 205n5, 221n29, 228n11
Figaro, 23, 42
Forman, D., 222n9

INDEX OF NAMES

Frege, G., 74
Freud, S., 17, 26–27, 204n1, 204n2
Fries, J. F., 228, 330n
Frilli, G., 211n22
Furlani, S., 209n1

Gadamer, H.-G., 126, 207n22, 224n20
Gadda, C. E., 82, 212n28, 215n50
Galilei, G., 155
Garve, C., 159
Gaspari, I., 207n23
Gassendi, P., 7
Geraets, T. F., 223n16
Guimaraes Rosa, J., 212n28
Giuspoli, P., 229n37

Halbig, C., 209n1
Harris, H. S., 223n16
Hartmann, K., 216n5, 218n11
Heidegger, M., 80, 98, 166, 213n36, 219n20
Henrich, D., 206n13, 215n49
Hobbes, T., 23, 41, 45–46, 91, 166, 195, 201n4, 207n23, 207n30, 208n31, 208n33
Hölderlin, F., 160, 205n5
Homer, 121, 211n19
Honneth, A., 217n10
Horkheimer, M., 117
Hotho, H. G., 224n23
Houlgate, S., 208n38, 209n1, 216n5, 217n5
Humboldt, W. von, 15
Hume, D., 23, 91, 119, 138, 144, 155, 161, 164, 168, 176–78, 182, 184, 201n4, 217n7, 217n8
Husserl, E., 24, 26–27, 44, 83, 92, 94, 204n1, 215n48

Ikäheimo, H., 208n34
Illetterati, L., 209n1, 229n33

Jacobi, F. H., 20, 109, 145, 150, 158, 184, 221n29, 221n35, 226n3
Jaeschke, W., 209n1
Johnson, S., 166
Jonson, B., 224n25
Joyce, J., 212n28, 224n25

Kemp Smith, N., 188
Kepler, J., 10

Kern, W., 220n25
Kierkegaard, S., 78
Kojève, A., 49, 197, 207n25
Ktenides, P., 222n9

Lacan, J., 41, 207n25
Lachterman, D. R., 212n29, 225n31
Lang, F., 82
La Rochefoucauld, F., 207n23
Lehmann, G., 188
Leibniz, G. W., 41, 74, 100, 143, 156
Livieri, P., 209n1
Locke, J., 143, 154, 155
Lolli, C., 111
Lugarini, L., 226n7
Lukàcs, G., 217n10
Luther, M., 155

Magrì, E., 220n23, 222n9, 229n38
Mahler, G., 3
Marconi, D., 212n29
Marcuse, H., 69
Marx, K., 31, 35, 117–18, 205n6, 213nn35–36
Masciarelli, P., 212n29
McDowell, J., 139, 206n17
Mendola, G., 209n1
Mephistopheles, 218n11
Monteverdi, C., 197
Melville, H., 53

Nabokov, V., 215n50
Nietzsche, F., 214n41
Nuzzo, A., 214n43, 219n19, 223n9, 229n34

Odysseus, 211n19
Orsini, F., 222n9, 209n1

Pascal, B., 207n23
Peperzak, A., 78, 206n12, 207n28, 213n33, 214n44, 222n5
Perelda, F., 209n1
Pico della Mirandola, 208n33
Pippin, R., 37–39, 206nn17–19
Plato, 35, 41, 55, 57, 65, 69, 74, 79, 112, 139, 196, 201n4, 211n20, 213n35, 214n41, 221n35
Plotinus, 55, 57, 71
Prauss, G., 226n10
Praxiteles, 198

INDEX OF NAMES

Proclus, 57
Pythagoras, 55

Queneau, R., 212n28

Rametta, G., 223n9, 225n30, 225n33
Ranchio, F., 222n9
Reinhold, K. L., 29, 153, 160, 205n5
Ricci, V., 222n9
Ricoeur, P., 15, 186, 223n17
Rosen, S. H., 45, 207n24, 207n29,
 217n6, 224n24
Rosenkranz, K., 127, 203n8, 224n24
Rousseau, J.-J., 4, 23, 35, 47, 192, 201n4,
 219n18
Russell, B., 225n31

Sanguinetti, F., 222n9
Saint Paul (Saul of Tarsus), 207n23
Santini, B., 209n1
Sartre, J.-P., 206n11, 215n50
Schelling, F. W. J., 78, 153, 160, 194,
 205n5, 210n5, 216n5
Schopenhauer, A., 153, 188
Schulze, G. E., 106
Siep, L., 33, 205n8, 206n9
Sietze, K. F. F., 127
Smith, A., 23–24, 44

Socrates, 15, 16, 79–80, 124, 183, 222n6
Soresi, S., 209n1, 223n17
Spinoza, B., 16, 30, 31, 41, 78, 83, 93,
 187, 194, 205n5, 207n23
Stendhal (Beyle, M.-H.) 218n12
Suchting, W. A., 223n16

Taminiaux, J., 208n32
Testa, I., 33, 205n8, 206n19, 222n19
Trendelenburg, A., 78, 216n5
Tugendhat, E., 206n13

Verra, V., 222n9

Weil, E., 41n9, 158
White, A., 216n5
Wiehl, R., 218n14
Wilder, B., 82
Winfield, R. D., 218n11
Wittgenstein, L., 20, 82, 206n13
Wolff, C., 143, 187

Yovel, Y., 225n30

Zahavi, D., 218n13
Ziglioli, L., 223n9
Züfle, M., 224n22